MW01256252

BEFORE GENDER

LOST STORIES FROM TRANS HISTORY, 1850–1950

Eli Erlick

BEACON PRESS, BOSTON

BEACON PRESS
Boston, Massachusetts
www.beacon.org

Beacon Press books
are published under the auspices of
the Unitarian Universalist Association of Congregations.

28 27 26 25   8 7 6 5 4 3 2 1

This book is printed on acid-free paper that meets the uncoated paper
ANSI/NISO specifications for permanence as revised in 1992.

Text design and composition by Kim Arney

Excerpt from *Transgender Warriors: Making History from Joan
of Arc to Dennis Rodman* (Boston: Beacon Press, 1996).
© by Leslie Feinberg. Reprinted with permission.

Library of Congress Cataloging-in-Publication Data
Names: Erlick, Eli, author.
Title: Before gender : lost stories from trans history, 1850-1950 / Eli Erlick.
Description: Boston : Beacon Press, [2025] | Includes bibliographical references. |
Summary: "An expansive exploration of the exciting lives of 30 trans people from
1850-1950 that radically changes everything you've been told about
transgender history" —Provided by publisher.
Identifiers: LCCN 2024050677 (print) | LCCN 2024050678 (ebook) |
ISBN 9780807017357 (hardcover ; alk. paperr) |
ISBN 9780807017340 (ebook ; alk. paper)
Subjects: LCSH: Transgender people—Biography. |
Transgender people—History.
Classification: LCC HQ77.7 .E75 2025 (print) | LCC HQ77.7 (ebook) |
DDC 306.76/80922—dc23/eng/20250219
LC record available at https://lccn.loc.gov/2024050677
LC ebook record available at https://lccn.loc.gov/2024050678

The authorized representative in the EU for product safety and
compliance is Easy Access System Europe 16879218, Mustamäe tee 50,
10621 Tallinn, Estonia: http://beacon.org/eu-contact

CONTENTS

REWRITING THE NARRATIVE

The narrative that we are in the midst of the first generation of trans children is so omnipresent as to be ambient. It is repeated ad nauseam in the media, online, by doctors, and by parents. Trans children, these various gatekeepers say in unison, have no history at all. [. . .] What happens if this consensus turns out to be baseless?

—JULES GILL-PETERSON, 2018[1]

No serious country should be telling its children that they were born with the wrong gender, a concept that was never heard in all of human history—nobody's ever heard of this, what's happening today. It was all when the radical left invented it just a few years ago. Under my leadership, this madness will end.

—DONALD TRUMP, 2023[2]

I n 1939 the sleepy British town of Great Yarmouth rumbled awake. National media picked up the story of two brothers, Mark and David Ferrow. The trans teens recently returned to their hometown after spending four years transitioning in nearby Maidstone. The siblings were far from extraordinary. Mark, the extroverted older brother, loved fine arts and literature. David, a shy young man, joined his father's book-selling business upon his return. The two grew more comfortable with themselves as they received overwhelming love and care in their small community. Mark and David found a way to thrive decades before the first trans kids were supposed to exist. Seventeen-year-old Mark and fifteen-year-old David did not have our modern language to describe themselves in 1939. The term *gender* only came into common usage around 1955.[3] Yet the trans siblings were far from alone. They were only a tiny part of the blossoming community defying gender norms.

Transgender people are nothing new. What is new, however, is the moral panic around gender identity. After opening up about my own trans identity at eight years old in 2003, I knew the idea that trans people have existed for only a few years was wrong. Calling us "new" erases our history. But exactly how much of our transgender past has been lost, forgotten, and destroyed? Who were the first documented children to transition? What means did activists have to resist society's extreme discomfort in discussing gender before our language developed? How did trans people live their everyday lives before they had terms to describe themselves? Which trans athletes participated in sports before sex testing? These questions led me to write *Before Gender*, which details thirty lost trans stories and what we can learn from them.

I started research for this book after a friend asked me the name of the first minor to medically transition. Amid the 2020s panic over trans youth healthcare, I realized there was no historical documentation to answer their question. Even Jules Gill-Peterson, the foremost expert on the history of trans children, argues that trans teens did not begin medically transitioning until the 1950s.[4] However, what I found was an entirely new history of transgender people.

I located Mark and David's full story after digging through British news and government archives. The teens are not only among the first known minors to transition, but they also invented creative and whimsical ways to label themselves. Mark told the *Daily Mirror* in 1939, "I feel I have worn these clothes all my life. I have always been a man at heart, and I am glad to be in trousers." He used remarkably modern phrases to tell the public about his transition. "I am glad to be through with it all. I don't think I could have faced up to it if there had not been some of the woman's power of endurance in me, though really, I suppose, I have always been a man." Testosterone was rarely used before 1939. With a mixture of surprise and excitement, I realized Mark's story represents the earliest known case of a minor transitioning with hormones.[5]

After I shared Mark and David's narrative online, millions of people read their history, saw their photos, and heard their story for the first time in over eighty years. I began sharing more stories of forgotten figures from trans history: a Black trans church leader whose segregated Florida town came together to mourn her death, an Indian snake charmer who hid her trans identity from the California press in the 1940s, and a trans boy who gained the support of his large family in 1862. Each of these stories inspired feelings of hope and familiarity for readers. Some showed their parents stories of familial support in the face of backlash and confusion. Others were excited for figures who once lived in the same regions as them. I knew this moment was a rare opportunity to share trans narratives that never made it into the history books.

The period from 1850 to 1950 is a unique era sandwiched between the explosion of mass media (newspapers, radio, and photographs) and the term *gender* (as opposed to *sex*) becoming popular in the 1950s. The division between the terms *gender*, *sex*, and *sexuality* represents the turning point when trans people became a related but ultimately separate population from those called *homosexuals* at the time. Sexologist Magnus Hirschfeld coined the German term *transsexualismus* (transsexualism) in 1923, although the term did not gain widespread usage until decades later.[6] It was only when David Oliver Cauldwell translated the word into *transsexual* in 1949 that we had an English name for the category describing the people in this book. The terms *transgender* and *trans* did not come into common usage until the 1990s. The period discussed in this book did not have a common language to describe trans struggles, yet trans people still existed everywhere from the largest cities to the most remote villages.

What do we gain from the stories of trans people who have not been sufficiently studied? I started writing this book believing I would find tidbits of interesting narratives that others would enjoy. However, after years of research, the following chapters will change our cultural understanding of queer, trans, and gender history. You will read about what may be the first mass queer and trans uprising, a riot against police in 1930 Berlin involving hundreds of people that was later erased from history by Nazis. Then there's a formerly enslaved Black trans woman, Sally-Tom, who is possibly the first trans person to have her sex legally changed in the US in the 1860s. One of Europe's greatest athletes, Stefan Pekar, transitioned in 1936, only for conservative bureaucrats to remove him from the record books. These are just a few of the interventions into erasure you will discover over the upcoming chapters.

The archive may not save us, but it will illuminate a path forward. We cannot challenge bad-faith arguments with history and rhetoric. The arguers do not intend to change their minds. However, those who bear witness to the vastness of history may be moved to fight for a better future—and to learn lessons from those who came before us. As Martinican author Aimé Césaire writes, "The shortest route to the future is always the one that involves the deepened understanding of the past."[7]

This introduction begins by reviewing the sections and groundbreaking narratives of this book. We then explore popular trans history and how lesser-known histories are lost, hidden, and destroyed. The following chapter explores today's debates over who is included as trans and how researchers use linguistic gymnastics to reduce the true extent of trans history. The introduction ends with an overview of discoveries that will rewrite transgender history forever.

THE ISSUES

There is no single right way to read this book. You can read cover to cover or you can begin with any narrative chapter since the chapters do not build on one another. Want to read a heartwarming story of a Tennessee trans man with the vocal support of his entire family, town, and county? Carl Crawford's narrative describes how he became the earliest known trans person to change his legal sex by court order. Interested in Roma culture or World War II? Albín Pleva's chapter uncovers details of a trans woman during the Porajmos (Romani Holocaust), which the Czech government continues to censor from history books. Curious about trans life in US-occupied Tokyo? Okiyo's chapter details her history and a trans-led riot she helped ignite in 1948. The sections cover four of the most debated aspects of the trans community today: youth, activism, employment, and sports.

"The Kids" highlights the stories of eight different young people, each of whom transitioned between the ages of five and sixteen. The section makes it clear that trans children have had familial and community support long before the concept of trans even existed. Many of the kids, like teenager Willie Ray, were celebrated by journalists, families, and officials across the world. Their treatment had both ups and downs; each pivoted upon their community's willingness to empathize with trans children before gender.

The next section follows nine of "The Activists" who worked at different levels of influence. Some were self-advocates. Others were national organizers. Not all of these activists embodied the policy-based advocacy we think of today. Many fought for their individual lives, like Mollie Wilson. She killed three men who tried to lynch her around 1884. Others, like Sadie Acosta, fought against government bureaucracy. She argued for her gender self-determination while incarcerated for refusing to sign a male draft card. Each activist narrative presents early trans advocacy that ranged from sparking large queer riots to correcting their legal sex.

"The Workers" tracks the lives of seven trans people who were forced to hide their trans status to find work. Some had rare occupations like snake charmer Elsie Marks. Others had more everyday jobs like John Berger, a florist trapped in St. Louis's most scandalous love triangle of 1893. Each offers a groundbreaking story of trans labor in the nineteenth or twentieth century. These narratives explore how trans people were forced into anonymity to keep their livelihoods. By exploring a range of professions, the featured narratives offer contemporary readers a diverse range of trans labor experiences that will change how we think about trans workers today.

Those transgressing gender roles have participated in sports for millennia. "The Athletes" goes back to the late nineteenth century through six stories of seven competitors in different sports. Many competitors played with others of their gender, like Frances Anderson, the world's greatest female billiards player of the 1910s. Others were forced onto the wrong teams like Léon Caurla and Pierre Brésolles, two trans boyfriends who played for France's women's running team in the 1940s. Some athletes, such as matador Agustín Rodríguez, played on both men's and women's teams. These stories are plentiful, and many of the trans athletes even knew one another.

POP HISTORY

Written history generally focuses on figures who are the most recognizable or prominent (as opposed to those who are disenfranchised, oppressed, or poor). Through these repeated narratives, we build the trans historical canon—what the public believes is a concrete, definitive timeline of transness. This timeline overlooks swaths of crucial figures and generally centers those with the most discernibly trans identities. This short section will provide an overview of the history and key terms that you should know. Following this brief introduction to trans history, I will review what is missing from these previous trans narratives and what we can do to reclaim the hidden past.

Canonical trans history may be summarized with a handful of (predominantly white) figures and events. There are only a few well-discussed trans individuals prior to the 1900s, such as Roman Empress Elagabalus and Joan of Arc. In the early twentieth century, celebrities such as sexologist Magnus Hirschfeld (who was not trans himself) made history by founding the first trans clinic in Berlin in 1919, the Institute for Sexual Science. Lili Elbe, one of the institute's patients, received one of the first vaginoplasties in 1930 before another historical "blank" period during World War II. Harry Benjamin, Christine Jorgensen, and John Money became household names in the 1950s and 1960s for bringing (limited) gender-affirming care to the United States. European trans celebrities like April Ashley, Coccinelle, and Jan Morris also entered the mainstream at that time. In the public imagination, it appears trans people only began organizing into groups that we would call *trans* today with the Stonewall riots in 1969 or when Sylvia Rivera and Marsha P. Johnson founded Street Transvestite Action Revolutionaries in 1970. Popular culture also saw an uptick in trans-related media when tennis player Renée Richards fought to compete as a woman in the 1976 US Open. However, some conservative pundits and politicians will point to more recent events like Laverne Cox gracing the cover of *Time* in 2014 or Caitlyn Jenner's 2015 *Vanity Fair* article as the true beginning of our history.[8] This historical canon certainly represents the pinnacles of visibility. Yet it leaves out key moments of influence, particularly outside the US and Europe. This book is meant not only to stitch together the massive gaps in public understanding of trans history but also to reveal how vibrant, exciting, and common trans life was during the 1850–1950 period.

Histories of the oppressed are not as neatly organized as they are often portrayed. Representation typically covers the moments that are, in actuality, mere plateaus of visibility. Most major texts on history overlook the long extent of the valleys below without diving into their depths. The distance between celebrities like Lili Elbe and Laverne Cox should not imply emptiness. Those less visible today were not necessarily less influential during their times. Some subjects in this book were considered famous enough to host large events and go on tour. Others overcame legal or cultural hurdles that the trans historical canon claims happened much later. As queer historians Mirjam Zadoff and Karolina Kühn explain, "To this day, we know only some of the pioneers of the queer emancipation movement. We know even less about the life of those who were persecuted, driven into exile, murdered—or simply remained invisible."[9] It is only through reaching deep into the ravines of our past that we learn the true extent of trans history.

Previous books on trans history tend to center—and sometimes construct—these highly visible plateaus. Susan Stryker's *Transgender History*, for instance, provides a thought-provoking read on many of the most influential moments of our timeline that are the most discussed today.[10] It is among the most popular trans history books ever published (and rightfully so). Books like these are crucial for learning about the best-known moments in transgender history. However, they also contribute to the construction of history itself by only focusing on the most visible individuals. What is left out of historical texts is as important as what is in them. Whether intentional or not, historians often erase our past in the process of writing it.

Erasure

While I researched this book, it became more evident than ever that the most influential single factor in erasure was race. Many recent scholars like C. Riley Snorton and Jules Gill-Peterson have pointed to the historical fixation on white, upper-class subjects in the US and Europe.[11] This is not necessarily the fault of researchers, however. Racism, anti-trans sentiment, nationalism, and economic austerity come from all around us. The Nazis infamously burned books from Magnus Hirschfeld's Institute for Sexual Science in 1933. The institute held the most comprehensive collections on trans identity in existence at the time. Although the institute was in Berlin, it contained writings on gender defiance from around the world. We will never recover all the burned texts, which also featured extensive African, Asian, and South American collections.

I personally struggled to obtain complete and accurate information from most countries outside of the US. North Americans and Europeans destroyed many archives from other nations, such as those in Japan in Oki-yo's home city of Osaka. Other records, like those from Mexico on Sadie Acosta, were never digitized due to a lack of public funding stemming from economic colonialism. My own methodology, which centers written text, is also biased. Many cultures prefer oral histories, which I rarely used in the following chapters. Western media, the single largest primary source of written material for this book, chronically overlooks nonwhite trans history. As South African trans activists Liesl Theron and Tshepo Ricki Kgositau point out, "Recorded history has remained largely silent about African trans people, with the exception of scandalized news stories of trans women who are portrayed as 'female imposters' committing fraud or trans people reduced to a spectacle to be humored."[12] To remedy this problem, I chose to center narratives of trans people of color in this book, even if their stories were more difficult to locate. Despite these additional efforts, most of the following chapters still focus on white trans people.

Misogyny also structures popular trans history as it intersects with race. Although trans women of the twentieth century were more frequently featured in the press, there is a tendency among recent history books to focus on people we may now call white trans men. There are at least a half dozen books published in the last twenty years that discuss the lives of white trans men during the 1850–1950 period. Apart from individual biographies, there are *zero* exclusively focused on trans women. Emily Skidmore's *True Sex: The Lives of Trans Men at the Turn of the Twentieth Century*, for instance, provides a thorough history of eighteen predominantly white trans men from 1876 to 1936.[13] It is detailed, thought-provoking, and timely. However, it does not offer insights into the treatment of trans people of color or women during the era. There is, of course, nothing wrong with focusing on the category of white trans men. But there is also a dire need for more research on trans women—particularly trans women of color—during this era.[14]

Among the most egregious errors that shape history is misgendering. Researchers chronically supplant trans identity with cisgender excuses for our existence. Before trans identity was better known, writers would often assume we transitioned for nefarious—or occasionally noble—purposes. Sometimes, cisgender men would pretend to be women to commit crimes. Other times, cisgender women would pretend to be men to obtain work or enter military service. However, I found that these excuses were overused. Many individuals expressed deeply held trans identities. For most of Western history, trans identity was so incomprehensible to the public that writers almost always attributed our identification to ulterior motives.

Texts that ascribe underlying causes for trans identity tend to erase, sensationalize, and misgender people we may now understand as trans. Cultural historian Kerry Segrave's 2018 *"Masquerading in Male Attire": Women Passing as Men in America, 1844–1920*, is a prime example. The book contains several short paragraphs about two individuals featured in this book (Willie Ray and Frank Williams).[15] However, the author does not mention the word *transgender* once. Instead, he misgenders each figure and claims they had underlying motives for transitioning. His book typifies the claims that our identities could only manifest through secondary justifications. He separates each chapter into sections on criminal intent, economics, mobility, love, and military participation, using examples found in newspaper archives. These five justifications—along with sexual fantasies—are the most frequent excuses historians use to misgender subjects. However, many of Segrave's figures were obviously transmasculine, declaring their identity even after it was no longer beneficial to them. In the process, Segrave erased over seventy years of trans history in his writing.

There is an old joke in the trans community that someone could murder a person for misgendering them, but historians would still call them by the wrong name, pronouns, and gender. This has happened several times.[16]

Amelio Robles Ávila, for instance, transitioned at age twenty-four in 1913. He joined the left-wing Zapatista army during the Mexican Revolution and was known as "El Colonel Robles." His nation, government, and peers respected his male identity. The Mexican government amended his birth certificate to male in the 1930s. He famously threatened to shoot anyone who challenged his identity and he even killed two aggressors who tried to uncover his anatomy in 1937. Amelio lived openly as a man for seventy-one years until his death in 1989. Yet writers, journalists, and researchers almost universally misgendered and deadnamed him until the 2000s. Like many trans male soldiers, commentators excused his identity as merely an attempt at joining the Zapatistas. It must have required an impressive level of willful ignorance to overlook the fact that he still identified as a man for almost *seventy years* after the revolution. Among the subjects of this project, I found that the "ulterior motive" form of erasure was the most common. It did not matter whether the individual was an obvious case of trans identity, such as Robles, or one that was less clear. The veracity of trans identity was almost always contested by writers and researchers until the past few decades.

In contrast to people like Robles, self-erasure is another means of losing track of historical figures' trans identities. The "self" in self-erasure is deceptive. Did these individuals truly desire to hide their identities or were their lives simply easier because they did? Most of the chapters follow individuals who were nonconsensually outed by the press, police, and courts. Only a few opted to go public about their identities on their own accord. Sandy Stone, considered a founder of transgender studies, argued that it was not until the late twentieth century that trans people came to seize upon visibility as a political tool. "The highest purpose of the transsexual is to erase him/herself, to fade into the 'normal' population as soon as possible," she wrote in her 1987 Posttranssexual Manifesto.[17] She suggested that "we can seize upon the textual violence inscribed in the transsexual body and turn it into a reconstructive force." Put more clearly: the 1980s became a tipping point in which trans people could share their stories to combat anti-trans violence, moving past the medical model of transsexualism that depicted the goal of transition as hiding one's identity. The era of self-erasure is certainly not over, but there are now more people open about their trans status than ever.

Activist, lawyer, and priest Pauli Murray (1910–1985) is one clear example of self-erasure. Like many figures you will read about in this book, he initially used creative terms to describe himself. In a 1937 note, he discussed his "inverted sex instinct," which he defined as "wearing pants, wanting to be one of the men, doing things that fellows do, [and] hating to be dominated by women unless I like them."[18] The civil rights icon requested to receive testosterone and abdominal surgery. He hypothesized that he felt he was a man due to undescended testicles.[19] To today's audience, this would be a clear demonstration of trans identity. However, Pauli's private efforts to receive hormones and surgery were largely overlooked until the 2010s, when restrictions were loosened on the personal papers of his Harvard archival collection. He never spoke publicly about his gender identity. Now, with access to his papers, well-known academics like education researcher Naomi Simmons-Thorne and cultural theorist Brittney Cooper have vocally argued for a change in pronoun usage for Pauli.[20] This change never happened on a wide scale. Pauli was even misgendered by the US Mint when he was featured on the quarter in 2024. Forms of self-erasure like Pauli's are particularly difficult because we can never know exactly how he would have identified, only that his self-described identity did not match the sex he was assigned at birth.

The more we reflect on our past, the better prepared we are to fight for our future. Dwelling on underreported and erased stories means grappling with how we fought for our freedoms in the past—and how much still needs to change. It is crucial that we constantly challenge popular histories so we can learn how others survived and thrived.

TRANS IDENTITY AND THE CLEOPATRA PROBLEM

Who exactly is included in the word *trans*? There will likely never be an agreeable solution to the debate on language. Some terms I use will certainly fall out of favor in only a few short years. Others will last for centuries. What is more important is identifying the tendencies and commonalities between different people from different eras. The question of trans status is particularly difficult when it comes to addressing those who lived before the term *gender*. Most broadly, I define *trans* as anyone identifying outside of their sex assigned at birth.[21] There are caveats, asterisks, and footnotes to this definition that will continue to be argued over for decades to come. I adhere to this broad definition to include stories of those who were more explicit about their identities (such as "I am a woman") to those who were less clear and were not able to provide words to their gendered actions. This leaves enough room for non-Western identities while excluding queer cisgender people. In this flexible understanding, I follow Susan Stryker and Emily Skidmore's definition of trans, in which someone pronounces themself outside of the Western gender binary.[22] This section will contend with how and why trans history existed before the term *transgender*.

Scholars, activists, and writers are frequently challenged over the historical extent of trans identity. That is, there is an ongoing debate over when the transgender community began and who may be categorized within it. Most people now agree that trans people do not need to medically transition to be trans. This means the term is based on language and description. Yet among the most common arguments against trans before gender is that the English word *trans(sexual)* did not exist until the 1940s and thus no trans people could have existed before then. I like to call this issue the Cleopatra problem. Cleopatra was a woman even though she lived over one thousand years before the word *woman* existed.[23] Does that mean we should refuse to call her a woman? How do we know she was a woman and why? Cisgender women had different gender roles two thousand years ago, just as the expectations for trans people differed. If you, like most people, agree that we may call Cleopatra a woman, then we may also call Mark and David Ferrow trans under the same logic. Women, like trans people, existed before the 1100s, when the word was coined.

Terms change over time, but the meanings behind them may be remarkably similar to one another.[24] This way of understanding history is often accused of "presentism" (applying contemporary values to past events). However, is trans actually a contemporary identity? We are ultimately engaging in presentism by using any language or term invented after the subject's lifetime. Historians do not treat any other term for a social category quite the same way as they do *trans*, reducing a large group so persistent throughout history to a purely modern phenomenon. Labeling these figures as *trans* should be a clear and concise solution to the Cleopatra problem and accusations of presentism. Yet this approach among trans scholars is still deemed controversial due to the volatility and specificity of the term *trans*—as though *woman* and *man* were not volatile terms themselves!

Why are historians so hesitant to call such unmistakably trans individuals *trans*? We can blame not only anti-trans prejudice but also cultural attitudes surrounding gender, history, and knowledge. Some of the rationales that erase trans people are typical historical interpretations, which consider presentism a cardinal sin of understanding the past. For example, at one point, the term *trans(sexual)* indicated a specific medical path that was impossible before the early 1900s. However, most people now know that not all trans people medically transition, and desiring gender-affirming healthcare is not a prerequisite for being trans. There is also the issue of self-identification. Today "transgender" is a category that someone identifies with. Historical figures, however, have no agency in what we call them. This again becomes part of the Cleopatra problem and misses the point that language changes over time. Historical erasure is not always intended to harm the trans community, but intent is not impact and the result is the same.

Trans historian Scott Larson provides an excellent example of benevolent erasure. While intending to point to the change in gender terminology over time, he instead excised millennia of trans history. Larson argues, "[Transgender] remains a modern category that cannot simply be retroactively applied. Moreover, gender is produced and challenged differently in different times and places. That is, the way in which gender was unmade and remade [. . .] was different from the ways that various transgender individuals and groups have sought to challenge gender categories in the twentieth and twenty-first centuries."[25] However, he proceeds to use the word *woman* when referring to Public Universal Friend, an eighteenth-century Quaker preacher who famously identified as genderless. According to Larson, Public Universal Friend described themself as "neither male nor female."

We again run into the Cleopatra problem. Public Universal Friend also existed under different norms than women today. By this same logic, one could not call them a woman either.

There is another form of "benevolent erasure" that presents a more complex debate among trans historians.[26] Labeling non-Western social roles as *transgender* could potentially erase Indigenous identities. Before Western Europeans began colonizing most of the world, Western Europe was one of the few regions with a strict gender binary. This binary was established as a global force through conquest, genocide, and the spread of Western European norms.

Colonization eradicated many traditional roles during the past six hundred years. Today some trans activists use certain Indigenous gender/sex roles to justify (white) trans existence. Others try to create solidarity between trans and colonized people through our mutual targeting via the gender binary. Many activists and scholars reject the comparison or labeling altogether. This book will take a cautious approach. The term *trans* originates in Western sexology and is problematic for perfectly describing social roles that do not neatly fit that category. However, I will still use the term when other roles are not named. Mollie Wilson, for instance, was a member of the Choctaw Nation, but did not appear to assume a traditional Choctaw gender role after leaving the territory as a teenager. On the other side is Muksamse'lapli, who appeared to assume a Klamath *t'wini꞉q* sex/gender role. There are more complicated cases. Okiyo, for example, used the Japanese term *danshō* to describe herself. The term is often interpreted as *trans woman* or *transfeminine* by contemporary scholars (including many danshō themselves). However, it does not directly translate since English does not have a perfectly analogous term. I take all these factors into consideration while applying a careful stance to the chapters focusing on non-Western figures.

The consequences of erasure

Who do we leave out by not addressing the Cleopatra problem? If we refuse to apply modern terms to past individuals or communities, then we could not call Oscar Wilde *gay* (first used in a modern context in the 1950s) or

Frida Kahlo *Latina* (first used to describe an ethnic gender category in the 1970s).[27] Taking this logic even further, the color orange did not exist until the thirteenth century (when the word was coined), and the first instance of manspreading was not until 2014 (when the action was named). Of course, very few make this argument about Wilde, Kahlo, orange, or manspreading because these categories are not perceived as new. The artificial divide between language and lived experiences undermines the impact of our historical arguments. Transgender is not a modern category but rather a modern word to describe an ever-present group of people.

There are clear dangers to denying the existence of trans people before gender. Like the Trump epigraph at the beginning of this introduction, the supposed novelty of trans identity is used against us. Trans people are far from the first group to experience this form of targeting through erasure. In the 1990s, American conservatives complained that being gay was simply "a new fad" harming children.[28] Similar critiques were leveled at the 1960s Black Power, feminist, free love, and civil rights movements. Of course, even if trans people did suddenly exist for the first time in the 1990s, that is not a reason to deny their self-determination. However, showing the persistence of trans identity throughout time helps others understand the transgender struggle and learn how trans people survived in the past.

Finally, I want to highlight some stylistic choices that I encourage others to use (unless the individual one is speaking or writing about requests otherwise). First, I removed deadnames and misgendering language and replaced them in brackets with the correct names and pronouns. I found there was absolutely no reason to deadname or misgender any of the figures in this book, a practice that is too often excused by academic authorities. Each section contains many references for those readers who would like to do further research (the only reason for including the names given at birth).

Next, there were several considerations while selecting chapter subjects. I carefully evaluated the possible ulterior motives for individuals identifying as a different gender than they were assigned at birth. Was it for economics, love, or jobs? Was it a disguise to escape persecution? These cases certainly happened. I cautiously reviewed each story to avoid including people who may have identified as cisgender today. To ensure these individuals were as close to today's definition of trans as possible, I considered each chapter through a test:

1. Did the individual declare themself to be a different gender from the one they were assigned at birth?
2. Did they lack a clear ulterior motive for transitioning (like taking on work traditionally done by men)?
3. If tested by a medical professional, were they found to not be intersex?[29]

Justifying trans existence in history this way, unfortunately, repeats some stereotypes about trans identities. The purpose of this test is to dispute the idea that transness is a recent trend, spreads like a disease, or is a "social contagion," as many fearmongering pundits would like you to believe.[30] I attempted to focus on the most compelling cases: those in which beliefs against trans identity hurt the subject's social status. Other "evidence" included choosing a new name, changing pronouns, and seeking medical transition. None of these are required to be transgender, of course, but they provide a parallel to the most common trans narratives today. Most—but not all—figures in this book changed their names and pronouns. Those who did not are no more or less trans.[31]

LESSONS FROM LOST TRANS HISTORY

Social leaders often cite philosopher George Santayana: "Those who cannot remember the past are condemned to repeat it."[32] But what if the presumption of linear progress is wrong? What if learning from history promises that we *could* repeat it? *Before Gender* is not a book about trans hardship. It also shares trans resistance, joy, thriving, excitement, and friendship long before we had today's terminology. Trans people found love, life, and opportunities in 1850–1950 that many today would not think was possible. It is important that we do not romanticize the past as a "better time," particularly for trans people of color. However, we may learn important lessons from the past for future forms of advocacy. Many of the figures you will read about even found the means to organize in ways that could help us today.

What do we learn from lesser-known trans history? Each section will grapple with an array of interventions into popular trans history. Spanning the four different narrative sections, I found the central question of this book answered in five categories: supportive communities, new "firsts," active trans resistance, community building, and survival-based deception.

Friendly reception

In 1913 a German newspaper discussed the growing number of trans people in Europe. "Such cases in which officials, on the basis of medical assessments, grant permission to men and women to wear the clothes of the opposite sex have increased significantly in recent times," the reporter wrote.[33] "The reason for this has less to do with greater frequency of such cases than with a growing awareness of their correct scientific understanding." Well over a century ago, the paper did not reduce trans people to the result of social contagion or moral decay (as they often are today). Instead, the reporter understood the increase in individuals to be the result of more understanding and support, which allowed individuals to express themselves. The support for trans people was one of the most surprising and delightful findings of *Before Gender*.

The historical positive reporting on trans people shows how manufactured the panic over trans identity is. Negative reporting on trans people has never been as central to media as it is today. Mainstream publications have recently adopted the strategy of "concern trolling," disingenuously displaying concern to undermine the agency of a community.[34] In 2022 alone, the *New York Times* used this tactic in over twenty thousand words of front-page stories discussing trans issues—mostly negative coverage about trans children.[35] The phenomenon of concern trolling allowed the newspaper to operate under the guise of journalistic objectivity while sowing seeds of doubt against the trans community. The moral panic over trans identity has now resulted in profound damage to the community—ranging from healthcare bans to violent attacks. Hopefully, by reflecting on the past, we may imagine paths forward for more uplifting narratives.

While some individuals featured in this book were certainly ridiculed, the majority had affirming or neutral reporting on their stories. This is not to say life was necessarily easier for people in 1850–1950. However, there was a positive interest in many of these narratives. Some were considered medical curiosities. Others, like Mark and David Ferrow, were publicly deemed as "brave" and "determined" for their transitions. The following chapters disrupt the idea of linear progress and instead often show *better* media treatment of trans individuals in the past than today.

Rural and Southern areas of the US were often quite warm to trans locals, contrary to how these regions are often represented. Willie Ray received extremely positive treatment in rural Kentucky. His story attracted so much sympathy that the governor pardoned him in 1890 after he stole a horse. Papers lauded the seventeen-year-old's blossoming celebrity, noting that soon after he transitioned, he "began at once to court all the attractive young women of the neighborhood, escorting them to church and to places of amusement and acquiring a local reputation as a beau."[36] Many other figures were similarly celebrated in urban and rural communities alike.

The US Midwest was also a hotbed of blossoming trans relationships. It is not frequently reported as a hub of queer and trans life. Yet around the turn of the century, it had flourishing communities of queer people so vocal that their presence would not be as visible again for a century. The *St. Louis Post-Dispatch* passionately defended trans man John Berger in 1895, arguing that he "is evidently irresponsible for [his] action so far as assuming male attire is concerned. [He] is afflicted, and has no control over the peculiar impulses [his] affliction brings."[37] Although the terms were pathologizing, the newspaper defended John's chosen dress as part of his understanding of himself as a man. The same paper wrote a glowing profile of Frank Williams in 1905. In 1909 it also celebrated an "astonishing number" of trans men who had moved to the area after several similar cases came to light.

Newspapers were unsurprisingly more sympathetic to white trans people—particularly young white trans men—than others.[38] But the tendency of reporters to demonize trans people of color and trans women contrasted with the actual community support. Georgia Black, for instance, was widely celebrated by her town but experienced neutral-to-negative reporting.

"By every law of society, Georgia Black should have died in disgrace and humiliation and been remembered as a sex pervert, a 'fairy' and a 'freak,'" *Ebony* magazine reported in 1951.[39] "But when Georgia Black died in Sanford, Florida, four months ago, both the white and colored community alike paid its solemn tribute." A Black trans woman in segregated Florida, Georgia was among the most admired people of her town. One of her neighbors explained in 1951: "I don't care what Georgia Black was. She nursed members of our family through birth, sickness and death. She was one of the best citizens in town." The chapters on Mollie Wilson and Okiyo also present similar cases.

Finally, supporting trans people is important but insufficient when we live in a society based on racial and class hierarchies. When there is oppression, there will be trans oppression. As you will read in Willie Ray's story, although he found support in his community, he continued to face persecution for trying to earn a livable income. He witnessed his father, who fought for the Union, struggle with poverty despite having fought to keep the country together. He worked harder than his peers yet was still forced into horse theft and bootlegging to make money. Without an end to inequity, trans people could not and cannot exist safely. This is the basis of intersectionality and why the trans movement was never solely about gender. Every aspect of life—social, political, and economic—must improve for trans people to thrive.

Rewriting the timeline of "firsts"

History is much less fixed and certain than society gives it credit for. We frequently hear stories of the first trans person to do *x, y,* or *z.* These claims are almost always wrong. During this project, I found numerous cases that exceeded some significant supposed "firsts" by decades. These irksome claims matter because they erase history. Calling a trans person the *first* is certainly important to garner interest in their history. However, it instills the idea that such events did not take place before that time. Historians Alex Bakker, Annette F. Timm, Michael Thomas Taylor, and Rainer Herrn explain, "Talking about the 'first case' also denies agency to earlier trans people, some of whom lived in parts of the world where these histories remain taboo."[40] Most individuals I located are likely not the firsts but simply the earliest known *for now*. These are some of the most significant findings from this book, promising to change the trajectory of trans history forever. The following chapters will tackle the false notions that Stonewall was the first queer/trans riot, Weimar German trans people were the first with governmental support to change their legal sex, the first minors to medically transition were in the 1950s (or the 2010s, according to some conservative pundits), and Christine Jorgensen was the first trans celebrity.

Stonewall is frequently considered "*the* emblematic event in modern lesbian and gay history."[41] In 1969 a police raid on the Stonewall Inn, a gay bar in New York City, led to physical resistance from hundreds of patrons and protesters. Thousands joined as the riots went on for over five days. It is the most recognizable queer and trans riot in history and is remembered with annual pride marches. It is frequently called "the first time LGBTQ people fought back" in public discussions.[42] More dedicated historians might cite the smaller Cooper Do-nuts Riot in 1959 Los Angeles, Compton's Cafeteria riot in 1966 San Francisco, or the Black Cat Tavern riot in 1967 Los Angeles (which was actually a civil demonstration and not a riot). This book highlights two separate riots thirty-nine and twenty-one years before Stonewall. The chapters will share the most detailed narratives of each uprising that has ever been published by bringing together dozens of legal, newspaper, and personal accounts, many of which have been hidden for decades.

The larger of the two riots is part of Gerda von Zobeltitz's story. The Rauchfangswerder riots took place on July 5–6, 1930. Around 300 queer and trans people from the activist group League for Human Rights faced 150 police officers and their 150 companions at a restaurant in Berlin's Rauchfangswerder neighborhood.[43] After a fight ensued, officers used trans woman Gerda von Zobeltitz's presence as an excuse for instigating the riot, deeming her mere presence as criminal. Writers have only published a few sentences on the Rauchfangswerder riots since 1930. Nazis destroyed much of the evidence in 1933 during their attack on the Institute for Sexual Science in Berlin. Using newly discovered archival materials, I located exciting details of the riot that have not been shared in over ninety years.

The second riot is featured in Okiyo's chapter. The Ueno Park riots began when police harassed a group of danshō, Japanese sex workers with identities paralleling today's trans women. On a chilly evening in November 1948, Tokyo's chief of police gathered a group of officials to harass the danshō. One of the workers, Okiyo, punched him squarely in the face, igniting the tensions into a riot. These rebellions, now described in detail in this book, are the two earliest known queer and trans uprisings.[44]

Another common myth contends the first trans people to gain legal permission to exist and change their documentation were in the Weimar Republic in the late 1900s to early 1930s.[45] Many researchers even cite the 1966 legal case *Matter of Anonymous v. Weiner* as the first attempt to change legal sex.[46] I found two major cases that radically shift this timeline. First, the Freedmen's Bureau, a government agency meant to facilitate Reconstruction, granted Sally-Tom permission to live as a woman in the late 1860s. Sally-Tom was a recently freed Black trans woman who lived openly as a woman until her death in 1908. Identification documents are a different question, however. Born in rural Tennessee in 1874, Carl Crawford changed his legal sex through court authorization in 1902. His mother, local officials, and community came together to support his transition. A judge accepted his petition to change his legal name and sex, granting what may be the first court ordered change of legal sex for a trans person. Although these cases did not set a legal precedent, they show an ad hoc path that many trans people took before gender to change their legal status. Both stories go far beyond their legal statuses to radically shift the narrative of transgender law before gender.

Another major source of "firsts" are medical breakthroughs. The date of the first gender-affirming operation is unknown and will never be recovered. Rudimentary genital surgeries have existed for millennia. Orchiectomies (castration) have been documented for thousands of years. Ancient Roman Galli and Scythian priests who were assigned male at birth performed orchiectomies on one another and wore clothing designed for women.[47] Mastectomies were first performed in the 1880s. As trans researchers often question, "What kind of surgery counts as surgery; are we speaking only of clinically sterile contexts common to Western medicine?"[48] Between the ancient origins of certain gender-affirming procedures and modern medical privacy laws, we will never know the names of the first recipients of most procedures.

Most of the individuals in this book did not receive surgery. However, I did find several instances that shift the popular timeline of trans history. As previously mentioned, Mark and David Ferrow are the earliest known minors to receive hormone replacement therapy. They were not the earliest to medically transition, however. While researching Gerda von Zobeltitz, I located a German surgeon, Ludwig Levy-Lenz, who operated from the same trans clinic she visited (the Institute for Sexual Science). He wrote an autobiography mentioning the story of an unnamed sixteen-year-old trans man who attempted to amputate his own breasts after being refused treatment. The trans teen had to have an emergency mastectomy in the late 1920s.[49] This would make him one of the earliest known minors to obtain chest surgery. These stories are chronically silenced yet crucial to emphasize the well-established benefits of transition.

As you have probably guessed, the people generally considered to be medical transition "firsts" are usually not. Lili Elbe and Dora Richter are often reported to be the first women to receive gender-affirming surgery in the early 1930s. Similarly, Michael Dillon is often incorrectly cited as the first trans man to receive a mastectomy and phalloplasty in 1946.[50] Sometimes mainstream publications claim trans celebrity Christine Jorgensen was the first to undergo gender-affirming surgery in 1951 (as the *New York Times* did in her 1989 obituary).[51] Again, while investigating Gerda von Zobeltitz's transition, I located the notes of another surgeon at the Institute for Sexual Science, most of which have never been published in English. The doctor, Richard Mühsam, performed an early type of vaginoplasty since at least 1920.[52] He was experimenting with testicular and ovarian transplants at around the same time. In 1912 he performed a hysterectomy and mastectomy on a twenty-five-year-old trans man who reported he "felt that these organs did not belong to [him]."[53] The patient was happy with his results and had his ovaries removed in 1921. Unfortunately, most recipients of the surgeries were not named. They could not share their own stories. One of the first subjects to have Mühsam's early form of vaginoplasty detransitioned to marry their wife, so I did not feature chapters on them. Like with the riots mentioned earlier, researchers will undoubtedly uncover even earlier named surgery recipients over time.

Other modern forms of trans surgery emerged in the early 1900s. Intersex trans man Karl M. Baer was among the first to receive a form of phalloplasty in 1906. He is often called "the first sex change [sic] operation in history" or the "first transgender person to undergo female-to-male (FTM) surgery."[54] However, if we include intersex people with varying forms of genitalia like Baer, there were numerous noted cases predating him by decades. Earlier forms of phalloplasty and vaginoplasty existed for intersex people we now may consider trans since at least the early 1800s.[55] There are likely even earlier examples of nonconsensual surgeries on intersex children. Again, these surgeries were rarely written into records as parents frequently hid intersex status from the public. The issue of trans surgery, like the word *trans* itself, is semantic and requires us to ask what exactly we mean by *trans surgery* in the first place.

Another similar myth credits Christine Jorgensen as "the first trans celebrity."[56] Jorgensen instantly acquired widespread media attention after stepping off a plane when returning from her surgery in Denmark in 1952. Although this book centers narratives that do not have enough (or any) attention today, several chapters focus on trans celebrities who lived decades before Jorgensen. Each was famous in their own time. Like surgery, a large part of the issue is the unclear definition of celebrity. Do they have to have international attention? National? Regional? Must they be famous solely for being trans? Several of the following chapters focus on celebrities of various levels of notoriety. Each of their histories was lost to time, politics, and shame.

Among the trans celebrities of the nineteenth century, teenage Willie Ray was frequently noted for his transition and general disregard for the law. In 1891, *The Tennessean* remarked, "Nearly every body in West Tennessee and the Kentucky 'Purchase' has heard of [him]."[57] Two days later, the *St. Louis Globe-Democrat* commented that his fame would soon reach the level of that of the notorious outlaw and Jesse James collaborator Belle Starr. Willie was far from the most well-known individual over the following chapters. Each of the featured narratives in "The Athletes" section achieved some level of international fame. Agustín Rodríguez was renowned for his transition and accomplishments as a matador. He went on to compete in several countries and make global headlines. Other figures like Elagabalus and Joan of Arc go back hundreds of years, usually achieving celebrity status through politics. Each trans celebrity's story shows the varied treatment of and fascination with trans culture before gender.

While researching, I noticed newspapers used a recurring phrase to describe trans people: "a singular case." Yet not one of them was. I cannot claim any of the events mentioned in this book are the "first." Several are currently the "first known" and others are "among the first." But many of these will be challenged as new stories emerge from the archives.

Resistance isn't futile

Studying history allows us to adopt certain social, political, and legal strategies that were successful in the past. From 1850 to 1950, many trans people rejected respectable forms of resistance, engaged in civil disobedience, and deceived authorities to gain autonomy that would otherwise not be granted.

Later in this book, you will read how Gerda von Zobeltitz's and Okiyo's respective riots influenced the public, police, and community relations. I found their collective actions had the largest impact on their communities. They inspired defiance, provoked discussion, and encouraged other queer and trans people to take action. However, these are protests most would not engage in today. Physical resistance is more dangerous than ever with militarized officers occupying most countries. Gerda and the League for Human Rights members could hit, kick, swing chairs, throw rocks, and toss mugs at police without being shot. In doing so, they rallied their community to push back against the police (many of whom would go on to become Nazi officers). Similarly, Okiyo was able to punch the Tokyo chief of police in the face in 1948. Her direct confrontation showed her community that it was possible to fight the authorities who constantly harassed, attacked, and killed them. Today these tactics would not be nearly as safe. Most likely, images and videos of the protests would be used for anti-trans propaganda (even more so than they were at the time). However, Gerda's and Okiyo's respective demonstrations show us the power of incitement. At what point did others join them and why? Was it the overwhelming anger at injustice? Fear for safety? These questions help us think about motivating others to activate their own communities. Actions ("riots") like the Martin Luther King Jr. assassination uprisings and George Floyd protests also show how physical revolts lead to ongoing movements. Countless groups emerged from these demonstrations and still impact the world today.

Several figures in this book engaged in more civil forms of disobedience. These rather respectable acts took place earlier than previously thought. In 1965 Dewey's restaurant in Philadelphia banned patrons from wearing clothing the staff perceived to be gender nonconforming. After turning away over 150 customers, three queer teenagers continued to sit in protest. They, along with a gay activist informing them of their rights, were arrested. Susan Stryker wrote that the lunch counter sit-in was "what appears be the first act of civil disobedience over antitransgender discrimination."[58] However, I found several other instances preceding the sit-in in the US and across the world (although not as part of the formal Civil Rights Movement of the 1950s and 1960s).

This book contains dozens of examples of early trans civil disobedience. Sadie Acosta, for example, publicly objected to her conscription into the US military in 1941. The sheriff threw her in prison for failing to register for military training after it was discovered she was assigned male at birth. The draft board gave her a physical examination and their doctor argued, "She is definitely a man." Sadie, on the other hand, protested to reporters: "I rather be a woman, so I am a woman."[59] In doing so, she called for the government to release women like her from conscription. She was eventually forced to sign the draft card. However, the twenty-nine-year-old translatina left her address off the document and escaped before anyone caught her. John Berger, Ray Leonard, and several other figures in this book undertook similar forms of disobedience against the legal system.

Another less common form of early trans activism was outing. In 1895, seventeen-year-old Effie Smith was caught in one of St. Louis's largest scandals of the century. Newspapers outed her boyfriend, Frank, and the police attempted to put him on trial for creating a space for queer youth. To direct legal attention away from Frank and her, she outed several powerful policemen, businessmen, and legal officials in the city. The ensuing scandal worked: the officers who harassed them were arrested and Effie received a lenient sentence. Although Effie is the only individual who used outing as a tactic in this book, many other queer and trans people relied on the approach at the time.[60]

These forms of noncompliance are memorable for embracing the illegality of their actions. Historical trans people like Sadie did not question if their disobedience was illegal. Instead, they asked *why* their demonstrations were illegal in the first place. Their efforts parallel fights against book censorship, trans healthcare, and abortion bans. Some teachers in the United States quit their jobs or left their states when the wave of 2020s book bans occurred. Others, however, fought back by actively sharing books they knew were against the new censorship policies.[61]

A blossoming community

It is common to see claims that the 1990s to the 2020s were the first time in history that trans people came together and organized. Even transgender historians cite the mid-twentieth century or Weimar Germany as the beginning of our community formation.[62] While trans identity is more visible than ever, trans communities popped up around the globe and supported each other for millennia. Several chapters in this book contain stories of trans people living, surviving, and thriving alongside one another. Many were friends, several organized together, and some were lovers.

Trans people have found one another for thousands of years. The Enarei were a group assigned male at birth who took on roles typically assigned to women in Scythia (today's Central and West Asia). Enarei typically adopted work similar to that of priests or sages beginning in the eighth century BCE. Greek historian Herodotus, who lived at the same time as the Enarei, described them as "women-men" afflicted by "female disease."[63] Like the Galli priests described earlier, they gathered and helped each other transition through customs, rituals, and orchiectomies. Nearly three millennia later Cercle Hermaphroditos was among the first US trans organizations. Founded in 1890, its anonymous members sought "to unite for defense against the world's bitter persecution."[64] These groups were an early way for trans people to build community before the emergence of more formal resources, direct action, and policy-driven organizations in the 1950s to 1970s.

Over the following chapters, you will read the stories of trans people who saw their communities grow. You will discover outgoing trans organizers like Maude Milbourne, trans event hosts like Gerda von Zobeltitz, and trans lovers like Léon Caurla and Pierre Brésolles. You will learn about trans brothers (Mark and David Ferrow), trans collaborators (Albín Pleva and Čeněk Vodák), and even trans teammates (Stefan Pekar and Zdeněk Koubek). Being trans did not have to be a lonely experience in the nineteenth and early twentieth centuries. In fact, the community blossomed in new and exciting ways during this period.

Lies, damned lies, and statistics

Finally, historians too often fail to take lying into account. Sympathetic researchers *want* to believe their subjects. Yet while researching for this book, I realized there was much more to consider than simply believing historical trans self-narratives. Many authors and researchers too readily accept historical reporters', doctors', and trans people's narratives at face value, overlooking the internal contradictions of their statements. This book, on the other hand, addresses every claim through a lens of doubt. Rewriting the popular narrative requires viewing discourse not as objective truth but as a piece of evidence. Highlighting how trans figures, along with authorities, deceived others may be controversial. However, trans people making up their own narratives often meant access to safety, healthcare, and respect from others. Many of the subjects in this book lied for survival and should never be blamed for trying to stay safe. The rampant anti-trans violence of 1850–1950, rooted in European systems of gender norms and punishment, is at the foundation of the problem. There should be no shame attached to staying alive through deceit. The so-called lies were often embellishments about legal issues and medical claims that trans people needed to survive.

First, it is crucial to remain skeptical of reporters in the past or present. Today we see reporters from respectable publications like the *New York Times* and *The Atlantic* quoting anti-transgender activists as authorities on trans issues. In the past, particularly during the "yellow journalism" period of the 1890s to 1930s, reporters frequently embellished narratives far beyond what was possible.[65] Newspapers would publish outrageous stories to drive up interest while competing for sales. Because several of these tall tales are mentioned in this book, I made a greater effort to fact-check them on all claims. Ann Storcy's chapter, for instance, featured several directly conflicting stories. Between 1885 and her death in 1904, newspapers reported that she was an Indigenous woman born in a Plains Native American region and was worshipped by the Potawatomi tribe as a goddess. Other papers reported she was a white French migrant who traveled the country and struck it rich in the Gold Rush. One confidently claimed her birth name was Monsieur D'Arcey, not realizing that *monsieur* translates to mister. I attempted to express doubt in each story while displaying the conflicting narratives to represent how others perceived the lives of each figure.

It is helpful to approach historic trans self-narratives by understanding the context in which they were written. In 1850–1950, trans people had to hide or lie about their histories to survive. Effie Smith, for example, was such a prolific liar that she escaped jail multiple times by weaving captivating tales. After police arrested the trans girl for "creating a disturbance" in 1893, the fourteen-year-old told the judge she had given birth to a baby and was abandoned by an unrequited lover. Sympathizing with her supposed struggle, the judge sentenced her to a short-term rehabilitation facility instead of jail. Several other trans people in this book lied for their survival with more believable fabrications, each still requiring doubt.

Similarly, several stories featured individuals who claimed their parents raised them differently from their assigned sex. I was surprised how common this excuse was, whether true or not. I could not find a single case in which I could confirm that parents were at the root of their gender expression—although I could not disprove the claim in most instances, either. The claims appeared to be a defense to gain sympathy and shift the blame onto family for one's gender transgressions. The strategy seemed to work as it consistently helped lessen punishments.

Another extremely common lie is false reporting of intersex conditions. These claims are frequently used to delegitimize trans healthcare as intersex people are viewed as more legitimate medical subjects (albeit often nonconsensual ones). It was customary for trans medical recipients to declare intersex conditions until only the past few decades. Historically, trans people were required to make these claims for their doctors to administer healthcare. Grappling with intersex claims is complicated because terms like *intersex* were not prevalent before the mid-twentieth century.

Sometimes trans people believed (or claimed to believe) their transness was an intersex condition within itself. Gerda von Zobeltitz, for instance, planned to tell Nazis that she had a psychological intersex condition if they confronted her. She used the now-pejorative term "mental hermaphroditism" to describe her sex. Although her doctors attested that she was not intersex, she believed this would prevent the Reich from executing her. Others reported external intersex conditions they simply did not have. Lucy Hicks Anderson, profiled at length in C. Riley Snorton's *Black on Both Sides*, also used the excuse. While on trial for perjury for stating she was a woman on legal documents, her attorney suggested that she claim she had "hidden organs" that could only be examined after her death. The strategy "offered up her corpse" in exchange for her freedom from jail.[66] Famously, Roberta Cowell (the most well-known British trans woman of the 1950s) swore to the press she had intersex conditions despite doctors publicly declaring she did not. She could only change her birth certificate by claiming intersex identity, so it made sense to do so.[67] Relatedly, the antiquated term *hermaphrodite* is often confused for *intersex* by modern researchers. Instead, during the 1850–1950 period, writers used the outdated word to describe anyone falling outside the gender norms, sometimes including queer cisgender people.

While it is necessary to believe trans people today, one would be amiss to uncritically accept historical accounts from anyone (trans or not). Future historians must take into consideration embellishments, falsehoods, and rumors.

Recovering the past

You will read more findings in the following narrative chapters. You will learn about the trans triumphs, romances, and tragedies that came before gender as they have never been told before. These stories are not only about trans history but also about how individuals lived in a time long before they were supposed to exist.

THE KIDS

I want to look like what I am but don't know what some one [sic] like me looks like. I mean, when people look at me I want them to think—there's one of those people that reasons, that is a philosopher, that has their own interpretation of happiness. That's what I am.

—LOU SULLIVAN, age fourteen, 1966[1]

Not meant to exist at all in the present tense of their childhoods, the ghostliness of trans children over the past one hundred years takes unique residence in the medical archive, hiding in plain sight, invisible to the inverse degree of being pervasively present, yet always slightly out of reach even as they come into discourse.

—JULES GILL-PETERSON[2]

Trans children have always existed. While this section covers trans children from 1866 to 1942, documentation of trans childhood goes back thousands of years. The infamous Roman empress Elagabalus was one of the earliest documented teenagers to transition. She led Rome between 218 and 222 after her coronation at age fourteen. While ruling the nation, she allegedly sought ways to medically transition. Contemporaneous sources explained, "The young monarch wanted a vagina implanted in [her] body by means of an incision."[3] Another anonymous Roman historian claimed Elagabalus succeeded in an orchiectomy but never received the genital surgery she sought.[4] In a different account from one of her contemporaries, when Elagabalus's lover called her "my lord," (masculine), she responded, "Don't call me lord, I am a lady."[5] The term *transgender* would not be invented for nearly two millennia.

Trans kids are not only our future; they are also our past and present, leading social movements throughout history. Not many people recognize that Sylvia Rivera was only seventeen and Marsha P. Johnson was only twenty-three when they took part in the Stonewall riots. Although many of the most iconic names in queer and trans history were rejected by their families, countless trans youth also received full support in the 1850–1950 period. The following chapters recount contradictory stories, with some news accounts celebrating transition as a courageous medical triumph while others disparaged trans youth as deceitful.

This section details seven stories of eight trans kids from across the world who transitioned between ages five (Masoud El Amaratly) and sixteen (Willie Ray). I decided to focus on this age group as they are the primary target of attacks on trans healthcare. Unlike many accounts of historical trans youth, however, I will not limit their stories to their childhood years. Each narrative will span a lifetime (or at least as much of a lifetime as I could locate). As you will read, many of these children grew into happy adults who were thriving members of their communities.

It makes sense why so many trans children's stories were lost, concealed, or destroyed. Young people were tightly controlled not only by the state but also by their parents. They were not as often sent to prison as trans adults, either. Courts typically compiled more records than private citizens. Trans kids were, however, sometimes subjects of the legal system. Thanks to the paper trail left by courts, we gain more insights into trans kids' lives and the process of regulating their gender expression. Consider this fifteen-year-old trans girl from Glasgow.[6] After police arrested young Francis Cairney in 1877 for soliciting and annoying people around her, a debate broke out in court over what type of charges she should receive:

> The BAILIE [bailiff]—It is a very distressing thing to see a female crying. (Laughter.) You stupid fellow, what made you dress yourself in this way?
>> Prisoner (crying)—I did not intend to do any harm.
> The BAILIE—What did you intend to be about when you put on these clothes? What do you do?
>> Prisoner—I work in the Adelphi Biscuit Factory.
> The BAILIE—Biscuit Factory! Well, I do not know, but some of the ladies might bake as well as you. There was no use, however, in your

putting on these clothes to get work there. I do not know what to do with the like[s] of you. What is the charge?

Superintendent DONALD—He is charged with disorderly conduct by importuning passengers.

The BAILIE—He is not charged with having dressed himself in female garb? That is a much heavier charge than merely disorderly conduct. It is a very dangerous custom for a man to dress himself in female clothing.

Superintendent DONALD—There is not a great deal in the charge. It seems to have been more of a frolic.

The BAILIE—This might have been a much graver charge, and if it had, I would have given you the experience of prison for such a time as you would not have easily forgotten it. Foolish fellow that you are. Do you plead guilty?

Prisoner—Yes, but not to speaking to anyone.

The BAILIE—No such frolic as this can be allowed. We sometimes look over foolish acts by young people, but this is serious. Take him away just now, I will take the case at the end of the Court.

When all the cases had been disposed of prisoner was again placed at the bar.

Superintendent DONALD—It was not known for some time after being apprehended whether he was really a man. (Laughter.)

The BAILIE—You must not do the like of this again. See that you have some idea of the dignity of being a man. Now, go away and get on your own clothes.

Prisoner's mother was in Court, and in a rather excited manner followed her [daughter] with [her] own clothes, which [she] put on in a side room, and subsequently left the office.

Like *hundreds* of other cases I located, Francis Cairney did not generate enough news to feature her in a chapter. Along with simply not having enough biographical information, there was insufficient evidence of her gender identity to make any conclusions. Most broadly, Francis's story tells us about the skepticism toward trans children—especially trans girls.

Imagine the humiliation and confusion bestowed on a nineteenth-century trans girl simply trying to express herself. There was very little community to turn to. An interaction like this could have coerced Francis into concealing her gender for the rest of her life.

Long before Francis, trans youth were changing history yet were erased from it. As Jules-Gill Peterson writes, "We do not know trans children's history because we have assumed they do not, generationally, belong in the trans past. The fact that trans children have been forced in the twenty-first century to fare without a history may itself be a major cause of the generational tension."[7] The assumption of trans children's novelty erases some of the most prominent names from history. Joan of Arc began dressing in clothing designed for men by age seventeen. Their attire and professed visions of saints eventually became the rationale for their capital punishment. While there is certainly room for argument around their gender, they undeniably transgressed 1420s gender roles in a way parallel to trans people today. Yet it was not until the 1996 publication of Leslie Feinberg's *Transgender Warriors* that the topic of Joan's transgender status became a more open debate among scholars. The idea of a trans saint was inconceivable until only recent years. It is cases like Joan's that show the need to review history and reconsider the impact of young trans people.

The consequences of rejection

The actions of trans children from the nineteenth and twentieth centuries reflect much of what we see today: familial and medical rejection led to increased hardships, while support allows for an easier path. Effie Smith's mother and brothers rejected her gender in the 1890s. She ran away from home and was repeatedly arrested, unhoused, and persecuted by the state. Contrast her story with that of Ray Leonard, whose parents and seven siblings accepted him wholeheartedly at age thirteen. He thrived, opened a store, and lived independently for sixty years until his outing. He had an extensive network of friends and community in several different states. Familial and medical acceptance helped trans children live happier and healthier lives.

Since the advent of trans medicine until the past few years, young transitioners typically concealed their transgender status from the public (the trans community calls this "going stealth"). This is exactly what I found: when given the option of hormones and surgery, young trans people generally did not stay involved in trans groups. Mark and David Ferrow, who transitioned in their mid-teens, received some media attention in 1939–1940 regarding their trans status. After that, they went stealth for the rest of their lives. They both married and had flourishing social lives.

Ludwig Levy-Lenz, a surgeon at the Institute for Sexual Science in the 1910s and 1920s, adamantly refused trans minors' requests for treatment. There were, however, dramatic exceptions that illustrate the imperative to provide young people with healthcare:

> A sixteen year old transvestian [boy] came to us to have [his] well-developed breasts amputated. [He] had had the luck, [he] said, to find a job as apprentice to a carpenter, and it was only [his] breasts which prevented [him] from working like the other apprentices.
>
> We refused to operate because we considered that at the age of sixteen the [boy's] mental development was not complete. A few days later, the patient was brought to us having lost a great deal of blood; in order to necessitate amputation, [he] had inflicted upon [himself] deep and severe cuts with a razor. We were able to save the [boy's] life by a blood transfusion, but I had to remove the breasts.[8]

We cannot know how many other trans people there were like the one Levy-Lenz operated on. Some died attempting their own surgeries and many others were lost to suicide. Familial and medical acceptance was just as necessary for trans youth in the nineteenth and twentieth centuries as it is today.

Segregated support

I could not locate many detailed stories of trans children of color that fit the criteria for a chapter in this book. As mentioned in the introduction, this does not mean there were fewer trans kids of color. It simply means there was less reporting on them. This tendency warrants exploring: Why was the support of and reporting on trans youth of color and trans girls less common and more negative from 1850 to 1950? I found that media presumed white trans boys were innocent bystanders to their own gender, and most journalists (a majority of whom were white) refused to report on trans youth of color.

Higher socioeconomic status allowed certain white trans children to access medicine before most trans children of color. As Gill-Peterson argues in *Histories of the Transgender Child*, doctors believed the narratives of some affluent trans children. In contrast, trans children of color, particularly Black trans girls, were pathologized for their gender identity. Gill-Peterson found that beginning in the 1950s, well-off white trans children often received gender medicine from their white doctors, while almost all trans children of color were turned away. Additionally, the most common form of research and reporting was on the exploits of white trans boys, who were generally perceived as innocent girls who simply wanted access to better wages. Some of these young white trans boys, such as Willie Ray (discussed later in this section), were even lauded for their heroic journeys of transition and debauchery. Interestingly, reporting on Willie became more negative as he aged, eventually landing him in jail in his twenties. Conversely, reporting on trans people of color and trans women was almost universally negative. Effie Smith, despite being only a teenager at the height of her fame, endured entirely negative press—but only if the journalist knew she was trans. After police arrested her for creating a disturbance at age fifteen, a local reporter assumed she was a cisgender girl. He summarized her case as "Though but Fifteen Years Old, She Has Drained the Cup of Sorrow and Misery. An Opportunity to Reform."[9] However, after she was outed two months later, nearby newspapers used terms like "insane" and a "prevaricator" to describe her.[10] This tendency was common among all trans women and people of color before and after their outing, regardless of age.

The media is still deeply segregated in the US. Today the largest publications are less likely to report positively on people of color. Only 24 percent of journalists are people of color.[11] These numbers were even lower from 1850 to 1950. The lack of reporting indicates little about the prevalence of trans children of color. For example, Georgia Black (featured in "The Activists" section) transitioned in 1907 around age fifteen in South Carolina. However, the bulk of her story occurred later in her life. Mollie Wilson's chapter will review her transition at age nineteen around 1884, and Sally-Tom's chapter briefly discusses her transition as a young person in the 1860s. The climax of these three Black trans women's narratives occurred too late in their lives to feature in this section. Translatina Sadie Acosta's chapter also briefly mentions her transition at age thirteen, although no records remain from her childhood. Ultimately, with the exception of Masoud El Amaratly, I moved the stories of children of color who transitioned before eighteen to different sections that better fit their narratives.

The other trans kids

The question of children's liberation is always on the horizon. At what point should young people have bodily autonomy? How young is too young? Should medical consent require parents' input? As you will read over the following chapters, trans kids' needs must be respected as soon as they are stated. These stories bridge the past with the present, highlighting the benefits of fostering a culture of self-determination, one in which young people can choose their own paths. Trans youth scare the political right for just this reason. If young people are allowed more agency, the conservative notions of family and ownership over children break down. If children are not property, instilling cultural norms through threat and coercion becomes much more difficult. Authors like Sophie Lewis and M. E. O'Brien have tackled this issue in their writings on restructuring the family. However, our society is still far away from systemically shifting to a culture of youth autonomy. The following stories will show how urgently our culture needs to change for future trans children.

With so many historical trans youth, it is amazing how cultural memory erases their incredible stories. Several kids from this section reached fame and fortune not *despite* their gender but *because* of it. These narratives again reveal how much more our society can do to uplift trans kids and support their self-determination. After all, children's liberation is necessary for trans liberation.

THE BROTHERS: MARK AND DAVID FERROW

In 1939 the sleepy seaside town of Great Yarmouth, England, found itself at the center of a national media spectacle. Fed up with prying questions, trans teen brothers Mark and David Ferrow spoke to the press about their genders for the first time. Unlike many sensationalized exposés of trans people, the boys were celebrated for their great accomplishment: becoming among the first men in England to medically transition. Their legacy would pave the way for British trans youth to obtain medical care for decades to come.

There was nothing remarkable about Mark and David's early childhood. The brothers were born to loving parents Ellen and George Ferrow, a stay-at-home mother and a bookseller. The pair grew up with their siblings, Rosa, James, and Malcolm.[12] Mark began to express his trans identity when he started puberty. He transitioned at age thirteen in 1934. David, two years younger, was soon to follow. The pair asked to change their names and be treated as boys. Their family quickly obliged. Believing a change of scenery would be positive for their sons' transitions, their parents sent the brothers to art school in Maidstone, 150 miles away. An anonymous, sympathetic local woman paid for all their travel, school, and medical expenses. While at the boarding school, the brothers were known only as boys and treated as such. They spent four years studying in Maidstone, happy to have their genders recognized by all.

The two boys medically transitioned in London at the recommendation of a doctor. Mark first began receiving testosterone in 1939 at age seventeen. David began shortly after, in 1940. There are no records of precisely where or how they transitioned, although Dr. Lennox Ross Broster at London's Charing Cross Hospital was among the most prolific trans healthcare providers at the time. The brothers were only fifteen and seventeen but had socially transitioned over four years earlier. Testosterone was first synthesized in Europe in 1935. It was not until 1937 that it first became available as pellets for consumers. Earlier hormone supplements existed but were not as effective and used animal extracts to achieve their effects. It is possible that Mark and David became the first transgender minors to transition with the new class of synthetic hormones—at least the first we know of.

Despite their incredible medical journey, the Ferrows only began to attract national attention after they came back to their hometown. They returned after four years to complete secondary school. Upon reappearing, they were faced with whispers about their gender identities. The pair grew exasperated and knew they had to be open about their gender to stop the rumors.

"People have gossiped so much that we want the facts to come out," Mark told a journalist shortly after turning seventeen in 1939. "I feel I have worn these clothes all my life. I have always been a man at heart, and I am glad to be in trousers." He further explained to the *Daily Mirror*, "I am glad to be through with it all. I don't think I could have faced up to it if there had not been some of the woman's power of endurance in me, though really, I suppose, I have always been a man."[13]

The two invented terms to help others understand their transition. "Though we have been girls, we have both felt men at heart," Mark explained. He would often tell others about the immense relief he felt from transitioning: "Even things like shaving, instead of irritating me, are a pleasure."

The brothers remained supported throughout their lives. There are no reports or indications that anyone refused to accept them for who they were. After becoming more open about their trans status, their neighbors increasingly admired the two. "David is sensitive but he is showing splendid courage," a family friend told a reporter asking about the brothers. "Instead of hiding indoors, he has decided to go out and show himself everywhere where he was in the habit of going before." Their community not only accepted them but also embraced their transition.

As for the brothers' post-transition habits, Mark and David could not be further apart. An adventurous artist, Mark traveled the country while showing off his paintings at galleries. David, quiet and timid, spoke less with reporters. He spent the rest of his life in Great Yarmouth. Inspired by the media attention, Mark wrote an account of his teen experiences. Unfortunately, the story has been lost to history and may no longer exist.

He continued to use the spotlight to show off his artwork and keen sense of humor. "People tell me I am rather an odd person," he told the *Yass Tribune*. "I am proud to be. I have a personality such as few others can have, I have a knowledge of male and female psychology that anyone may envy."

Unlike many stories of trans childhood, Mark and David's lives were well reported in a remarkably upbeat tone. The Ferrows' transition was not presented as an attack on "traditional values" as it often is today. Instead, the boys were celebrated as an example of medical progress. "Vanished Sisters Return as Boys" one 1939 headline read. Another called them the "Two Sisters Who Grew into Brothers." The shockingly affirmative language shows us a time before transgender was understood as a category. Shortly after they transitioned, one of their neighbors said, "People will soon get used to the brothers." "Used to" is perhaps an understatement, as both became distinguished members of their towns upon their return.

The Ferrows lived long, happy adult lives. Mark and David spent most of their years with less media attention than during their childhood. Interestingly, the 1939 and 1940 articles were the only times their gender was mentioned, despite the pair making the news for decades to come. The brothers lived the rest of their lives relatively stealth—without most others knowing they were trans. Retellings of trans kids' stories often end in their teens. For the Ferrows, however, their transition was only the beginning.

World War II affected the whole Ferrow family. Only a week after the boys' transitions made the news, the UK joined World War II. This major declaration overwhelmed all other news coverage, meaning there was less reporting on Mark and David. The Ferrows next appeared in papers during the Blitz. Early on April 8, 1941, Great Yarmouth roared awake once again. Axis planes dropped two parachute bombs on the brothers' neighborhood.[14] The explosives caused immense damage to the streets, almost immediately demolishing ninety-nine homes and businesses. Mark jumped into the action and began extinguishing nearby fires. George William Dye, a local bricklayer, then began organizing the official rescue. He called for volunteers to dig an elderly man and woman out of the depths of debris while volunteers hosed down the fires. Mark immediately stepped forward to help. After thirty minutes, the smoldering rubble suddenly burst into flames again. Deep, suffocating smoke poured onto Mark and two other rescue workers. The rancid smell of burning homes filled the air. The three tied handkerchiefs around their faces and did not waver in their search. A fireman pointed his hose toward the debris, but the inferno was so hot that he could only begin to cool an adjacent section of the street. Mark bravely continued to dig as a heavy rush of steam lashed his face. Soaked, smoky, and burned, the Norwich Rescue Squad ordered the volunteers to immediately rest after digging out the elders from the destruction. The Axis dropped between four and five thousand bombs on the United Kingdom throughout the night.

Mark earned the prestigious King's Commendation for Brave Conduct medal for recognition of his work.[15] Great Yarmouth lost 109 residents to German bombings that year alone. Mark and David's neighborhood was in ruin, but their whole family survived the attack.

Mark and David's older brother, James, enlisted to fight the Axis in 1939. While Mark was rebuilding his neighborhood, James fought with British troops in Japanese-occupied Malaysia. In February 1942 the Imperial Japanese Army captured the twenty-two-year-old and he became a prisoner of war. The military held the young man as a captive in Thailand. Fearing the worst, British officials declared him a casualty of the war in August 1943.[16] The Ferrows had no sign of James until September 1945. Upon liberation of his camp, the military declared him officially dead shortly after what would have been his twenty-sixth birthday.

James's death represented the beginning of Mark's adulthood. Always more outgoing and adventurous than David, Mark was celebrated for his civic, artistic, and social endeavors. Never without his trademark pipe, he traveled the country and settled in Leicester. Five foot ten, outgoing, and stylish, he attracted the attention of many women but quickly married Edna Hall in 1942.[17] The two lived together for the rest of their lives.

Mark's artwork received much praise over the years. He joined the Kirby Muxloe Players theater troupe as a writer. There, he turned British folktales into plays. He never gave up painting, either. He created well-known portraits of ballerina Margot Fonteyn and Leicester's mayor. The renowned National Portrait Gallery continues to sell prints of his 1988 oil painting of famed cricketer David Gower to this day. He also took up jobs at a tube factory and a marriage counselor's office to support his art. Mark died in 1991 at age sixty-eight, six months after Edna. The paintings from his galleries are still strewn about England to this day.[18]

David lived in his hometown for the rest of his life and became a local icon. The Ferrows' street was left in ruin in the months following the Blitz, and Mark left the town soon after the German bombing. David, always staying closer to home, remained in Great Yarmouth during the rebuilding. He sold books like his father, starting almost immediately after his return to Great Yarmouth at age fifteen. After World War II, he opened a book-shop on his home street, but it eventually outgrew the storefront. He then expanded his book collection to over thirty thousand titles and opened a shop closer to the town center. David had a daughter, Jan, who supported his work. The whole town adored him. A local pottery organization still sells tankards of his face. He ran his prosperous bookshop until his death in 2006, sixty-eight years after transitioning.[19]

The brothers' legacy transcends their times, media, and country. When I initially posted online about the Ferrows, several people reached out to tell me they knew David before he died. They had no idea about his trans status and recalled a happy older man helping them at his bookstore. While there have been no publications on their trans stories for over eighty years, their contributions to trans community should not be forgotten. Neither should their town's unconditional celebration of their transition. They paved the way for a whole new generation of trans youth, artists, and residents of Great Yarmouth to live their lives to the fullest.

THE OUTLAW: EFFIE SMITH

Effie Smith was always a fighter. After publicly transitioning in the early 1890s, the teenage trans girl had adventures Hollywood could only dream of. Her escapades through the Midwest brought her fame, fortune, and heartbreak in one of the most astonishing trans stories of her era. Escaping from lockup several times, becoming an unwitting accomplice to murder, and finding herself at the center of one of St. Louis's greatest scandals of the nineteenth century, Effie was a true trans rebel whose journey transcended her years. As a girl with nearly as many aliases as arrests, deciphering the full story of her exploits took years of tracking her many identities. This chapter represents the first time her narrative has been published in over 120 years. Yet, the St. Louis outlaw stirred such shocking controversy that her adventures became the subject of national debates.

Effie's life, including her early childhood, was relatively well reported for her time. Born in Kansas in January 1878, Effie came from humble beginnings. Jennie R. Smith raised her daughter in Wichita alongside three brothers. Her father died when she was young. Around 1887, Jennie first noticed Effie's gender-defiant behavior when she began wearing clothing designed for girls. According to her mother, it was also at nine years old that Effie began to "tell her the most preposterous stories."[20] Even Jennie did not know the source of her daughter's fondness for inventing incredible accounts of her own life. "When asked why [she] did it [she] could not tell," Effie's mother explained to reporters. The young girl had a true talent for tall tales and gave herself countless, often conflicting, backstories. What did seem to have some semblance of truth, however, was her self-reports of girlhood. Her gender was one of the only aspects of her identity to not change over time.

The outlaw gained so much notoriety in her teenage years that reporters flocked to those close to her for answers. The media frequently described the slender trans girl with vivid details of her beauty. They often contrasted her pale skin with her dark eyes and jet-black hair, suggesting she carried herself with the confidence of ten women. She was, in fact, so feminine she would be arrested for wearing clothing designed for men at least *three times* in her life.

Effie's penchant for crime and tall tales seemingly transfixed all who heard of her exploits. How did this small trans girl from seemingly humble beginnings become an infamous outlaw? With dozens of accounts of Effie's past, we can piece together a picaresque history through the voices of her friends, family, lovers, enemies, and, of course, Effie herself.

The early years

Effie first found her path toward independence through her work around Wichita. Child labor was considered a cheap and abundant resource at the time.[21] Effie began as a messenger for a Western Union telegraph office before transferring to a publishing company in 1891. Her boss called her an "unusually bright" and hard worker.[22] However, she was underpaid and allegedly stole almost anything not nailed to the floor. On November 12, police discovered the room where thirteen-year-old Effie stashed her goods. The young girl filled her secret headquarters with "bedclothes, furniture, stationary and almost everything else found loose." There were so many stolen items that reporters surmised she had been working with a crew. She gleefully admitted to collaborating with a group of young thieves who stole from nearby offices of wealthy businesses. She allegedly slipped away from her unsupportive mother to spend time with friends in the room when she found a free moment. Each of her associates used an alias, and she claimed not to know their names. The thirteen-year-old spent two months in jail before the case was dismissed on the condition that she would stay out of trouble for two years. She did not.

In early 1892, when Effie turned fourteen, she began working at the Beacon book bindery, where she continued until March 29 of that year.[23] One day the bookkeeper was out sick and did not pay her. Frustrated, Effie returned home and told her mother she was going to a theater. Instead, she fled to Kansas City two hundred miles away and began wearing clothing designed for women full-time. There, she socialized in opium parlors before moving on to Chicago.

Effie had adventures in the Windy City for several months until she was arrested again. She and an accomplice, James Janes, were caught shoplifting in Chicago that November. The two trans girls made national news for their dress and creative heist method: a spring-loaded box that could instantly hide merchandise with the slightest touch. The box had a string tied around it to make it look like a parcel delivery rather than a shoplifting machine. The pair traveled the city with their large two-foot-by-ten-inch cardboard box. They decided to expropriate extravagant clothing teenagers could not typically afford. They first heisted clothing from the Leader, a large department store, before arriving at the massive Mandel Brothers shop. The pair rushed into the towering building and sped toward the women's section. Their hurried entry caught the attention of clerks, who called the police. The two managed to make it out of the store and into their third shop, the Fair. There, officers caught up with the girls and arrested them. Upon opening the shoplifting box, they found a trove of luxurious silk stockings and gorgeous gloves.[24] Officials returned the clothing to the stores. The teens reportedly had planned to pilfer the famous Marshall Field store later but did not get the chance. The following day, the two were tried, convicted, and released after paying a fine of seventy-five dollars. There were no reports if they had successfully used the box before, but the trick nevertheless caught the attention of police—and newspapers around the country. The *Chicago Tribune* called their scheme "one of the cleverest methods of shoplifting that have come to the notice of the police for some time."[25] Somehow, Effie only became craftier from there.

The murder of Edgar Shields

Effie did not appear in papers for several months until she moved to St. Louis that summer. Shortly before her return to national infamy, she claimed to have become an unwilling accomplice to murder. If she is to be believed, the fifteen-year-old traveled to play cards with another trans woman, Meva Monroe, and their friend Edwin Russell on August 8, 1893.[26] They were joined by their victim, nineteen-year-old Edgar Shields. After arriving in an open carriage, the four began gambling and sipping beer. Edwin, Edgar's cousin, sprinkled snuff into Edgar's drink. Effie claimed the cocktail sent him into convulsions (it should be noted that snuff typically does not have this effect and is often chewed). Meva and Edwin informed the landlady that they would bring him to a doctor as they dragged his body into their wagon. The group instead drove to a cabin in rural Missouri. Edwin fastened window weights around Edgar and dropped him in a river with the help of the man who owned the cabin. Effie was horrified but had no power to protest. Edwin threatened to kill her if she spoke up.

Effie claimed Edwin stole a sizable roll of money from Edgar's clothing, a possible motive for the murder. The trio took their carriage back to

St. Louis and arrived early in the morning. Effie stayed quiet for over two years until Edwin and Meva no longer lived in the city.

Allegedly traumatized by the series of events, Effie went on a bender of drinking, arrests, and fights. The fifteen-year-old fled St. Louis and traveled north to Alton, Illinois, the following day. Shortly after arriving, young boys began harassing her on the street. She wore clothing designed for men (which could have kept her safer while traveling). The police took notice and arrested her for "suspicion that [she] was a girl in man's attire."[27] Once Effie proved she was assigned male at birth, she traveled to Upper Alton, where she was arrested *again* for the same reason. Disheartened by the events, she returned to St. Louis.

Effie's month seemed to decline by the hour as police arrested the young woman just one day after her August 11 release from Alton. She yelled at men across the street while wearing a long, stunning white dress on the warm Saturday evening. She may have been soliciting sex work clients or stereotyped for her femininity. Police took notice and decided to question her. "Where are you going?" asked Officer Birmingham of St. Louis.[28] "I'm going to hell," she replied. "Don't you want to come along?" The officer promptly arrested her for "being a disreputable woman." He dragged her to jail, seemingly unamused by her joke. However, the court quickly released her that Monday as they could not identify her. They knew neither of the murder nor her assigned sex.

Four days later, St. Louis police arrested the fifteen-year-old again for frequenting saloons and creating a disturbance. A reporter documenting her trial was struck by her harrowing story, intense beauty, and fashionable style. Neither the judge nor the reporter knew she was trans and sympathized with the incredible tale she spun. The reporter described her case as an "opportunity to reform."[29] One could only imagine the report if the journalist knew about her gender.

As the clerk called up Effie's name, she marched forward to the front of the room. Those present "were surprised to see a tall, well formed girl, bareheaded, with short raven black hair reaching to her shoulders and regal carriage, step from the cage." Her deep eyes swept across the room, and she stopped at the court railing. She sat in her dark, calf-length skirt, complemented her by cloak, and smiled. After hearing the prosecution's testimony, she prepared to lie for her life.

"With the air of a queen," the observant reporter explained, Effie spun a tale "of a peculiar sadness." She claimed her father died when she was five and living in Wichita. She left school at thirteen and worked in a dry goods store. She told the court she became pregnant by her boss, who did not return her love for him. She left Wichita to find anonymity in Kansas City, where she could start anew (this may have been true). She was left without money or a home after having her supposed child in the new town. The young woman eventually found a roommate, who died mere months after becoming her best friend. She claimed to then have fallen in love with a railroad man who took her to St. Louis, where she was arrested at the saloon. She cried to the judge:

> Oh, I am so tired—tired of drink and—and everything, and if I could only quit them all and be a good girl I would do it. But I could not quit drinking as long as I am going around, but if I was locked up in some home until I forgot the taste I know I would quit and never return to this life again. Can't you send me somewhere?

Her tale paralleled her actual journey with some embellishments along the way. The story was so powerful and captivating that the judge immediately believed her. "Well, suppose you are sent to the House of the Good Shepherd," he said. Effie immediately affirmed his proposal: "That's the place I want to go." She walked out of the courtroom with a smile on her face and a flash of her flame-red stockings. The police and court did not have a clue who she was or what she may have known about Edgar Shields's murder earlier that month. But this would not be the last time they heard from Effie Smith.

Escape from the workhouse

Following Edgar's killing and her trial, Effie spent less than a month in the House of the Good Shepherd. She appeared not to realize that the house was run like a slave camp (as contemporary scholars often describe it) until after arriving. Although Good Shepherd institutions were touted as rehabilitative, the people sent there were "sentenced to religious-run, but state-sanctioned, prison systems of slave labor and abuse."[30] Unsurprisingly, no prison could contain the immense weight of Effie's audacity. She climbed over the surrounding twelve-foot wall and bolted from the large building. The young trans girl successfully escaped the institution. However, she soon learned she was unsafe no matter how far she fled.

Tired of the arrests, Effie went on the run. In mid-October 1893, about six weeks after her capture in St. Louis, she fled to Peoria, Illinois. Without shelter or financial means, she contacted the police for help returning to Chicago. Instead of assisting her, they promptly detained the young woman for being unhoused.[31] She spun another elaborate tale in which she was abandoned by a lover in St. Louis before being robbed in Decatur, Illinois. This time, her narrative did not move the court. The judge sentenced her to thirty days in the Peoria workhouse, another forced labor camp where she was made to do laundry and kitchen work with other women. Nine days into her sentence, she climbed the barbed-wire fence and stole a boat to paddle down the nearby river. Pearl Jennings, another detainee, joined her escape. The two decided to travel to Springfield in a desperate flight from their captors.[32]

Superintendent Joe Boardman decided to hunt Effie and Pearl as soon as officials realized the women were missing. He enlisted locals throughout Illinois to help him in the search for the outlaws. Meanwhile, the escapees discarded their boat in Pekin, around ten miles south of Peoria, on October 26. The year 1893 was one of the coldest years in Illinois history, but the pair scavenged food and made their way twenty miles down the chilly railroad tracks on foot. They set up camp in the forest, heated only by their open fire. After a night's rest, the two continued on foot for another frigid twenty miles. Despite the long journey, their troubles had just begun.

Superintendent Boardman figured the pair were headed toward Springfield and boarded a train to Havana, Illinois. To his luck, locals in the nearby town of Kilbourne recognized Effie and Pearl. After nearly fifty miles of travel, local police recaptured the women on October 28. Boardman went to Havana to request assistance but was met by his targets who had already been detained by authorities. It turned out Effie's chic sense of style finally betrayed her: locals tracked her by her distinguished, deep red Mother Hubbard dress and fashionable hat. Boardman locked Effie and Pearl in a caboose overnight while returning to Peoria. On their way back to the workhouse, an attendant gave them women's clothes but she grew suspicious of Effie. She told Boardman, "I believe that 'Effie' Smith is a man!"[33] After an examination, they sent her to a men's labor camp, where she was forced to manufacture brooms.

Effie provided a masculine name to the officials and initially claimed to be eighteen (which meant she would not become a ward of the state). As they discovered her genitalia, they also learned more about Effie's past. One local reporter covering the case explained, "Only fifteen years of age[, she] has had enough experience during the past six months to entitle [her] to be at least thirty." The reporter appeared astounded at Effie's slight build, soprano voice, and beautifully arched eyebrows. The teen explained she had a mother and three brothers back in Wichita, whom she left of her own volition (this part appeared to be true). She then began weaving another captivating tale to the officials. "Ever since I was 9 years of age, I have been in the habit of periodically donning female attire," she said. She claimed a woman from Kansas City asked her to wear women's clothing so they could live together with her husband, as though it were not Effie's own desire. She explained she worked as a waitress and then needed to continue wearing feminine attire to keep her job. Effie claimed her mother did not care for her and would not answer her letters, so it was her only option for living. This tall tale again helped her gain sympathy from officials, and they released her in early November without additional charges.

The girl in boys' clothing

Effie made her way to Davenport, Iowa, following her discharge. She had family in the city and had visited before. She claimed she sold her women's clothing in Springfield while traveling (although there is no evidence of this, and Springfield is in the opposite direction of Davenport from Peoria). She then donned male apparel and journeyed to Davenport. Shortly after arriving, police took notice of the young woman in misfit clothes.

This time, they believed she was a male impersonator. They sent her to jail for her clothing on November 16, 1893, in what must have felt like mere moments after her last confinement. This marked her third arrest for donning clothing designed for men.

A local journalist met her and was sympathetic to her struggle. Believing she was a cis girl, he contended her masculine costume "didn't fit—in fact, the disguise was a pretty poor one."[34] He noted the heavy shoes blistering her feet, adding to her desperation. "In the foolish attempt to make herself look more boy-like the girl has shaved herself a couple times during the past week," he wrote. He even called for donations of women's clothing: "It is hoped that some of the charitably disposed women of Davenport will see that the unfortunate is provided with the clothing she needs."

Effie invented another fascinating story on the spot. She claimed she was originally from Chicago, where her father trained stage actors. She dressed as a boy to seek work and was traveling after a former lover, Claude van Sickle, cheated on her (there is no evidence Claude existed and she never mentioned him again). The two split and she had to live in a dangerous home. She admitted she was arrested in Peoria. However, she claimed it was for driving a wagon too fast. The young woman then explained she managed to escape Peoria for Springfield, where she began donning clothing designed for men after selling her dress for five dollars. She traveled to Davenport to see her aunt, A. P. Alexander (who actually lived there).

The police chief from nearby Rock Island arrived in Davenport to inspect Effie after the reporter's visit. Recognizing the infamous teenage outlaw, the officers realized she told people in Rock Island an entirely different backstory than what she shared in Peoria. One reporter declared, "Effie is one of the most engaging liars that has been harbored by our police station for some time. [She] has no use for the truth where a lie can by any means be made to answer." The authorities decided not to charge Effie and released her the following afternoon. She traveled to Geneseo, Illinois, from which she departed back to St. Louis.

One week later, Eunice Foster wrote a letter to the Davenport newspaper stating she was A. P. Alexander's sister and one of Effie's relatives. Foster explained that Effie had a love of tall tales, that her father was dead, and that she was truly from Wichita. Alexander had moved away from Davenport, leaving Effie without a host. Reflecting on the ordeal, a reporter noted Effie "will long be remembered as the most accomplished female impersonator and all-around prevaricator that the police force has had any experience with."[35] The letter appeared to be genuine.

Nurse Effie

In 1894 Effie stayed out of the public eye and allegedly performed legal work in Chicago. After reading hostile articles in the *Wichita Beacon* about Effie, someone called F. F. Ford (later named by the paper as Frank F. Ford) wrote a mysterious letter about Effie's "reform." On June 10, the individual mailed the upbeat note to the paper. The editors published it three weeks later:

In my professional career I have met with many things that have called me to the hospitals and in one of the largest of these I have of late seen a slender [girl] gliding around ministering to the sick and doing what [she] could to alleviate the sufferings of poor unfortunates. No female nurse is more gentle and patient: no doctor or friend is more cordially welcomed by the inmates than [she]. And yet this self same [girl] has been in prison, has been written up in your papers, and [her] name has been handled with care by more than one.

But now no one needs to be afraid nor ashamed to claim [Effie] Smith as their friend. The saints in heaven have sometimes sinned. The nobi[l]lity in this [girl] will some day live down the misdeeds of the past, and in the character of nurse [she] will be blessed where ever [she] goes. [Her] effeminate voice and gentle manners will some day be remembered as a blessing and the training and good breeding [she] displays now shows but too plainly that [she] was not the natural youth when [she] was a well known character to the police. No one would think that the pale, soft spoken [lass] who comforts not only the sick, but their heart broken mothers and sisters, was once a prisoner . . . in the Peoria jail. One man in the ward who has the reputation of being the most surly, rude, man around, has said when anything was wanted, to let that little muse tell him and it

would be done, . . . for when [she] asked you[, she] asked you as if you
were [her] equal and not a thing. Three times I have seen this [girl], once
in a flashy costume laughing, swearing, smoking cigarettes, but twice I
have seen [her] in a white apron moving hither and thither, now smoothing
a pillow and at now telling some weeping friend to be of good cheer, the
darkest hour is just before dawn. And when I think of such a miraculous
change I truly think "God moves in a mysterious way His wonders to
perform."

    Yours truly,

    F. F. FORD[36]

The letter would appear genuine and decisive at first glance. The *Beacon*
provided no commentary on the note other than reiterating its claims as
fact. However, after exhaustive searching, I found no evidence of a Frank
F. Ford living in Chicago in 1894. It is entirely possible the letter was genuine, and the man simply did not appear in any newspapers, phone books,
census records, or other archival materials from Chicago around that year.
However, it would not be unreasonable to speculate Effie wrote the letter
herself. "Frank" was one of her aliases around that time (although "Frank
F. Ford" does not appear again in her story). Comparing her to a saint—a
far-fetched portrayal—also suggests that the letter was not authentic.

Effie later reported she joined a brothel in Chicago by mid-1894. The
house was not just any regular space: it specialized in bringing together
"female impersonators." The label was generally given to people we would
now call trans women and drag queens. The establishment had ten individuals working under Madame Holland, who protected Effie over the
following months.[37] Effie later told reporters the workers were all about
eighteen, although she was only sixteen when she joined. She did not
mention her duties in the brothel, but teenage sex work was common at
the time, and there was a significant demand for trans women. Holland was
an experienced house leader operating similar establishments for years. In
1894 the madam took Effie to Indianapolis to establish a similar brothel.
However, police swiftly closed their Indiana location so they moved near
Forest Park in St. Louis.

St. Louis's Oscar Wilde

For several months, Effie's name did not grace midwestern newspapers. It would appear as though her successive arrests left an impression on her. Yet considering Effie's temperament, it was only a matter of time until trouble found her.

In 1894 Effie moved back to St. Louis and began seeing Frank Ellsworth Dacons, a local publisher who was notorious for supporting young queer and trans people with his wealth. He was a decade older than Effie and provided her with community and luxuries she would otherwise not have had access to. He edited *The Young Americans*, a monthly periodical for the twelve-to-twenty demographic. He ran the covertly queer publication since 1888 and boasted thirty thousand subscribers. He also claimed it was the official newsletter of the Order of the Coming Men, a secret male society with one hundred thousand members, and the Boys' Correspondence Club of All Nations, which helped connect boys and men from around the world.

Frank's downfall came from the outrage over his many queer friends and lovers. And perhaps, most of all, his end came from one trans teenager: Effie Smith. Frank rented a space in the famous McLean office building on Fourth and Market streets in St. Louis. There, queer and trans people could mingle, drink, and be merry together. The McLean building was particularly convenient for its central downtown location and notable scenery. Workers erected the large five-story structure in 1875 to much fanfare as the building was considered an architectural feat, mixing neoclassical and Victorian styles. Statues lined the windows and a dome towered at the top, jutting over two hundred feet into the air. Frank safeguarded his room by spreading soap over the outer windows, stuffing cloth into the keyhole, and nailing the transom shut. There was no way to peer inside. The press dubbed this innovative space his "den of vice and vileness."[38]

The scandal began on February 25, 1895, when police arrested Effie for carrying a loaded revolver. They forced her into the House of the Good Shepherd again. During this time, Frank attempted to visit her and provide her with food. She was incarcerated until March 6, when she finally arrived for her trial. Her attorney advanced a "novel theory that a revolver in the hands of such a shy, delicate and effemin[a]te [girl] as Smith was in no sense of the word a deadly weapon."[39] The lawyer believed Effie's slim stature was her best defense—she stood at five foot eight and weighed only 125 pounds. Effie also claimed she was about to leave town and was thus entitled to the weapon. The judge did not buy her excuse. He fined Effie twenty-five dollars but stayed the fine. Frank attempted to raise money to keep her out of the workhouse, where she was supposed to be sent back to for an extended stay. Instead, desperate for leniency, Effie told the authorities about Edgar Shields's killing in 1893. It is possible all or none of her account of the murder was true. However, the narrative was plausible enough that officers were forced to investigate. Officials released Effie several days later on account of her so-called "queer confession."[40] Police could ultimately not corroborate or disprove her dramatic tale.

As St. Louis forces dug further into the Shields case, authorities began to receive separate reports of Dacons's activities. Everything came crashing down when one of Frank's femme lovers, Tony Berner, attempted suicide. Police asserted that eighteen-year-old Tony tried to kill themself after receiving an April 18 letter from Frank. The *St. Louis Post-Dispatch* compared the scandalous note to Oscar Wilde's writings to Alfred Douglas. Tony's father quickly passed the letter to the chief of police, who recognized Frank's handwriting from the letters he sent to Effie.

Tony and Effie were on friendly terms and knew one another well. Both were aware they dated Frank at the same time. Like Effie, Tony often wore clothing designed for women. However, they never changed their name or pronouns (why I use they/them for them). According to one reporter, Tony was also quite vain and "strongly addicted to having [themself] photographed."[41] In fact, Tony went to the photographer at least once a week, where they playfully wore costumes of various genders.

Law enforcement brought Effie into court, where she had no issue admitting to having dated Frank. She named two police officers who were also part of Frank's circle, immediately provoking outrage throughout the city. Tony then named four well-known businessmen and numerous male officials who had also had sex with men. The *St. Louis Post-Democrat* released the relatively vanilla letter on May 19, 1895.[42]

MY DEAREST TONY—Why do you not come to see me? I have waited for you, oh, so many evenings, and yet you do not come. Do not treat me this way, my dear Tony. You dear, sweet boy, if you only knew how often I think of you and how much I wish to see you, you would be with me every evening. Can't you come to me, Tony, my dear, and let me have a talk with you? I am so lonesome here all alone all the time, and you are such good company.

Drop me a note and tell me that you will come to me Thursday evening after 9 or on Saturday evening after 8, anyhow. Do not stay away from me any longer than that, or I'll die, sure. Come to me at my office at any time any day, and if I happen to be out leave a note in the door saying when you will return or when and where you will see me.

Now, please don't disappoint me, Tony. Be good to me. Above all other things burn up this letter as soon as you have read it, so as to prevent the possibility of any person but yourself reading it. Will you do this? Be good to yourself, now, Tony, dear boy, and be good to me.

Don't tell any one you know me, excepting merely as a passing acquaintance, and come as soon as possible to see me. I have something to say. I remain your most loving and affectionate friend,

FRANK.

Tony was not the only one to receive a love letter from Frank that month. Effie was arrested for wearing women's attire shortly before Tony's attempted suicide. While searching her, police found another eight-page letter Frank had sent to her. A reporter described it as "the most sickening letter I ever saw or heard of, every sentence teeming with an unnatural love and hinting broadly at things which dispelled all doubts as to the character of the writer." In modern terms, one can only imagine the letter was a sensual joy to read. Effie was sent to the workhouse to pay her twenty-five-dollar fine. The papers never published the long letter.

The Frank Dacons scandal broke on May 18 and immediately found its way into dozens of news outlets across the state. Tony was apparently nonchalant about their "crimes," which were punishable by years in prison if convicted. The teenager nostalgically reflected on their time with Frank in his "school for scandal." Journalists were surprised to find that Tony was far from alone. "No less than a dozen men of the same stripe [. . .] are in a sort of clique, dine together, discuss their unnatural crimes and are companions in sin." In other words, Frank operated a sort of queer and trans social club long before such a thing was supposed to exist.

The press dubbed Frank "St. Louis' Oscar Wilde."[43] Reporters declared him "the high priest and head offender" of the "Oscar Wilde cult." The word *homosexual* did not gain popularity until the early twentieth century, and the main point of reference for those in the 1890s was Oscar Wilde and his sensationalized trial in 1895. Many reporters believed queerness was purely a form of moral depravity. Unlike Wilde, though, Frank escaped prosecution for his many affairs. His trial was held by the press rather than judges.

Intrigued by the scandal, two men from the *Post-Dispatch* attempted to knock down Frank's door in the McLean building. Frank finally let them speak to him after they began charging at the entryway. He denied everything, despite the evidence and love letters to Effie and Tony. Frank claimed Tony sought revenge after the editor learned of incriminating information about the teenager. While explaining this to reporters, a banker stood in Frank's room, arguing for his loan back after learning Frank was queer. Frank fled the city that same evening, leaving a letter behind for Effie.

> My Dear [Effie]—I am going to leave for parts unknown. It is the best thing to do under the circumstances, don't you think so?
> My life is a living hell * * * but keep a stiff upper lip, dear, I will be with you soon. At least I will write. Your Little Queen,
> Frankie

The officers Effie named were marched to court for a McCarthyite hearing within twenty-four hours of the scandal breaking. They were brought before a grand jury and would face charges if found guilty. This, of course, brings up ethical questions about outing. Was it right for Effie to out these policemen? The officers were on the same force that terrorized queer and trans people of the era. Would sending them to prison make the world a safer place?

The *St. Louis Post-Dispatch* predicted at least one of the officers would be fired as he was already on suspension for unreported reasons (perhaps confirming Effie and Tony's accounts).[44]

Frank was declared missing the next day. A local reporter dug through the absent editor's apartment. In the mess, he found news clippings about hypnotism, counterfeiting, and "female impersonators." He also had letters from Effie:

MY "DEAR EDITOR"—What is the nature of my offense? Another whole week and I did not hear a word. I think you are offended, dear. Are you not? I wish I could see you. * * * Otto Neusel, of whom I have spoken, and who called on you first, did another errand for me. He has left letters in the quarry for me from some of my friends who didn't dare to openly acknowledge their relation to me, but who are friends nevertheless. They have kept me posted concerning certain matters.

I cannot remain in St. Louis. I will return to my old friends and I cannot let them know I regard you as a friend, but I will write to you. Don't worry about me. You say you can't live without me. You must try. * * * The day I am released I want you to come to Mrs. Holland's and I will tell you all about my intentions. I will get out on the 17th of May. I wish you would get my articles at Barnum's Hotel. I have a great female attire there. Pay my bill and get it. I get so tired of trying to exist sometimes.

I had thought to conduct myself as a civilized human being for a year, and if at the end of that time I was satisfied that I could behave myself, I would go home to my mother. Frank, I wish sometimes I were dead. You know what kind of a family and home I gave up. I sold my home and family for notoriety, a fancy wardrobe and "R." and now that I want to trade back again I find it impossible.

Say, Frank, after what the papers have said the people think we are anything but on friendly terms. It is a good thing for us. Now, get my traps and meet me, dear.

It is unclear if Frank ever picked up Effie's clothing from her swanky hotel. Barnum was the finest lodging in Missouri then, and it is plausible he could have been caught there. He fled far away to Michigan, presumably to avoid arrest.

As the scandal snowballed, Effie made it known she was not pleased with Tony Berner for outing Frank. "Why that little idiot," she said, "the sooner [they] kills [themself] the better, and if [they] were locked in a cell with me I would help [them] do it."[45] She also continued to wedge herself against Frank despite her letter being published days earlier claiming the animosity between the two was a front to their benefit. "Why[,] that man is not in our class at all," she told the *Post-Dispatch*. "We never recognized him except as a tool. Of course, when we came here we were strangers, and we had to have some one to introduce us. We used Dacons for that purpose." The reporter did not question her assertion and placed the blame on Frank. The court eventually sent Effie to the workhouse for three months, although her exact charges were never published. She was released on September 7, 1895, a day before police sent John Berger (subject of the chapter "The Florist") to the same holding cell that they detained Effie in.[46]

Frank hid for over a year before landing in Van Buren County, Michigan, that October. There, he met his family, with whom he had lost touch.[47] His father died from pneumonia weeks before he arrived, so he returned to pay his respects. Earlier, Frank had employed the infamous Pinkerton detective agency to find his family, spending hundreds of dollars to track them down. He learned he had three siblings he did not know about. He also discovered his mother, whom he believed to be deceased, was still alive. While it was exciting to find his family, the scandal ruined the young editor's career. Frank stayed out of the public eye for the rest of his life.[48]

Mexico, Missouri

Although Effie did not tell Frank where she was going in the letter, we know the young woman traveled to Mexico, Missouri, after her release. The seventeen-year-old hid her trans status from the town for several months. She changed her name to Inez Hoyt, occasionally going by Inez Fate. Effie turned up in newspapers again five months later, on October 22, 1895, for her next jail stint. The young woman allegedly stole a gold watch and clothing from her landlord, Hannah Wilson. She spent the following two months in a women's jail. While awaiting the grand jury, the St. Louis police heard of her incarceration and thought she may be connected to an unrelated murder. Detective Gocking, who knew Effie, arrived in early January.[49]

"Hello, Effie!" the detective smirked, calling her by her chosen name.

"How do you do, Gocking?" Effie responded.

Mexico's sheriff interrupted the two, "Do you know her?"

"I rather guess I do," the detective replied. He turned back to Effie. "Well, Effie, old boy, how are you?"

"Oh, pretty well," she joked. "How did you know me?" Gocking did not reply. Instead, he took the sheriff aside and informed him that Effie had been assigned male at birth. The sheriff refused to believe Gocking. He needed more convincing. Effie waited in her cell wearing a brazenly feminine silk dress, diamond earrings, and fancy rings while the two sheriffs debated her sex.

Furious at Effie's attire, Gocking demanded the sheriff put Effie into men's clothes. The sheriff conceded and forced her into a male prison that same day. She was sent to a large cell with men, "several of whom had fallen violently in love with [her]," according to one report.[50]

By the end of the month, officials dragged Effie to Jefferson City to face trial. On January 20, 1895, the judge sentenced her to two years in the Workhouse, St. Louis's most notorious labor camp. For the first time in her life, she spent over a year behind bars. There, Effie was forced to work hard labor alongside cis men from all walks of life. The detainees often worked for ten hours a day in manacles as either slaves or indentured debtors (depending on their sentence). The people of the St. Louis penitentiary typically spent their days splitting rocks in a quarry off the Mississippi River. The city used their unpaid labor to pave its roads. St. Louis did not end this workhouse system, which remained largely unchanged for nearly 180 years, until 2021, when activists won their battle to shutter the jail.[51]

The state released Effie under the "three-fourths" law (most offenders had to serve only three-quarters of their sentence).[52] She left the jail on July 29, 1897, ten days after her minimum sentence. There are no reports on her time at the Workhouse, although the conditions were unanimously brutal to prisoners. There were few records of Effie after her release.

The later early years

Effie kept to herself more than ever following her departure from the Work-house. Here, Effie's story seems to end. It is possible she moved or changed her name again. Her various aliases vanished from St. Louis's public records. Someone going by Effie's deadname and matching her age and description stole thousands of dollars' worth of chickens in Missouri in 1900. Several other individuals with her aliases were outlaws, thieves, and bandits of various stripes. I could not confirm that any of them was the notorious trans girl.

Effie Smith's story teeters between tragedy and adventure, a parable of familial opposition to trans identity. Her exploits—and her struggles—were exciting enough for several lifetimes. If nothing else, her frequent arrests, houselessness, and persecution show us what happens when families do not support trans kids. Even with these hardships, she still found humor and joy in her life. Whether going by Effie, F. E., Inez, or any other name, she mastered the art of queer escapade like no other.

THE SINGER: MASOUD EL AMARATLY

When I first heard Masoud El Amaratly sing, I knew there had to be a story behind such an immaculate, melancholic voice. First inscribed into the grooves of a phonograph record in 1925, Masoud's songs are among the earliest known recordings of a trans person. Masoud El Amaratly was a *mustarjil* (an Arabic term meaning "becoming man").[53] Encouraged by the public's wide acceptance of him and his music, he became one of Iraq's greatest folk singers. His story marks a hidden yet transformative part of West Asian trans history. Between his supportive upbringing, international fame, and shocking 1944 murder, Masoud El Amaratly's life reveals a history much more supportive than the conservative stereotypes of Iraq.

Masoud was born in or around 1897 in Al-Kahla of the Al-Muntafiq emirate in the Ottoman Empire, today's southern Iraqi marshlands.[54] He was part of an Ahwari farming community near the Tigris River, where he herded livestock on the sheik's farm. He was a member of the Shammar, the most populous tribe in modern Iraq. His mother, Moula Saad, cared for his family while his father farmed. From a young age, Masoud enjoyed singing, which he developed and honed through the boredom and toil of farmwork.[55] Even as a child, he became locally famous for his voice. He would sing all night into the morning as spectators celebrated his informal performances. With glossy brown hair and dark skin, the young farm boy would soon garner vast audiences to witness his unmistakable talent.

There are conflicting reports of exactly when Masoud transitioned, with some noting as young as five or six while others suggesting as old as eighteen or nineteen—sometime in the 1900s or 1910s. There are some clues as to which story is true. Professor Salman Kayoush at Baghdad University, one of the few contemporary scholars studying Masoud, believes that Masoud began his transition as a young child but only began living full-time as a man/mustarjil in his late teens. Transition was not an all-or-nothing decision for Masoud, akin to transition in the West today.[56]

Mustarjils like Masoud had lives parallel to trans men. They were assigned female at birth and lived as men. In the patriarchal Ahwari society, male children were more celebrated and respected than girls, meaning mustarjil's transition elevated their social status. However, it was not only patriarchy that led to acceptance but also respect for the gendered desires of the individuals. Some mustarjil married men, while most married women. Some did not marry at all. Regardless, their societies considered their genders legitimate and respectable.

English writer Wilfred Thesiger, having lived in Iraq in the early 1950s, was among the first to bring the concept of mustarjil to the Western world. In his prominent 1964 ethnographic book *The Marsh Arabs*, he recounts speaking with another mustarjil near Masoud's hometown. His local informant, Amara bin Thuqub, clarified that mustarjil were common in the region.

"A mustarjil is born a woman," Amara explained. "She cannot help that; but she has the heart of a man, so she lives like a man."

"Do men accept her?"

"Certainly. We eat with her and she may sit in the *mudhif*. When she dies, we fire off our rifles to honour her. We never do that for a woman. In Majid's village there is one who fought bravely in the war against Haji Sulaiman."[57]

Thesiger met many other mustarjil over the years, including a twelve-year-old. He also met people we may now understand as trans women. One even requested Thesiger amputate her penis ("cut this off and turn me into a proper woman"). Like the mustarjil, she was accepted by her community and worked with other women. Amara again expressed sympathy, "Could they not do it for [her] in Basra? Except for that, [she] really is a woman, poor thing."[58] These gender roles did not exactly align with contemporary notions of trans men and women but offer striking parallels to today's trans community.

The most popular account of Masoud's transition suggests it happened out of desperation. Sheik Mohammed bin Aribi's wife, Fatna, allegedly wanted to marry Masoud to one of her male servants. She feared her son, Allawi, dishonored the family by spending too much time with the poor farm boy—Allawi and Masoud had grown close.[59] Masoud ran away instead of being misgendered and married to a man. He first traveled to his mother in the nearby town of Majar al-Kabir. There, Masoud's voice attracted the attention of Sheik Khazaal bin Faleh al-Sayhud. Al-Sayhud put Masoud under his protection until the sheik was banished for partying too late into the night. Masoud spent a short time playing to local audiences before returning to his hometown.

Iraqi journalist Amer Badr Hassoun attributes some of Masoud's solemn lyrics to these stories of fear and loss associated with his rural hometown. Hassoun uses Masoud's song "Ya Sakina" ("Oh Sakina") as an example. Masoud's lyrics reminisce about his lost friendship with Allawi.

I wished from God, to be with you
My friend, we face everything, to be with you
Let's endure the hatred, to be with you
I swear by the dawn and those who forgot me
After "Allawi" Mohammed, they forgot me
I cry over the separation, they forgot me
After his eyes, sadness is my duty[60]

Losing Allawi was far from Masoud's only childhood trauma. In 1916, around age eighteen, the young man returned to herding the sheik's sheep.

One day, two men decided to harass Masoud while he was singing to the herd. The teenage trans boy defended himself, singlehandedly beating the men. He tied them up and dragged them by the rope to the sheik's home. Tired of being misgendered, he emphasized that he was a man and had to be treated as such.[61] The men apologized and claimed Masoud's entrancing voice seduced them. The townspeople then celebrated Masoud for his bravery. The young man lived as his gender thereafter.

The Ottoman Empire's defeat in World War I led to great upheaval in Iraqi life. Britain began occupying Iraq shortly after the beginning of the war.[62] European officials proposed annexing Iraq's territory as a British or Indian colony. However, the Iraqi Revolt of 1920, in which over one hundred thousand protesters around the country took part, proved it would be too difficult to fully subsume Iraq into another territory. Instead, British politicians established Mandatory Iraq in 1921. They installed King Faisal I, who permitted Britain to seize some of the nation's land and resources. Over seven million people died in West Asia during the war and resulting famine. Masoud's land would never be the same. Unsurprisingly, Abudiya poetry (one of Masoud's styles from this time) is often compared to the blues.[63] Masoud also spearheaded *rifi* (rural) music, a genre parallel to folk or soul, which similarly developed from violence and struggle. After witnessing war, poverty, death, and grief, Masoud sang with the power of the thousands of Ahwari who came before him.

Escape to Baghdad

In 1925 music agent Isa Ibn Huwaila scoured the southern Iraqi countryside to find a singer to take to Baghdad with him. Predictably, he quickly located Masoud and brought him to the city for his first recordings. At this point, Masoud did not know how to read or write but played music from the heart.[64]

Masoud created his album on the British His Master's Voice label (now known as HMV).[65] His songs were recorded onto gramophone (phonograph) shellac discs at the beginning of the electric recording age.[66] He was paid thirty-two Indian rupees for his first four songs ($11.60 at the time, equivalent to $206 in 2024). His label distributed the music nationally and it grew to such high demand that the record company called him back to raise his per-song fee from eight rupees to 150, a lavish sum at the time.[67] Many of his songs had allusions to his gender identity, such as "The Sacrifice of the Cloak." Others would reference friends and family ("Oh Sakina"). The record company brought him back to the studio for a new album no fewer than five times between 1926 and 1934.

Masoud sang in restaurants and cafés, quickly gaining notoriety. According to Amer Badr Hassoun, his "grief fueled [his] singing talent and accelerated [his] poetic maturity."[68] Although he was young in the 1920s, elders recognized many of his traditional songs from their home territories. He combined classic instruments with the haunting echoes of his voice and creative lyrics. As he progressed in his career, he recorded dozens of tracks, many of which survive today.

Masoud married a maid named Ashnina in his youth. The exact year is not known as such records were lost or destroyed during the various wars and occupations of Iraq. Masoud quickly began singing live to home listeners when the first radio station in Iraq, Radio Baghdad, launched in 1936. Masoud notably performed with several Jewish musicians. Muslim-Jewish tensions were not exacerbated until the British ceded Palestinian Land to European Jews in 1948, four years after Masoud's death.

In the 1930s and 1940s, Masoud ventured throughout West Asia. From the late 1930s and early 1940s, he traveled from Aleppo, Syria, to Lebanon. He recorded at least two more albums during his journeys and played with many local musicians.

Wife and death

After leaving Ashnina, Masoud married Kamila. This choice turned into a grave mistake. Masoud died on October 9, 1944, allegedly from a dinner Kamila poisoned. A later rumor circulated that Kamila killed him because she found out he was trans.[69] Another legend claims he died of pulmonary tuberculosis. However, the actual cause was most likely that Kamila killed him for his money, which Masoud's family repeatedly alleged. Masoud's brother Sa'id was adamant that Kamila poisoned him. "Mr. Hamad Al-Alaq, the musician who accompanied Masoud and composed some of his songs, recalled that Masoud died from poisoned food at the last party he attended. It was Masoud's brother Sa'id who accused Kamila (Masoud's wife) out of greed for his brother's belongings, a gold necklace, and 40 dinars. He filed a complaint with the court, and Kamila was arrested. She was imprisoned for nine months after the investigation," Masoud's friend and brother-in-law, singer Kariri Al-Salman, agreed with Sa'id's story.[70]

Masoud's fashion and musical styles did not change much as he aged. One of his family members described him in his final years as "dark-skinned, very dark, with a wrinkled face, a notch in one of his nostrils, always wearing a headband with a white scarf underneath."[71] His music likewise remained dedicated to the marshes of his homeland.

Masoud is still relatively well-known in Iraq. The famed southern Iraqi singer Saadoun Jaber portrayed him on a short television special in 1996.[72] More recently, Professor Salman Kayoush brought Masoud's music onto UTV, one of Iraq's most popular television channels. The host described Masoud's singing as "a world of sadness," while Salman explained his gender identity: "He is Masoud and loved by the community. In return for his service to Allah, we call him Masoud."[73] Salman argues that the British stole so many documents from Iraq that it is possible we will learn more about Masoud when they are returned.

THE SHOEMAKER: RAY LEONARD

Ray Leonard was born on Valentine's Day 1849 in rural Maine to Joseph Leonard, thirty-eight, and Irish immigrant Catharine "Rowie" Leonard, eighteen. He was the oldest of eight siblings and grew up extremely close to his family. The young trans man moved around the East Coast over his early years, making a living from the family shoe store. When Ray turned thirteen, he transitioned with the enthusiastic support of his parents and siblings. *They immediately accepted him.* It was not clear if the support was rooted in their happiness for Ray's contentment as a boy or traditional misogyny. Male children came with increased social standing and job opportunities, so either reason (or both) was possible. Regardless, he did not wear women's attire again for decades.[74]

Ray spent his early years moving between Philadelphia and Maine. As his siblings grew older, they began to relocate throughout the states. Ray realized he would become the man of the house and would one day take over his father's business. He then joined his father Joseph's shoemaking store, where he would work for the rest of his life.

The entire family looked up to Ray's father. The former sailor supported their large household with his shoe shop. Many newspapers wrote glowing reviews of the store, complimenting Joseph and Ray's friendliness and craftsmanship. A local newspaper even remarked that the father and son "bore a remarkable resemblance." Both were upstanding community members and had many friends wherever they lived.

In 1885 the family decided they would try their luck in Nevada. Ray and his parents relocated to the state together. There is not much documentation from their time in the Southwest, but government records show that Ray's mother died in 1886. He and his father moved to Oregon three years later. The newly admitted state offered white men many opportunities due to the US government's policies excluding Black communities and displacing Native Americans (for more on Indigenous trans experiences in Oregon, see the chapter on Muksamse'lapli).

Local Oregon newspapers celebrated the opening of Joseph Leonard & Son, their shoe shop.[75] The pair quickly became beloved community members in their town of Lebanon. Shortly after arriving, Ray met his first reported love.[76] He and another man allegedly competed for her affection. At one point, as local legend has it, their rivalry almost led to a duel. Ray briefly dated the woman before losing interest.

Joseph died in 1894 at age eighty-three. Devastated, Ray would not let the coroner touch his father's body until he prepared it for burial.[77] After the funeral, townspeople often found Ray at the cemetery, reminiscing next to his father's headstone. He did not quit shoemaking and continued to grow their store, eventually changing his business name to "Ray Leonard, Shoemaker," as he came to accept his father's passing.

Ray lived a relatively typical life over the following years. He was in a horse and buggy accident in 1902.[78] He expanded his shop several times. He went hunting and fishing with other men in the town. He laughed with his friends over stories of the Old West during their evening gatherings. His doctor appeared to be the only one to know his trans status, which he helped Ray hide from the public for over two decades. But, as a rather introverted man, Ray still spent most of his time inside, working away. His bedroom was in the back of his shop, and he remained there except for meals.[79]

Ray became more religious as he aged. He decided to join the Christian Science Church, which focused on the healing element of religion. He often joked with local townspeople, "Christian Science is all right when I'm well, but it ain't worth a damn when I'm sick."[80] He saw no contradiction between his religion and his gender.

In 1911 everything changed. The sixty-two-year-old became quite ill. He complained of headaches and often had to close his shop early. The spiritual healing did nothing to ease his pain. On the night of September 25, locals found Ray wandering around town while disoriented. His concerned neighbors detained the aging man and a local judge assigned him to an asylum.

It was customary to bathe each patient as they came in. He protested that he had just bathed, but it was a required part of treatment. His attendant, Mr. P. H. Grub, immediately realized Ray was trans after he undressed. The hospital worker ran to the institution's superintendent and doctor to out him to the staff. The workers sent Ray to the female ward against his protests.

The small town of Lebanon was swiftly caught in a national scandal. Headlines from small, local papers to the *Los Angeles Times* paraded Ray's name as though he had killed someone. Until then, nobody suspected Ray was trans: he had an angular face, balding head, and hairy chin. The surprise rocked the town.

Reporters were curious about the man. A paper from Salem, Oregon, described him at length: "[He] resembles a man in many respects. [He] has a scant beard, [his] features are masculine, so are [his] manners, and [his] language. [His] conduct, say the physicians, is clean, and there is nothing to indicate that [he] is in any way degenerate. [He] is suffering from a mental impairment caused by the secluded life [he] has led."[81] That is, doctors blamed Ray's declining mental health on his choice to isolate himself. It is unclear if he decided to become sequestered to protect his identity or for another reason.

Ray's life made a fascinating story to readers. He transitioned forty-nine years earlier and was happily living as a man. While this may be a common experience today, there were very few people at the time who so publicly transgressed gender. Newspapers continued printing Ray's story and the famous frontier doctor Mary Canaga Rowland became acquainted with the new celebrity in town. Ray would plead with Mary to recognize his gender, "Look at me, Dr. Rowland, do you think I have one feminine feature?"[82] The doctor later confessed, "I had to admit that [he] certainly looked like a man."

Although Ray was "violently opposed to entering the woman's ward," he arrived in the unit on September 27, 1911.[83] His supposed caretakers then dragged him to an asylum in Salem, where his health improved. He returned to Lebanon, but authorities forced him to wear clothing designed for women. He quickly petitioned the court to continue wearing clothes that he felt comfortable in, although nothing came of the case. He would conceal pants under his dresses despite the risk of arrest. Sympathetic to the elder man, articles did not mention residents reporting his minor transgressions to the authorities.[84]

He spent the following decade like any other: working in his shoe shop and spending time with the other men in town. His old customers returned as soon as it reopened, although a few men avoided it for a time. Some of Ray's neighbors would tease his former lover by yelling into her ear trumpet that Ray was a woman. "Why the old !@#*!" she would jokingly retort.[85] Ray's small business thrived even after he was outed. Like his parents, his community supported him. Many confidently refused to misgender him. In 1917 Ray moved his work into the former Lebanon public library building to grow his shoemaking business even more.[86]

Ray's final census record in 1920 shows that he continued to describe his gender as male, even after being outed.[87] He was dedicated to his work until he died from kidney disease on January 13, 1921, at age seventy-three. His physician marked his death certificate as male, even with the whole town aware of his gendered past. The Oregon State records list him as female, however. He was buried next to his father in Lebanon, where they rest side-by-side to this day.[88]

THE LOVER: MABEL STANLEY

How many men does it take to capture a young trans woman in 1888? Evidently, the answer is twenty-six. Mabel Stanley, a marvelously mischievous trans girl, was among the many trans youth supported by their families in the nineteenth century. After transitioning around the age of nine, she was able to live openly as a woman for nearly two decades before the law caught up with her.

Mabel was born in Boston on April 9, 1861, to George Warren Norcross and Maria Estella Dudley.[89] Her early life was rather typical for a poor downtown Bostonian in the 1860s. She had one sibling, George Russell, born around 1868 when she was six. Her small family was industrious but economically precarious. Her father worked as a teamster while her mother stayed at home to raise their children.

Mabel reported knowing she was trans at an incredibly young age. She never desired clothing designed for boys as a child. However, her parents first forced her into them when she was about seven or eight. Early childhood clothing was predominantly gender-neutral in the mid-nineteenth century. Both young boys and girls were adorned in dresses. Mabel distinctly remembered being compelled to don boy's attire after resisting it for many years. The act of transitioning a young boy to traditional boy's clothes, known as breeching, was seen as an exciting rite of passage toward manhood in the Western world. Mabel, on the other hand, understood it as an unacceptable infringement on her girlhood.[90]

Mabel's family sent her to live with the Cordin family in South Boston around 1871. During this time with her extended family, she transitioned and was only known as a girl. She took up a new name, and her deadname disappeared from government records.

The blossoming young woman clearly developed a strong desire for love. At age seventeen, she was courted by a man named Leon King.[91] She loved the man dearly, and he had significantly changed her life. She moved out and married him in a ceremony in Boston. She claimed King did not discover her assigned sex until after they were married. Though, this is often an excuse given by trans people at the time to protect those around them. They stayed together for three years before separating. The *Boston Globe* reported her marriage "created a stir" after she was outed, although it did not go into detail.[92]

As a five-foot-three trans girl with delicate features, Mabel remained stealth through the 1870s. Records show her father died from pneumonia in nearby Watertown in 1879. It is unclear if they were still in touch after years of living apart.

The young woman lived peacefully for over fifteen years, taking up housework—and theft—for income. It is not clear exactly where or how she lived. Perhaps she wanted it this way: her public anonymity made her less likely to be caught or harassed. A person going by Mabel Stanley was arrested for "night walking" in 1884.[93] Another Mabel Stanley was held on a two-hundred-dollar bond for "being idle and disorderly" in 1885. A newspaper advertised a clairvoyant with the same name a month later. However, it is uncertain if any or all of these three reports concern the same Mabel Stanley who transitioned fourteen years prior. The Boston courts could not locate these archival records, so we may never know if these reports are about the same woman.

Finally, our Mabel was arrested for pickpocketing near Boston in April 1887. It was there that officials revealed her assigned sex to the newspapers, leading to a series of increasingly public brushes with the law. First, the young woman fled to Rhode Island, allegedly to escape the charges. With her thick black hair twisted into a French roll, Mabel took up work as a domestic servant in Auburn (now a neighborhood in Providence). She did housework and cooking so she could live independently over the following months.

Mabel's undoing began with what may have been a simple prank. The twenty-seven-year-old woman would hide behind dark bushes at night and pop out, scaring women and children passing by. It is unclear if she knew these individuals. She reportedly also "accosted men in a loose nature."[94]

However, the news articles did not provide details of these escapades. It is possible she was soliciting sex buyers or simply yelling at or flirting with them. Nineteenth-century newspapers used the word *accosted* as a euphemism for soliciting but also to describe harassment, self-defense, and "disturbing the peace." Any woman accused of flirting could be prosecuted for it. At the time, police had even freer rein on arresting people than they do today.

Mabel's flirtatious disposition ultimately led to her downfall. On a September afternoon in 1888, she approached a man named Kimmerman to explain her interest in him. She "admitted to him in very bashful tones that she had been smitten with him and would like to become better acquainted." The two agreed to a walking date in Auburn the following night. Kimmerman, suspecting she may be the person scaring the women, hatched a plan to capture her. They would meet at Fenner Pond (near today's Roger Williams Park). Kimmerman's two friends would then grab her there and take her to authorities. However, the friends were too loud when it came time for her capture. She caught them running toward her, threw off her heels, and fled into the night.

Mabel escaped the men but became a topic of heated discussion in the neighborhood. Women and children were reportedly scared to leave their houses after sunset. Local officials realized they would need to capture her to have the townspeople feel safe once again, so Sheriff Viall contacted another man who knew Mabel and had him secure a date with her. This morally dubious technique would later be known as a "honeytrap." For the time, it was an innovative (albeit sinister) strategy to catch a woman. Viall lined up twenty-five men on the road out of town to stop her.

At 10 p.m., Mabel appeared, and the sheriff immediately grabbed her. She struggled and shrieked but could not break free of his grip. The sheriff momentarily "felt he was a brute." A pang of guilt came over him for overpowering the tiny woman. He lessened his grip on her throat, and she nearly escaped. However, two other men seized her and paraded her back to her home. Far from the "deceptive trans woman" archetype that we often see in media, it was the cisgender men who tricked the trans woman into harm's way.

For unknown reasons, she divulged that she was assigned male at birth. Her captors were shocked at her assigned sex. Mabel wept into her brown dress and overskirt. She begged for release, claiming she simply dressed that way as she preferred feminine work. She lied to the authorities and asserted she had only worn dresses since July of that year (a statement she would later contradict in court).

Despite her pleas, the police dragged her to jail in Olneyville. She was arraigned near midnight. The following day, authorities took her to the Eighth District Court. She pleaded guilty to charges of "being a lewd and wanton person in speech and behavior." She was sentenced to three years in a state workhouse and fined $7.20 on September 27, 1888. Her arrest record simply noted her offense as "lewd, wanton, & lascivious." She was ultimately persecuted for being a sexually free trans woman. That is, authorities charged her for her flirtations with men. Whether she engaged in sex work or not, her longing to be wanted clearly threatened the moralizing public and led to her arrest. She was captured for her capacity to love—her desire for the men who tricked her.

There was a small but notable commotion about Mabel's gender. Even reporters remarked that her figure "was that of a woman in every respect." Her story spread in newspapers across states from Pennsylvania to Alabama. After her arrest, however, she stayed far away from publicity.

According to the Rhode Island State Institutional Records, she departed the workhouse on September 22, 1890, a year before her official release date.[95] Her chosen name would not appear in any paper again. Now almost thirty, Mabel moved back to Boston, where she lived with her mother and brother. She joined her mother's work as a laundress while her brother supplemented their income by posting advertisements for businesses around the city. The family moved throughout the city over the following years. In 1897 her brother died from alcohol poisoning, leaving the family with even less income.[96]

Mabel lived many of her later years on Waltham Street in the South End of Boston, continuing her laundry work. Her mother died from myocarditis in 1916 at age eighty-two, and Mabel moved near Bunker Hill to become a decorator.[97] There are no reports or government records available for Mabel after 1917. She may have moved, died, or taken up a new name. While official reports of her story end here, her full narrative of longing for love should never be forgotten.

THE GIRL BANDIT: EMMA HEINRICH

The police never knew what to do with fourteen-year-old Emma Heinrich, dubbed "The Girl Bandit of Passaic County." In 1906 New Jersey officials fiercely debated whether to send the thieving trans teen to jail, to a youth home, or back to her family.[98] Unsure about their course of action, the authorities took to the press to get answers. But Emma Heinrich's story reveals much more than an accomplished trans girl bandit. She was a migrant and used her crimes to build community. She embraced her "tomboy" label as a trans girl who refused social or legal norms. Emma's narrative shows us how how nineteenth-century trans girls could explore their identities between, beyond, and before gender.

Emma was born in February 1891 in Germany to Charles Heinrich.[99] Her father worked as a blacksmith, while her older sister cared for her and her brothers, Charles and Richard. She immigrated to suburban New Jersey around 1899, residing in a German immigrant quarter called Plauderville.[100] She claimed to have transitioned as a young child and always had the name Emma, although no records from her early childhood appear to exist. Journalists reported that she went to school in both Passaic and Garfield in Bergen County.[101] Her mother died when she was young, but her father and siblings were always supportive of her gender identity and expression. They identified her as "Emma" on her census forms and did not misgender her in the press. Up to her teenage years, Emma refused to define herself by gender, loving hats adorned with flowers and jackets designed for boys. Her ambivalence toward her gender presentation helped her command respect while affirming her status as a girl.

Newspapers did not report precisely when Emma formed her gang. However, we know she attracted the interest of several boys in the neighborhood during her early teenage years. With a friendly freckled face and radiant red hair tied up with a ribbon, the young bandit attracted the attention of many boys around her.

Emma's first named accomplices were John Laksock, eleven, and John Doolick, fourteen. Apparently, her glare was so powerful that John Doolick "lost all will power when she cast her stern eyes upon him."[102] A local newspaper described her as the "Female Fagin," an antagonist from Charles Dickens's *Oliver Twist* who teaches children to live lives of crime. She would call up the boys on a whim and entice them into committing break-ins with her.

Late on October 31, 1905, Emma and her gang began a long string of robberies. They stole cigars, "great quantities" of tobacco, and five gold rings from a store (worth around $1,785 in 2024).[103] Halloween night was widely celebrated in Passaic, and the holiday events provided the perfect cover for their heist to go undetected. The following evening, the gang stole alcohol, tobacco, and other valuables from a saloon. The trio used a skylight to enter and plunder the bar. One estimate put their loot at an astonishing fifty bottles of alcohol, which they resold to a local man.

The "tomboy burglar"

The police first caught Emma on November 13, 1905. She stole a coat worth $4.50 ($161 in 2024) from a clothing store in Passaic in October and was later spotted in it by an officer, who arrested her while she held a basket containing a large beefsteak. She carried the steak with her to the county jail and admitted she knew the coat was stolen but swore she was not the one who committed the theft. Her uncle paid for the coat and the judge dismissed the case. However, police and officials remained curious about her "boyish nature."[104] Her father explained, "She is a Tom boy [. . .] she invariably associates with boys and leads a reckless sort of existence." This seemed to satisfy the officials, who let her go. She immediately returned to stealing.

Police were unaware that the Halloween robberies were connected until the early morning of November 21, 1905.[105] Emma's gang sneaked into a grocery store through an unlocked window above the back door. They nearly escaped, but Officer Michael Dorany heard muffled voices through the walls at 2 a.m. Knowing the store owners were gone, he approached the building and saw Emma and John Laksock in the act. The policeman hid behind the front door until they left the shop. He swiftly arrested the pair and searched their bodies. They held $4.35 from the till along with several other small items. John Doolick had fled the scene earlier, but Emma and the other John implicated him in the robbery. All three were interrogated so officers could understand how they accomplished such a successful heist.

While she was in holding, Laksock and Doolick turned against Emma and claimed she was the mastermind behind the scheme. They admitted to having plundered many stores in the area by using their small bodies to enter locked buildings. While searching their homes, the police seized the rings they stole on Halloween. The judge held the three without bail, and they became a small media spectacle. It was unusual for such young individuals to be involved in complicated break-ins—and for a girl to lead a gang. The press then dubbed Emma the "tomboy burglar," and she sat in jail for nearly a month.[106]

Emma's case finally reached juvenile court on December 14. She was only fourteen and considered not entirely liable for her many crimes. However, Charles Heinrich attested that she was persistent in her behaviors and should be sent to an institution.[107] After listening to testimony, the callous Judge Scott sent John Laksock to the New Jersey State Reform School for Boys in Jamesburg. John Doolick was deemed too young to understand his offenses and was placed on probation with his parents. The judge sent Emma to the notorious State Home for Girls in Trenton. Emma burst into tears when hearing her sentencing, pleading for mercy. Judge Scott did not yield. "You are the worst girl I ever saw," he scolded during sentencing.[108]

The press continued to debate Emma's girlhood. One journalist described the fourteen-year-old as "muscular as any boy her size and equally masculine in her language."[109] She allegedly boxed and pitched baseball. The reporter guessed this was a way for her to command respect from the boys of her gang. She continued to enjoy both men's and women's fashions, which did not help with the questioning. However, when the sentencing came, a reporter claimed, "She lost her masculine aspect and pleaded with the judge to let her go." The judge refused.

The State Home for Girls was infamous for its brutality on residents. It is unclear if Emma knew its reputation, but the *New York Times* ran an article three years later detailing the institution's horrific abuses. The girls were whipped with leather as punishment. Some were put in a tiny windowless room known as "the 'dark' dungeon," for days at a time.[110] The administration persistently beat and berated the residents. During Emma's stay, she allegedly "had broken every rule of the institution."[111] Her personal experiences in the home were not documented but were undoubtedly abusive.

Emma on trial

With the new year came new information. On January 1, 1906, a doctor declared that the "bold girl" was assigned male at birth.[112] It is unclear exactly how Emma was exposed, but it is not inconceivable Emma outed herself due to the appalling conditions in her confinement. Upon the discovery of her sex, an attendant from the girls' home swiftly brought Emma back to the county jail. The case was so unusual that the *Boston Globe* covered Emma's story:

> "We can't keep her at the home," said the attendant to Sheriff Bergen.
>
> "Why not?" asked the sheriff, vexed that he should have the case of the girl again. "She's bad, I know, but you must have many such there."
>
> "No," said the attendant, calmly, "none like her. She's a boy."
>
> "What!" yelled the sheriff, jumping from his chair.
>
> "Undoubtedly a boy," Dr. McBride, the county physician, reported to Sheriff Bergen, a little while later.
>
> "What do you mean, going around dressed like this?" the angry sheriff cried, seizing Emma's skirts, the same she wore when she went to Trenton.

Emma considered the event blasé. "I don't know. I was never dressed any other way that I can remember," she claimed, while refusing to give them any other name. Media attention exploded over the mystery of Emma's past. "Emma was the object of curiosity when she was before the courts recently, and the curious interest taken in the child will be doubled now," a reporter explained on the day of her outing.[113] Emma was confined to the women's section of the jail as she waited for Judge Scott to return to court.

After another three days, the judge offered Emma a retrial. She accepted and waited three weeks in jail. Emma's stepmother and brother finally came to court to support her. They demanded her release. The judge decided the best way to deal with Emma was to discharge her to her family on the condition that she wear masculine clothing. Emma protested the single demand. As a local paper reported, "'Emma' doesn't want to wear trousers; 'she' objects to separation from dresses and ribbons—'she' wants to continue to be a girl."[114] Just shy of her fifteenth birthday, Emma was out of jail again.

Emma's story is perhaps a warning that basic tolerance of gender identity is not enough. Acceptance is not the same as support. Emma's family may have accepted her gender identity but clearly did not provide her with the necessary sustenance to keep her out of trouble. Or, perhaps, it is a testament to economic precarity. It is unclear exactly what Emma did with her stolen money. However, her father supported at least four people at a time. It is possible Emma felt she needed to steal to live. Whatever lessons you take away from Emma's story, it is satisfying to know that she had fun along the way.

Emma stayed out of the spotlight for over a year. It is possible she was caught stealing in Yonkers, New York, in March 1907, when newspapers identified her as the culprit. However, the culprit gave a different first name, so it is conceivable that it was a case of mistaken identity.[115] At this point, Emma's trail runs cold. Emma Heinrich is not an unusual name. Records show dozens born in 1891. There is no certainty about which could be her. Perhaps as more archival documents are restored and digitized, we will learn what finally happened to Emma, the girl bandit.

THE HORSE THIEF: WILLIE RAY

In the early 1890s, a Tennessee teenager made headlines for his remarkable adventures: a young trans boy with a penchant for intensive farm labor—and repeated horse theft. After transitioning at age sixteen, Willie spent decades as a cowboy, wrangler, farmer, servant, and whisky smuggler throughout the Midwest and South. With various aliases and identities, nobody has uncovered the breadth of Willie's story until today.[116]

Willie Ray was born on August 23, 1873, to Joseph and Susan Rankin in northwest Tennessee, on the Kentucky border.[117] He grew up with three full siblings and two half siblings in Weakley County, a rural farming community. His father fought for the Union in the Sixth Tennessee Infantry Regiment but struggled to make ends meet after discharge. Joseph worked as a farmhand while Willie's mother kept the home. The family was part of the Cumberland Presbyterian Church throughout the 1880s while living in Milan (about thirty miles from where Willie was born). The church was relatively progressive on gender and did not enforce norms as strict as other sects.[118]

Willie's story is not only one of a transgender child but also a lesson on the inequities of capitalism. By his teens, Willie had seen the underbelly of his industrialized nation. He witnessed his family's poverty unchanged by their toiling labor. Joseph Rankin struggled to find a well-paying job despite his tireless work and years of service to the Union Army. His service did not alleviate his economic precarity. Pensions were then provided only for soldiers who were killed or disabled in the Civil War, leaving his family only making the bare minimum to survive. When Joseph was born into a farming family, 70 percent of all US jobs were in agriculture.[119] This dropped to 43 percent by the time Willie transitioned in 1889. Farm owners reaped the benefits of new technology and industries while the shifting economic system strained farming communities like Willie's. It did not take long for Willie to gain a passion for stealing from the wealthy who benefitted from his exploited labor.

Willie's life took twists and turns between a governor's pardon, whisky smuggling, and several love affairs deserving of their own films. During the height of his infamy, one Tennessee newspaper even commented, "The strange [boy] is in possession of more deviltry than any female in the South."[120] He became one of the most famous men in the state at the time (trans or cis), making him among the most well-known trans men of the nineteenth century before fading into the depths of the archives.

Willie's media presence tells us much about the consequences of visibility. Reporters did not know what to make of trans men during Willie's era and thus did not generate panic or concern about it. In fact, they found creative ways of describing the young man. "Nature sometimes doesn't know her business thoroughly and gets conflicting elements mixed in the same body," a paper commented on Willie in early 1892.[121] "[Willie] seems to have lived in a perpetual protest against the feminine form with which [he] is endowed." Another journalist was convinced the young man could win anyone over with his charm. "With attractive features, a glib tongue, a sweet mellow voice and winsome eyes, beautiful shaped hands with long tapering fingers the youth at once attracts attention and always succeeds in making a fine impression on the first acquaintance."[122] Willie, like many other young white trans boys of his era, was respected—if not glamorized—in the media.

Kentucky

Willie's life became increasingly complicated as he entered his teens. His twin, Annie, married in 1888 as a child bride to an older man who variably reported his age as anywhere between fifteen and twenty-eight at the time.[123] His father died the same year. The ambitious trans teen would make headlines spreading his name around the country soon after these life-changing events.

Willie transitioned on his sixteenth birthday in August 1889. After living peacefully as a farmhand for months, he was thrust into the news for stealing a horse (the first of several similar thefts). But it was not the stealing that fascinated the impoverished region as much as his manner of dress.

Willie's notoriety began shortly after he moved to Union City, Tennessee, sometime in late 1889 or early 1890. There, he spent his time drinking and smoking with the other men, finally able to live his life openly as a boy.[124] Like many trans people today, the teenager experimented with his name. He first called himself Charles E. Jones before changing it to Ed Jones. It is not known why he picked the name, which also belonged to his younger brother, Ed Rankin. The young man found different farm jobs around the region before the wealthy landowner Thomas Spiller hired him in Weakley County.

Willie toiled on the Spiller farm for three months until he tired of the strenuous work and low pay. Farmwork during the cold months of winter was far from pleasant. In March 1890 the young man rode off with one of his employer's horses and sold the animal to a stable owner over the Kentucky border. He received eighty dollars (equivalent to around $2,700 in 2024) in return. Following a series of telegrams about the crime, a constable matched Willie's description with the horse thief. The officer swiftly arrested the young trans man. Willie requested to be sent to Martin, Tennessee, for processing. After traveling back into Tennessee, the officer was apparently "astonished" to learn that Willie was assigned female at birth when locals identified him. Shocked, the constable released him, presumably under the impression that he was a woman and women could not be thieves (both incorrect assumptions, of course). The sixteen-year-old fled back to Kentucky while the horse buyer continued to pursue him for selling him stolen property. Willie was rearrested in Hickman and sent to the county jail.

Reporters began to dig into his fascinating life. They initially passed off his attire as a disguise to evade capture or find employment. They thought he would change back into petticoats after the horse's owner found him. The reality was much more complicated as he treaded the line between safety and survival over the following decades.

The *Akron Beacon Journal* soon discovered that after Willie transitioned, he "began at once to court all the attractive young women of the neighborhood, escorting them to church and to places of amusement and acquiring a local reputation as a beau."[125] Headlines called him the "young lady tramp" and "a Tennessee beauty who tired of petticoats." One young woman told a reporter he "was the nicest boy in the country." Despite the onslaught of relatively positive reports, Willie was still sentenced to two years in a Kentucky penitentiary by a Hickman court for stealing the horse. During his stay, he demanded wardens allow him to wear pants, to which they complied.

Kentucky governor Simon Bolivar Buckner pardoned Willie on September 9, 1890. He was in jail for a total of six months (one quarter of his sentence). Pardons were only applied to a small portion of the incarcerated population at the time, which leaves us to wonder how exactly the young trans man's story reached the governor so soon after his arrest.[126] Reporters were also astonished to see him in men's clothing within a week of his release. Bewildered by Willie's defiance, one journalist remarked he "immediately donned male attire again and declares [he] intends to wear man's clothes evermore."[127] The pardon only emboldened him, marking the mere beginning of his escapades.

Tennessee

Following his six-month stint in Kentucky, Willie traveled back to Martin, Tennessee. The young man wore a well-fitting sack suit but left town after people realized his identity. He then traveled ten miles east to Dresden, where a local magistrate recognized and arrested him for his attire on October 3, 1890. Authorities dragged him to Union City. The teenager stood trial in district court, while the press both romanticized his story again. The *Nashville Banner* provided some of the only negative commentary, arguing, "There has been considerable misplaced gushing sympathy for [him]."[128] Willie became something of a folk hero legend. The state targeted him for nothing other than how he looked, and he was willing to risk it all to be himself.

Within weeks of his second arrest, Willie's deadname was again plastered in newspapers—this time even more widespread than his first outing. Outlets from Los Angeles to New York speculated various reasons for him dressing in men's clothing. Now seventeen years old, the young man attempted to rationalize his gender expression with an economic motivation to reporters.

> I prefer to wear men's clothes for the same reason that first led me to put them on. They insure [sic] me employment wherever I go. Were I to come into this community dressed as a woman and ask to be allowed to do a hard day's washing for fifty cents, I would neither get the work nor be allowed to stop in the house without being indorsed [sic] by a responsible person, or showing a pocketful of recommendations to satisfy the household of my respectability. But if I come rigged as a man I get plenty of work at one dollar a day and no questions asked. I discovered a good while ago that it doesn't pay to be a woman. Women are no good.[129]

Willie's explanation was tailored to the public. That is, he formulated an explanation that would make sense to the general population under the logic of making an income. It made sense for the teenager to switch his language to fit their economic (and misogynistic) reasoning, knowing they may understand excuses aligning with their preexisting beliefs. Yet if he truly only dressed in men's clothes for money, why would he continue to wear them even after he was outed? Why would he wear them while in jail with no place to hide? He would go on to falsely announce in 1892 and 1893 that he planned to stop wearing clothes designed for men. His self-narrative is a paradigm of how the fear of anti-trans persecution led many trans people to erase themselves.

There are no reports of exactly how Willie's Dresden trial went. He was either immediately freed or released within weeks, as the young man moved to Crockett County, Tennessee to work as a farmhand shortly after his legal trouble. The seventeen-year-old then hid his identity for over nine months while trying to earn a living. Willie's time in the rural county was not lonely. He allegedly began a long streak of heartbreaking as he dated several farmers' daughters at once.[130] None of them knew about the others. He even proposed to three of them and planned on becoming engaged to a fourth woman by the time he was caught. The *Los Angeles Times* described him as "playing the old Harry [. . .] with the most attractive young women in the surrounding country."[131] Each of the farmers' daughters reported that Willie treated them well. He escorted them to church, took them on exciting dates, and even told his favorites "of a 'vine-clad cottage by the sea.'"[132] His proposals, however, were soon cut short.

That August, Willie wanted a suit. The young man, about to turn eighteen, decided to forge his employer's name on a money order. Officials caught him in his new suit and threw him in the local jail. The grand jury quickly acquitted the young man, an act that reporters suspected was due to the discovery of his assigned sex while he was detained. A journalist cynically remarked, "The history of this erratic creature's career has many pages of humor as well as evil."[133]

Just a month later, Willie tested his luck again. He allegedly stole another horse, on which he rode away in the dark of night from Memphis. He began his journey out of the area late on September 21, 1891, but was immediately suspected as there were reports of a woman dressed in men's clothing departing the city that night. The black horse belonged to W. P. Dunnavant, a wealthy banker and businessman from Memphis.[134] This horse theft generated so much reporting on Willie that *The Tennessean* remarked, "Nearly every body in West Tennessee and the Kentucky 'Purchase' has heard of [him]."[135] Some papers speculated that he would finally serve a full sentence upon capture. However, others considered his "usual good luck" when it came to the charges being dropped.

The *St. Louis Globe-Democrat* predicted Willie would charm his way out of jail, "as a boy [he] is said to be exceedingly gentlemanly and manly in [his] intercourse with the people with whom [he] mingles, and no one would suspect for a moment they were in the company of a crook. The young ladies go dead in love with [him], papas and mamas all like [him]." Counties began fighting over who could claim Willie's legacy. Papers from around the Midwest noted "several envious counties claim the honor of [Willie Ray's] notoriety."[136] They correctly located his birth town of Martin, Tennessee, and gave Weakley County the credit. The young trans man had a golden tongue and could seemingly escape any perilous situation in better condition than he entered it.

Police again caught Willie in Gates, Tennessee, shortly after the theft of another horse. It was never established that he was the thief, but the truth of the theft did not matter. The media appeared certain he was to blame for the steed's disappearance. Newspapers did not circulate reports on his trial. The young trans man was again either immediately released or received only a short sentence. Landowner W. A. Wray reported he employed Willie under the pseudonym Will Osborn twenty miles south of Gates that October, just days after the trial. Willie had gone to Wray's wife and convinced her to hire him as a farmhand. His labor had been of "perfect satisfaction."[137] However, the Wrays discovered his trans status and fired him for no reason other than his gender. They would soon learn he was the notorious Willie Ray and spoke with journalists about their experience with the hardworking thief.

This time, Willie did not steal a horse (which is notable!). Instead, after two months of working for the Wrays, Willie left by train. *The Tennessean*, which at this point treated him like a modern celebrity, noted he "will have a dashing, jolly good time Christmas dancing luncheon floor breakdowns with the girls in some out of way district." The papers left him alone for the following months of an unseasonably warm Tennessee winter.

During his short-lived anonymity, Willie fled twenty miles south and took up the name Willie Craig. He began working with another farmer, C. M. Alexander, within days of leaving the Wray farm. The young man laid low there for eight months, until around his nineteenth birthday that August. There were reportedly no issues with Willie's work until his new boss discovered his assigned sex and fired him. Willie moved to the nearby home of W. W. Melton, where a local reporter, the sheriff, and other spectators interviewed him after his sex was again discovered in September 1892. Willie's audience did not appear to realize his true identity as the notorious horse thief, but they were still captivated by his harrowing albeit fictional story of loss and heartbreak.

As an excuse for adopting his male identity, Willie spun a romantic tale meant to appeal to heteronormative gender ideals. A journalist explained, "The reason for [his] disguise is that [he] had two lovers, Sam Beasley, of Union City, and Lee Steed, of Martin, and that the latter was killed by the former at Marion about three years ago. About the same time [his] father died and [his] mother broke up house-keeping, and [he] being thrown on [his] own resources and at the same time being troubled over the death of [his] lover, decided [he] could make a better support and easier bear up under [his] troubles by assuming male attire and mixing and mingling with the sterner sex."[138] While I could not locate any evidence that either of these men ever existed, there were elements of truth in his statements, such as his father dying and his mother working as a housekeeper. Perhaps keeping lies parallel to the truth is how Willie stayed free for so long. This incident was among his last well-documented stories before he escaped Tennessee for good.

Willie agreed to never wear clothing designed for men again (another promise he would not keep for long). What he did achieve was relative privacy for a time. His name rarely reached major newspapers for the following decade, and there were only short, infrequent reports on his whereabouts in Tennessee.

Willie stayed with his mother, Susan, occasionally in the 1890s. He eventually worked with her as a servant in the house of William Stanley in 1900. Stanley was a notoriously liberal early settler of Obion County, Tennessee.[139] He owned large swaths of land and had money to spare. He attended the same church as Willie and his mother, which is possibly how they connected. Susan's monthly widow's pension was a mere twelve dollars in 1900, meaning she could not live off it alone. It is unclear how long they stayed with the Stanleys as Willie had a colorful, parallel life across state lines at the time.

Mississippi

Willie moved to Mississippi in 1895. He worked on a farm and laid low in rural Prentiss County in relative anonymity. He was an avid tobacco chewer and had a reputation as a hard worker there. Every Saturday afternoon, he took a trip to Booneville on horseback. After regular work for seven years, Willie finally opened his own farm on rented land in 1902. This is where his Mississippi troubles began.

Officials caught Willie again for his love of women. He had apparently graduated from farmers' daughters to farmers' wives. In July 1903, weeks short of his thirtieth birthday, another young farmer, James Gatlin, caught Willie having sex with his wife, Fannie. The furious farmer beat Willie to a pulp. He "got after Ray with a horsewhip," a weapon strong enough to easily blind someone.[140] The local circuit court swiftly charged James with assault and battery. He was tried and held in jail on a $250 bond, which he could not pay.

Reporters noted Willie's blackened eyes and bandaged head when he arrived in court to testify against Gatlin. Instead of hiding his identity this time, he used it in a uniquely strategic manner: he outed himself on the witness stand. Willie felt obligated to disclose his history to dispute the allegations that he had sex with Fannie. At the time, it was considered impossible for two women to have sex. This meant the beating was not justified in the eyes of the court. One reporter described the tactic: "The aforesaid farmer with blood in his eye and a shotgun in his hand, was on a mission of settling the matter according to the ethics that prevail in this section of the country, and for urgent self protection Willie was obliged to own up and reveal the fact that [he] was a woman."[141] The obligation to confess may have outed him, but there were never reports of Gatlin attacking Willie again.

Willie realized being out did not mean he had to pretend he was a woman. As noted in several southern newspapers, "Authorities attempted to force [Willie] to don female attire, but upon investigation found that there is no state law forbidding a woman from masquerading in male attire, or vice versa." In fact, after Willie outed himself, one paper noted "half a dozen rosy-cheeked girls" fell in love with the young man. Another outlet celebrated Willie as an "industrious, capable, intelligent and peaceful citizen" in his Mississippi community. He was not charged and instead admired as a trans "Lothario" by the media. Willie continued to date Fannie for years to come. He moved in with her and her children and was listed as female but as her "partner" on his 1910 census record.[142]

Mississippi began enacting laws banning alcohol earlier than other states. It was the first state to ratify the Eighteenth Amendment for national prohibition in 1918 and the last to repeal prohibition laws in 1966. Willie, who never closely adhered to laws or social norms, began selling alcohol in Booneville almost immediately after the first prohibition laws came into place in 1907. In September of that year, he was convicted and fined a hundred dollars for selling alcohol. The court also sentenced him to thirty days in jail but suspended his punishment as they believed his promise to abandon the alcohol trade.[143] Willie did not sell alcohol again. Or, at least, he was never caught.

Willie continued manual labor while living on Fannie's farm. James, Fannie's husband, was no longer in the picture, and Willie helped raise Fannie's young children, Ules and Ethel, as his own. He continued to run the farm with his new children for some time before Fannie married another man, Joe D. Lauderdale, later that decade.

At this point, Willie's trail runs cold: no census records, arrests, or news articles could be located by any name he previously used after 1910. It is likely he changed his name or died around this time. With nothing to connect the aliases, there is no way to know where or how he lived for the remainder of his life. Annie, Willie's twin, died in 1938. She was survived by eight children, most of whom also took up farm labor. Fannie died in 1958.[144]

THE ACTIVISTS

I rather be a woman, so I am a woman.

—SADIE ACOSTA, 1941[1]

In 1970 Sylvia Rivera and Marsha P. Johnson cofounded Street Transvestite Action Revolutionaries. It is widely considered to be the first transgender activist organization started by the first trans activists.[2] Except, trans organizing actually goes back much further. This section features activists from the 1860s to 1950, revealing a much longer trajectory of trans organizing than previously established in media or academia. Some of the following chapters feature activists organized in formal groups while others operated in courts, churches, or spontaneous outbursts. These narratives radically change what we know about transgender uprisings, organizations, and policy.

Transgender activism is often denounced as a product of modernity. That is, trans advocacy is perceived to be the result of decadence, moral decline, or extremism existing only in our contemporary world. Sometimes, even trans activists and scholars will claim that trans advocacy is only possible due to medical breakthroughs or the wide reach of the internet.[3] However, this is far from what you will learn from the following underreported trans advocates. While transgender healthcare and digital culture are crucial to today's trans movement, gender activism existed long before transition medicine or the internet. People fought for name changes, freedom of expression, and self-determination before the first web forum or shot of estrogen.

Several of the "firsts" discussed in the introduction are featured in this section. The first known government approval to transition (Sally-Tom), legal sex change in court (Carl Crawford), queer and trans riot (Gerda von Zobeltitz), and trans elected official (Maude Milbourne) are each activist narratives that follow a remarkable history of resistance. Some activists engaged in polite civil disobedience, such as Sadie Acosta's refusal to sign her male draft card. Others opted to take less respectable routes, such as Okiyo, who punched a police chief in the face. Each event demonstrates a pathway for future activists to build a better future: to gain public support while fighting for ourselves and others.

Activism

What is activism? Most activism in this section is not quite like today's organizing. Some of the figures worked to ease their own living conditions, while others focused on queer and trans people as a whole population. Some, like Sally-Tom, were accidental activists. Sally-Tom found herself as a witness in a late 1860s court case and was able to advocate for herself to gain government approval to live as a woman. Her small act, along with several other cases of individual action, reveals a trend. Authorities held trans people to arbitrary standards that led to—and perhaps forced—self-advocacy. We have resisted much longer than the past few years; our resistance did not begin in the 1990s or even at the 1969 Stonewall uprising.

Unique among these early trans activists is the formation of experimental, coalitional groups intended to protect one another from the law. Certain mutual protection groups emerged in vastly different cultures, regions, and religions. In Tokyo, for instance, Okiyo led a group of danshō (transfeminine sex workers) to protect one another, sparking the Ueno Park riots. For Maude Milbourne, this looked like a broad group of gender transgressive individuals organizing under the label of "dress reformers" across the US. They wanted to remove draconian dress laws limiting what one could wear based on their perceived sex. Georgia Black found a vastly different way to organize. She led her Black church group to take on so much community service in her segregated town that even white residents felt a need to defend her.

Simply existing as a trans person in the 1850–1950 period meant that one had to be an activist to some degree. To announce one's gender is a form of self-advocacy. In this sense, every chapter in this book features an activist. Of course, mere self-pronouncement is not the central conflict of the following chapters, in which trans people had to petition, fight, and even kill to survive. Each of these stories shares a time long before gender in which trans people found their own unique paths toward self-determination.

THE FREED WOMAN: SALLY-TOM

Sally-Tom was one of the first people in the US to have her gender recognized by a legal governing body long before sex was included in regular documentation. Sally was a formerly enslaved Black trans woman who became an incidental activist. Unlike many others at the time, she was open about her gender in public. In fact, she may be the first trans person in US history to have her gender recognized by any governmental institution. Around 1869, the Georgia Freedmen's Bureau approved her decision to live as a woman. Although no photographs or recordings of Sally exist, local journalists wrote vivid details of her life and struggles.

Sally was born in Georgia around 1839.[4] According to the reporters documenting her case, she lived in rural Randolph County. Georgia birth records for whites did not begin until 1875, and public records of people of color (except for slave sales) were even less common. It is unlikely Sally had any records before the 1860s. The Kendrick family enslaved her and forced her to perform plantation work up to the end of the Civil War when she was about twenty-six.

Sally-Tom sought new freedoms with her emancipation. The end of the Civil War brought economic opportunity for formerly enslaved people. Many of the over four hundred thousand formerly enslaved people in Georgia stayed on their plantations. Sally, on the other hand, left for the city of Albany, Georgia.

Although she adopted paid work, Sally was still subjected to slave-like conditions. Former Confederate major Thomas Walker first hired her. She became his cook, gardener, cotton cutter, and wood chopper. During her early years as Walker's employee, Sally-Tom began living more openly as a woman. She was seen running errands in a men's shirt buttoned to white pants with a feminine white apron meant to contour her body. She also donned a sailor's hat.

While Sally-Tom worked for Walker, Georgia entered the Reconstruction era with the aid of the Bureau of Refugees, Freedmen, and Abandoned Lands (popularly called the Freedmen's Bureau). The agency intended to help transition Black communities out of slavery through a constellation of offices throughout the Southern states. Yet their councils were divisive. They forced Black women to work and attempted to convince families to do plantation labor again. On the other hand, they distributed food, encouraged education, and helped settle legal disputes. The councils began to close in 1870 and are seldom heard of today as they failed to truly emancipate the Southern Black population.

Around 1869, officials brought Sally-Tom into the local bureau office as a witness to a case. The branch leader was much more interested in her than the matter she was brought in for.

An unnamed reporter noted the bureau leader "inquired minutely into [her] life and habits, found out all about [her], and after due deliberation solemnly laid down the law that [she] could either be a man or woman as [she] preferred, but [she] had to be of one sex only as far as wearing apparel was concerned."[5] Interestingly, the reporter initially used it/its pronouns for Sally-Tom in the article before switching to she/her pronouns when he described the Freedmen's Bureau giving its approval for her to live as a woman.

Respectability politics generally did not favor trans people in the nineteenth century. However, Sally took advantage of the gender binary. By embodying the shame of being forced to live between genders, the council offered her a choice to live as male or female, depending on her wishes.

The reporter pondered, "Here was a dilemma, a position that few human beings are placed in, to decide at once whether to be a man or woman for all one's future life. To toil among the men or live in the more quiet manner of the gentler sex and be one of them." The answer was clear: "Sally-Tom was not too long in deciding. [She] had good taste and determined henceforth to lead a new life and become a woman. She changed her sex, donned feminine garments and since that day for over twenty years has passed as female." Interestingly, the reporter seemed to accept Sally's changed gender and pronouns. After transitioning, Sally-Tom wore a brimmed straw hat that became her new, distinguished look.

If Sally were white, it is possible her gender would have been prosecuted. Cross-dressing laws began emerging in the 1840s, but in the wake of Reconstruction, the Freedmen's Bureau had significant jurisdiction over the Black population and frequently made decisions that would avoid inciting more conflict.[6] There is no way to know what each court member thought, but cultural attitudes undoubtedly influenced Sally-Tom's case.

Sally refused to discuss her life with reporters, so we do not have a single word of her self-narrative. Those who knew her described her to papers at length, however. With a high and crackly voice, Sally reportedly hid behind her straw hat and left events before conflict arose. Her decision to avoid media made sense from the perspective of self-preservation; she likely did not want to draw attention to herself during such a violent era of increasing lynchings and attacks on the Black population.

Thomas Walker died in early 1877, and Sally continued to undertake similar work. She hired herself out for tasks like cooking and gardening. One man who hired her to be his chef decided to let her go because he was uncomfortable with her Black gender-nonconforming presence. She would hold his baby in her lap, as most female cooks did at the time, surprising him with her gentle demeanor. Intuitive, she left before he had a chance to officially fire her.

About twenty years after Sally's gender became official, white-owned newspapers reported on her with mixed reactions. They used slurs against her but appeared amazed at her confidence in transitioning. The 1889 articles referred to Sally as a "hermaphrodite" (now considered a slur for *intersex*). At the time, the term was typically used to describe any queer person, typically those who were gender nonconforming.[7]

It is possible "Sally-Tom" was simply a nickname as no records with that name appeared on Georgia's registries in the nineteenth century. Other local commentators used the term *Sally-Tom* to describe indecision or conflict within a single body. Sally was a feminine name and Tom was masculine, after all. Commentators also began to use the term *Sally-Tom* to describe conservatives and President Grover Cleveland when they had unfavorable policies to the South or whites, similar to how we use *flip-flop*, *centrist*, or *traitorous* today. One 1893 commentator explained, "A 'Sally-Tom' Democrat is a sort of political hermaphrodite—half Democrat and half something else."[8] The term appeared to emerge around the same time newspapers reported on Sally-Tom's case, so it is unclear if one Sally-Tom led to another or if the names were unrelated. The articles on Sally-Tom did not describe her as "*a* Sally-Tom," and the articles on her independently used the name, indicating it was the multi-gender name she used for herself.

Sally-Tom's obituary confirmed the 1889 article on her. She died on March 4, 1908, likely around the age of sixty-nine (although the obituary claimed she was "about 80 years old.").[9] An unnamed reporter published the death notice in the *Waycross Journal* and revealed that nobody in her community knew she was trans. It was not until a doctor revealed her assigned sex that her neighbors learned about her gendered past. "After living here for the past 50 years as a woman, death revealed the fact that Sallie Tom, about 80 years old, was in reality a man," the reporter wrote. "No cause for the deception can be ascertained. Postmortem examination was made yesterday, the negro having died the day before." Sally-Tom shied away from media and public life, hence the lack of reporting for two decades. Her cause of death was never printed, and no death records for that week are available in Ware County.

The obituary also revealed she lived in a small room in the Black neighborhood of Hazzard Hill, Waycross. The 1889 and 1908 news articles would mean she lived in the cities at overlapping times. It is unclear if she picked up seasonal work in one location or the other—or why reporters could not agree on where she was located. Waycross was over one hundred miles from Albany, but living in two places for seasonal work was not uncommon at the time.

Waycross was considered among the most religious towns in the state during the early 1900s, another reason why Sally may have wanted to avoid attracting attention. Even her neighborhood, Hazzard Hill, was named after a reverend.[10]

There would likely be many more details of Sally-Tom if she were white. White reporters seldom reported on internal Black affairs, and white people owned nearly all the newspapers at the time (historical Black newspaper indexes yielded no information on Sally-Tom). It was usually crime or law that drew the reporters to similar cases. Perhaps there would be more information had she been prosecuted by the Freedmen's Bureau. However, the acceptance of her gender was notable enough for a few news stories in the South and Midwest. We will never know the complete account of Sally-Tom. But even from these small fragments, we know her incredible narrative was an important moment in trans history that has been overlooked until now.

THE COUNTESS: GERDA VON ZOBELTITZ

"A German Baron Now a Countess by Court Degree" rang 1912 headlines across the United States.[11] Born into German nobility, Countess Gerda von Zobeltitz was among the first to receive a *Transvestitenschein*, popularly known as a "transvestite pass," during the Weimar era. Her history goes much further than her legal status, however. She was also a trans activist, beloved tailor, and ignitor of the Rauchfangswerder riots, one of the first pre-Stonewall queer uprisings, which occurred in Berlin in 1930. Despite these compelling aspects of her story, there are almost no English-language publications about Gerda. Her name remains all but unknown in the history books.[12] After publicly transitioning as a young adult, Gerda lived a life of revolutionary activism, resistance, and community building that deserves more appreciation.

Gerda was born in the Weissensee quarter of the Pankow borough in Berlin on July 9, 1891.[13] The von Zobeltitz family came from Saxon nobility and can trace its roots back to the medieval era. The family was relatively famous and even owned an eighteenth-century palace in Glinka, Poland. Their coat of arms furnished the architectural adornments around the property and featured a sable atop a helmet, itself atop a German coat of arms. Sables, known for their grace and luxurious fur, were the root of the von Zobeltitz name (*zobel* meaning sable and *titz* being a common suffix rooted in the term for "ruler of the people"). This name seemed fitting for Gerda, a lover of fine textiles and leader among trans people during the early twentieth century.

Gerda knew she was trans from a very young age and was fortunate to have access to her family's fine tailor shop. Her story helps us understand a history far beyond her own: a time of queer and trans resistance long before the modern movement.

Little of Gerda's own writing remains. However, shortly after participating in the 1930 Rauchfangswerder riots, she wrote a brief autobiography in the well-circulated *Die Freundin* magazine, a periodical for queer and trans people (with a focus on those who love women). It is important to remember that while Gerda preferred the German term *Transvestit* to describe herself, the term does not translate directly to today's pejorative *transvestite* (or *cross-dresser*) but is closer to *transgender* or *nonbinary*. Her short paragraph offers most of what we know about her childhood:

> The World of Transvestites
>
> I was born the son of a merchant, and at the age of about 7 I noticed my *Transvestit* tendencies. At that time, my parents owned a laundry store, which allowed me to own beautiful embroidered linen, which I often wore under my pants during the day, in secret, of course. Once my mother caught me in the act and gave me a good beating. But it didn't help, the urge always came back, and I had to restore the girls' undergarments again and again, whether I wanted to or not. After 15 years of not feeling the urge to change my clothes, the urge has now reawakened again. For some years now, I have been living with a friend who absolutely had no desire [for me] to do so, and despite the fact that we understand each other very well in all other things, it makes life in the house hell for me.
>
> Which of our sisters has been through a similar experience? I would be happy if the readers of our dear "Freundin" [girlfriend] could tell us about it.
>
> Gerda.[14]

Early transition

In February 1912, police arrested Gerda for cross-dressing in Berlin.[15] The news report on her trans status noted that she did not dress for criminal intent, which was considered the primary motive of non-normative gender expression by authorities at the time. The paper also commented that she "had always felt the urge to wear women's clothing, and had learned to fashion [her] own clothing and hats with tremendous expertise."[16] Trying to avoid more arrests, Gerda met famed sexologist Magnus Hirschfeld in 1912. He and physician Ernst Burchard performed a medical assessment on her, determining that she had an "uncontrollable tendency" to dress in women's clothing and was not intersex.[17]

On August 6, 1912, Gerda received her Transvestitenschein, which helped her avoid arrest when questioned by police. The following year, she again made the news after the Potsdam military recruitment commission called her in for service. They did not force her to serve on account of her trans status, providing her with additional legal legitimacy as a woman.

The *Berliner Börsen-Courier* newspaper commented on her situation during this time of burgeoning trans culture in Germany. Worries over what we would now call "social contagion" of trans identity existed in the 1910s. In a sympathetic article that could have been written today, the journalist found "such cases in which officials, on the basis of medical assessments, grant permission to men and women to wear the clothes of the opposite sex have increased significantly in recent times. The reason for this has less to do with greater frequency of such cases than with a growing awareness of their correct scientific understanding."[18] However, the right-wing media at the time alleged that the increase in trans people was a (typically Jewish) plot to destroy the German population. These reactionary pundits pathologized the increased understanding and dedication to self-expression, much like the 2020s panic over trans people.

Gerda received a glowing profile in the Austrian newspaper *Das interessante Blatt* in 1913, providing us with her clearest known photo see page 2 in the insert). In it, she wears a long, dark fur-trimmed coat with fashionable heels and a decorated cloche hat. Her shoes tip slightly out of her dress to show their feminine buckle. The unnamed writer captioned the image "the youth in women's clothes."[19] The reporters celebrated her transition, declaring that "nature has made [her] the famous third gender."[20]

Police arrested the young woman again in 1914. This time, her skirt was allegedly so short that it caused crowds to form around her. The Potsdam district president warned her they would revoke her Transvestitenschein if she continued to wear such clothing. There are no reports of her skirt causing such a commotion again. However, two years later, Gerda found herself in trouble once more. In fall 1916, Gerda's great-uncle Hanns von Zobeltitz petitioned for the removal of her Transvestitenschein. Historian Katja Koblitz speculated his actions were derived from conservative familial shame.[21] During the hearing, Hanns attested that his line of von Zobeltitz nobility was more widely recognized and thus the courts should listen to him over her. Gerda's penchant for newsworthy escapades certainly did not help with Hanns's annoyance, either. He cited two examples of Gerda attracting unwanted attention when petitioning the court to deny her the freedom to express herself. The results were dealt with through internal letters. It remains unclear if her pass was ever officially revoked.

Shortly before the legal battle, Gerda began partaking in a string of marriages. She first wed Charlotte Valeska Theophile Paulig, a sailor twelve years her senior, on August 29, 1916.[22] Gerda's wedding certificate listed her birth name and declared she was male, although she continued to use "Gerda" for the rest of her life. She again married on Valentine's Day, 1919, to Helene Elisabeth Emma Abel.[23] She then married another woman, Ida Marie Mörbitz, on December 30 of that same year.[24]

There was never an official reason for why she married so many times. One eyewitness alleged that she actually had no desire for women—which aligns with Hirschfeld and Burchard's assessment. Instead, the women wanted the noble surname "von Zobeltitz" as their own. One interviewee in Koblitz's research also mentioned that Gerda would occasionally go to gay clubs and have men over (although this does not negate the potential for her to love women). It is possible there was an exchange for the "von" title, although we may never know exactly what for.

The Rauchfangswerder riots

Among the most groundbreaking elements of Gerda's story came on July 5, 1930. She allegedly instigated a large queer and trans riot virtually unknown in the English-speaking world. The uprising framed the relationship between the German people and the police for years to come. I call these the Rauchfangswerder riots.[25] The riots were just a sample of increasing anti-queer police violence in the final years of the Weimar Republic. What separates Rauchfangswerder from similar riots of the era is the explicit targeting of queer and trans people, brazen self-defense, and large number of participants.

The Rauchfangswerder riots began with a peaceful queer steamboat trip in Berlin organized by the queer organization Bund für Menschenrecht (BfM, or League for Human Rights). The league was among the largest queer/trans organization in Germany since its founding in 1920. The group specialized in both educational and social events, some of which Gerda attended.[26]

In June 1930, *Die Freundin* (the same magazine Gerda shared her story in) featured an advertisement for the BfM's annual boat trip (see page 2 of the insert). Unbeknownst to the organizers, the small notice would lead to a monumental event for their group—and the thousands of queer and trans people in Berlin. The quarter-page ad helps us understand the peaceful background of the riots:

> *Your girlfriend and you are hereby invited to our great moonlight steamboat ride with a summer night dance in the wonderful Waldhaus-Restaurant Rauchfangswerder at Zeuthener Lake*
>
> > *2 bands on board and in the hall*
> > *Departure in the evening 9 o'clock*
> > *from the Michaelkirchbrücke*
> > *Saturday, July 5*
>
> *Tickets in advance guests 2.50 Mk., members 1.50 Mk. in the office Neue Jakobstraße 9 and at our events in Florida (Tuesday and Saturday). Gentlemen in women's clothing and ladies in men's clothing are not permitted to travel.*
>
> *We invite you to the Berlin chapter of the B.f.M., e. V.*[27]

As a so-called "gentleman in women's clothing," Gerda was not officially allowed on the trip. It is unclear if she hid her trans status or if the organizers let her attend on an ad hoc basis. She was well-known and liked among the community so it is unlikely she would go unnoticed. It is possible Gerda's Transvestitenschein helped her convince organizers to let her attend. Her pass meant the police were not officially allowed to arrest her for her attire (although they often chose to ignore orders).

The policy against transgender participation arrived from a complicated history within the queer and trans movements. At the time, trans and gender-nonconforming people (*Transvestiten*) were considered representatives of the broader movement of what were then called *homosexuals, inverts,* or *sexual intermediaries.* Many respectable gay people, particularly those we would now call cisgender gay men, considered the existence of trans people to negatively reflect on them as they were within the same community. Instead of working toward more public support for trans people, some spaces barred them from participating entirely. This form of respectability politics made it so trans people could not often attend queer events. Gerda was something of an exception because of her nobility and Transvestitenschein, making her among the most privileged of the trans Weimar Germans.

In this case, however, the anti-trans policy stemmed from the fear of police retaliation rather than the more typical active hostility against trans people. The BfM was highly supportive of trans people (at least for their time). Lotte Hahm, a frequent contributor to *Die Freundin* and famous BfM member, was assigned female at birth and renowned for their dapper suits.[28] They even led multiple trans groups in Berlin and organized trans and gender-nonconforming people within the BfM.[29] But fear was too strong of a force for the group that faced immense pressure to hide their identities, and the clothing ban for the trip to Rauchfangswerder was not lifted.

The police later argued the league ignited the riot due to Gerda's mere presence at the restaurant. If we are to believe the police's excuses for provoking the skirmish, the policy was there for a reason. This is not to excuse the BfM's anti-trans rule or to blame Gerda. Rather, it is useful to understand the context in which the police could evoke such fear among queer and trans people that BfM organizers would ban their own friends from an event.

Following over eight months of preparation, the excursion set off as planned. The cruise departed from Berlin's historic Michaelkirchbrücke (Michael's Church Bridge) without any problems on Saturday evening. The steamboat voyaged down the scenic Spree River as queer people of various genders mingled and watched the scenery pass by. According to attendee and BfM secretary Paul Weber, the ship was "in perfect peace and harmony."[30] At around seventy degrees Fahrenheit and without a drop of rain outside, the boat sped toward its destination in ideal conditions for a social night.

Multiple reports note Gerda was the only openly trans person on the trip, which included a mixed group of around three hundred other queer people, most of who remain unnamed. Following the river cruise, the boat arrived at eleven in the evening. The group disembarked onto the long Rauchfangswerder dock before entering the scenic Waldhaus-Restaurant (Forest House Restaurant) just feet from the shore. The venue was in southeastern Berlin and overlooked the picturesque river. The restaurant was so admired that it continued to be a popular cruise destination until the 1980s. Its large cream-colored facade stood tall above the shoreline, wedged between the nape of the deep forest and the tranquil Zeuthener Lake. The large restaurant provided ample room for the BfM members to dine, dance, and mingle in and outside the building.[31]

The conflict began before the boat reached shore. The BfM reserved Waldhaus's great hall while a police sports group reserved a smaller room. Around 150 officers were in attendance, joined by another 150 of their friends and relatives for a total of 300 (around the same number as the league). The police group arrived at eight in the evening, before the BfM's cruise departed. The restaurant staff let them know about the BfM gathering and the police were immediately upset that their room was smaller.

Major Erwin Sander, the head of the police gathering, personally reserved the lesser room. The police, however, claimed that the establishment mistreated the officers in a case of reverse discrimination. They alleged that Waldhaus gave the BfM unfair preference over them by allowing BfM to use the larger hall. However, Friedrich Radszuweit, *Die Freundin* publisher, gay activist, and former BfM chair, contested the claim:

> If, as Major Sander says, the police were annoyed that they were assigned the small hall while the League was given the beautiful large hall, it should be pointed out once again that the League had already secured

the large hall in October 1929 by written contract with the owner of the restaurant and had also rented the steamer for this trip in February 1930. So it was not, as various newspapers reported contrary to the truth, that the League suddenly appeared in Rauchfangswerder and claimed the large hall.[32]

BfM secretary Weber similarly alleged it was police chauvinism that led them to the attacks as "revenge for the fact that the homosexuals, of all people, were given the beautiful hall and the Schupo officials had to make do with a hall furnished with garden chairs."[33]

The police immediately began insulting the queer crowd as the BfM disembarked. The officers belonged to the Schutzpolizei, the "protection police" (commonly called the Schupo). Many of these uniformed patrolmen went on to be—or were already—Nazi Party members.[34] They were a group notoriously antagonistic to the queer struggle. However, Gerda and the league managed to enter the great hall without any fights breaking out.

Erwin Sander shamelessly fueled provocations between the groups as he continued returning to the league's beer tap to steal their alcohol. The hostility escalated as he became violently intoxicated. Noticing the major's increasingly rude behavior, the restaurant's host feared escalation and alerted the Berlin *Überfallkommando* (akin to a riot squad). Sander requested that the squad depart as soon as they arrived. However, unnamed Berlin officials commanded them to stay. Both groups of officers then joined together to insult the BfM, calling the queer crowd "gay pigs" and "abnormal scum." The restaurant's landlord, Fritz Krause, confirmed the attacks started escalating due to initial police harassment, but he could ultimately do little about it.

At this point, an unnamed officer took off his pants and mooned the group. Friedrich Radszuweit was particularly disgusted at this mockery: "What was the purpose of this officer's actions? Did he expect a friendly attack from the homosexuals on his naked buttocks? If so, he must have realized that he was mistaken, because homosexual men are not like the other pigs that constantly wallow in mud." Another Schupo officer fiddled with his fly. "Size 8 for me!" he shouted at the group. The Überfallkommando departed but the tensions and provocations continued until three o'clock in the morning. The officers finally retreated to their steamboat but ominously delayed their departure for half an hour before finally setting off on the river.

Now feeling safer, more BfM members left their hall and socialized in the adjacent garden and riverbank. However, the Schupo steamboat suddenly reversed course. According to Sander, a fight broke out between the officers remaining in Rauchfangswerder and the BfM. The police also told the *Berliner Lokal-Anzeiger* that members of the league attacked the lingering officers, forcefully beating them to the ground.[35] Sander claimed that they turned around to retrieve these three remaining Schupo. However, the BfM members allege the return was to attack their group, not to rescue the officers. Regardless, the result was the same: the Rauchfangswerder riots had begun.

League members began tossing rocks and sand at the boat and officers as they returned to shore (BfM officials did not deny this allegation). Sander led the police force in running off the boat and indiscriminately beating attendees. The major reached the group of league attendees and immediately punched a board member. The unrest fully ensued. A queer rioter returned the favor and hit Sander in the testicles with a chair leg.[36] Others tossed beer steins at Sander. More officers stormed into the hall, grabbed chairs, and threw them at the event attendees and restaurant workers. The brawl escalated and participants threw coffee cups, beer, and fence slats at one another. Even secretary Weber, a famous pacifist, said, "It goes without saying that some of our people fought back, because after all, not only the police officers have the right to fight, but other people as well."[37] The rioters followed his philosophy: refusing to defend one another was akin to committing violence themselves.

Multiple journalists reported the alarming lengths some of the Schupo went to attack the queer attendees. Some read more like cartoon violence than an actual riot. "An officer grabbed a large woven basket of coffee cups and smashed them individually over the heads of the members of League standing at the buffet," one reporter noted. The BfM members then escalated the fight. One rioter grazed patrol officer Waldom with a knife, and constable Gilsing was so badly injured that he had to be taken to the nearby Köpenicker Hospital. The Schupo finally choked and beat the hostess before fleeing back onto the steamboat to escape the queer people fighting back. Sander departed with a bruised and bloodied face.[38]

The Schupo were mostly gone but the riot was far from over. Despite the violence around them, the league continued to dance and socialize with one another. However, the Überfallkommando returned to the scene after being alerted to the commotion. The riot officers entered the great hall and interrupted the BfM's celebration. "Here we clean up: [those] who resist get beaten!" one shouted to the group. An attendee demanded the officers speak more respectfully to the BfM. The request for basic dignity provoked the officers and they began to attack the group again. In one report, the squad also attacked some remaining Schupo officers and other patrons. There is little documentation of what forms of force the Überfallkommando used or how the league resisted at this point in the night. However, a newspaper report three days later claimed "bleeding faces could be seen everywhere."[39]

Several papers alleged the Schupo and Überfallkommando fought one another throughout the night, but others deny this allegation. The discrepancy may have come from patrons confusing the groups or accidental in-fighting between officers. Alternatively, the Schupo could have planted the story to blame the riot squad for the incident. Regardless, *Vorwärts*, a Social Democratic Party newspaper sympathetic to the BfM, pointed to Sander's claim that the fight between officers was "pulled from thin air."[40] The *Vorwärts* reporters alleged the inter-police battle was tabloid reporting, but the rest of the story was accurate.

As the sun began to rise behind the clouds at about four in the morning, the BfM slowly exited Waldhaus and walked to their steamboat. Injured and bleeding, the members still attempted to obtain the police officers' information so they could lodge a complaint. The remaining officers refused and also departed.

The league eventually filed grievances against the police, but, much like today, reporting the police to the police rarely leads to satisfactory results. Over the following weeks, the police justified their actions centrally around Gerda's attendance. They attested that she, as a trans woman, instigated the fights by her mere attendance. They also complained that sex workers came to the event, which required intervention. Sander even claimed, "It was not the Schupo, but the public garden that felt bothered by the presence of the [league] members."[41] This incident, however, would have occurred *after* the officer had already harassed and complained about the league. Radszuweit admitted that there was a woman in the garden, a Ms. Schmidt, who felt uncomfortable with the BfM's queer presence. However, he jokingly retorted, "Ms. Schmidt and her kind apparently don't realize that they themselves have a sexual orientation. Otherwise, they wouldn't have been able to bear children. I could list many more amusing remarks here, but I will refrain from doing so because the printer's ink is too valuable for so much stupidity."

On July 30, three weeks after the events, Friedrich Radszuweit remained furious about the police's behavior. Like today, many newspapers published police descriptions of events without questioning their veracity. Journalists from around the country reported on the riot as though it were celebrity gossip. A paper from Ebersberg, hundreds of miles south of Berlin, shared the relatively sympathetic headline "When Police Officers Fight against 'Human Rights'" three days after the riot ended.[42] Different papers shared varying perspectives on the uprising, ranging from amused to enraged. Some were entirely sympathetic to the police while others took a more critical approach.

Friedrich claimed he had located forty-four news articles about the riots, many with sensationalistic headlines like "Homosexuals Beat Police Officers!" and "The Schupo Were Really Innocent." He provided a scathing article in *Die Freundin* to denounce the police riot. He contested Sander's assertion that the hall was filled with trans people: "Either Major Sander is deliberately lying to cover up his people and his scandalous behavior, or he was so drunk that he could no longer distinguish between a woman and a man." Radszuweit's writing helped tease the absurdity of policing. However, he did not question the principle that significant trans attendance is sufficient cause for police beatings, casting out trans people like Gerda from his "community." While witty and creative, Radszuweit was still notoriously skeptical of—and bigoted against—feminine men, trans people, and sex workers.[43]

Radszuweit, who would later write appeals to Nazi Party leaders, believed the system of policing could merely be reformed. He concluded his remarks on the Rauchfangswerder riots with confidence in the morality of more sympathetic officers: "The day will come when even these fools will have to recognize the homosexual people of Germany as equal. The day will come when even police officers realize that their salaries are also paid from the tax money of homosexuals." Radszuweit unexpectedly died in 1932 and did not witness the Nazi seizure of the German policing apparatus the following year.[44] The public prosecutor's office announced their findings in March 1931, dropping all charges by claiming the officers acted in self-defense.

Following the Rauchfangswerder riots, trans activist Marie Weis wrote that the BfM and similar cisgender-led associations "are not only unsuitable for achieving the social and economic recognition of transvestites, but that these kinds of associations compromise transgender people in the most serious way."[45] She cited the Rauchfangswerder attack as the prime example of their failure to help trans people. Marie believed that the BfM scapegoated trans people like Gerda for the riot. She then promoted the D'Eon Association as an alternative organization led by and for the trans community. The independent group of activists, launched in October 1929, quickly gained membership.[46] Magnus Hirschfeld's Institute for Sexual Science provided the D'Eon Association a room in their building that same year. It is unknown if Gerda joined the group as their membership rolls were not public and likely destroyed in the infamous 1933 Nazi book burnings.[47]

Erwin Sander, a German World War I veteran, became a Nazi general in 1935. He won several major awards from the Third Reich for his war crimes. He quickly rose through the ranks to become a special liaison to Hitler's headquarters. Sander notably oversaw the slaughter of the Jewish population in Ternopil in 1942 when he began leading the city's occupying force. The massacre began as soon as he took over command on July 4. His troops "systematically searched the city" for the Jewish population, brought

the men to assembly locations, and shot them.[48] As Sander marched through
Russian territory, he reflected on the paradox of Nazi religiosity in a letter
to spiritual leader Dietrich Bonhoeffer:

> These persons must be done away with in this manner because otherwise
> German soldiers would have to forfeit their lives. . . . We cannot give
> special consideration to the civilian population's store of provisions . . .
> including seed potatoes . . . if we are in need of them. We have had to
> burn down many a village in the last three weeks out of military ne-
> cessity. . . . And to us soldiers the promise comes from the Sermon on
> the Mount, "blessed are the merciful, for they will receive mercy." The
> contradictions are enormous.[49]

Echoing the Nazis' logic, the police who incited the Rauchfangswerder
riots adopted a scarcity mentality joined by supremacist beliefs. The idea of
a superior form of humanity dictated his actions throughout his life, leading
to everything from the Rauchfangswerder riots to his participation in genocide. Sander would fight for the Nazis until the bitter end, commanding
the 245th Infantry Division to protect Berlin's canals against the Canadian
military in 1944. Canadian forces eventually captured and interrogated him
in the Netherlands.[50] Despite overseeing various atrocities, Sander was
released by the Allies after the war. He died in Berlin in 1962 at age seventy.

The point of highlighting Sander is not to make him out as the individual perpetrator or ignitor of violence during the Rauchfangswerder
riots. Hundreds of officers and their companions took part in beating the
queer crowd just as hundreds of queer cruise attendees took part in the
resistance. None of the police stopped Sander from harassing and beating
the BfM members. There were no individual offenders but a collective
struggle between the state and the queer population. Blaming one individual
does not get at the underlying philosophy behind their actions. The entire
system of policing was responsible.

By the time of Berlin's reunification the Waldhaus building fell into
disrepair and was demolished in 2005. Its ice cellar is all that remains,

marked by two pieces of laminated paper mounted on a post where the restaurant once stood. There are no memorials, commemorative holidays, or books about the Rauchfangswerder riots. Perhaps this is a testament to just how much transgender history Nazis destroyed. I could locate only a handful of the forty-four articles Friedrich Radszuweit claimed to have found about the riots. Nazis burned many of the documents related to Gerda and the riots during the "1933 destruction" of the Institute for Sexual Science. There were other moments of queer resistance in Weimar and Nazi Germany but few that were so well archived as Rauchfangswerder. These moments from Gerda's lifetime only provide a small glimpse into the radical protests of the Weimar era.

The later life of Gerda von Zobeltitz

Hitler was sworn in as the chancellor of Germany in January 1933. Although many queer and trans people fled the country, Gerda opted to stay. Defiant in the face of authority, she also refused to detransition following the Nazis seizing power. Koblitz notes, "All contemporary witnesses emphasize that Gerda von Zobeltitz always wore women's clothes during the Nazi era and let herself be addressed as Gerda or Ms. von Zobeltitz."[51] Gerda was not afraid. One neighbor reported his family was scared "the Nazis would put [her] up against the wall because of [her] wearing women's clothes."[52] Ultimately, the Reich disregarded her social transgressions.

There are different theories as to how Gerda survived the Nazi regime. She told her neighbors she would claim she was intersex due to Hirschfeld's theory that transgender identity was an intersex condition within itself. He used the theory that transness was actually "mental hermaphroditism" (now a pejorative phrase) to help his patients receive their Transvestitenschein, even though the idea was not generally part of his larger theory of gender.[53] Gerda was confident she could convince authorities she was biologically predisposed to wearing women's clothing. She believed they would not persecute her for her transness if her gender was a medical condition. However, the real reason the Nazis let her live was much simpler. Gustav Tuszewitzki, who knew Gerda, explained: "She was a 'von' and the Nazis did nothing to the nobility." This aligns with past findings that the Nazi regime did not target certain wealthy, powerful "Aryan" trans individuals for death as often as other trans community members.[54]

Gerda kept to herself during the early 1940s, as she reportedly hated the Nazi regime. She even owned three Saint Bernards, which she named Voralarm, Alarm, and Entwarnung (Pre-Alarm, Alarm, and All Clear) to keep people away during Hitler's reign. She was eventually called in to join the Volkssturm (a militia of citizens forced into service) in September 1944. It is unclear if she was forced to participate in any Nazi events, as the war ended soon after.

Gerda continued working as a seamstress, specializing in women's luxury apparel after the war. Many community members did not know she was trans, and she did not go out of her way to tell them. She did, however, correct people who called her by her deadname.

Gerda died in a car accident in 1963. With failing eyesight, she reportedly walked directly into oncoming traffic. Her wife at the time, Margarethe von Zobeltitz, lived in Gerda's apartment until her death in 1985.

Gerda's story only recently came back into the public eye in Germany following Katja Koblitz's groundbreaking research. In 2015 the Berlin State Office for Equal Treatment and Against Discrimination also published a short two-page recognition of Gerda in their brochure of outstanding LGBTQ Germans.[55] Hopefully, this chapter will help inspire people in the English-speaking world to understand the long history of trans resistance before Stonewall. Gerda is only one of many queer and trans people who fought back against police brutality during her lifetime. There are endless stories of queer struggle that will continue to come to light as the movement marches on.

THE PETITIONER: CARL CRAWFORD

Carl Goodwin Crawford's narrative shows us a moving tale of love, life, and law. As of this writing, he is the earliest known non-intersex trans person to change his legal sex through court-based advocacy. Uncovered while researching this book, Carl's heartwarming story radically shifts the transgender legal timeline while also demonstrating an abundance of support for his identity in the early 1900s. However, Carl's story goes much further than his name and transition. He had unwavering advocacy from his loving mother, wife, and family during his transition. Between three marriages, an incredible family history, and a history-making court case, Carl Crawford is a self-described "mental, moral and spiritual man" to remember.[56]

Carl was born in rural Tennessee on October 22, 1874.[57] His mother, Louisa Elizabeth Tipton, raised him alone with his brother, Amos, and his sister, Flora. He never knew his father, Crawford, very well. However, when he transitioned, Carl took his father's first name as his last.

Carl's family history was key to his fight for legal gender determination. It all started when fourteen-year-old Louisa Elizabeth Griswold married twenty-four-year-old Stephan Palmer Tipton in 1854, almost exactly twenty years before Carl was born. Although Carl never met Stephan, the Tipton family's heritage would frame Carl's influence in his town for the rest of his life. Carl's neighbors considered him Stephan's son despite the two having no biological relationship. It made sense for the family to do so: Stephan (sometimes spelled Stephen) was initially a prosperous man. The Tipton family was instrumental in founding Grundy County and received 2,886 acres that the government stole from the Cherokee Nation. (The Indian Removal Act of 1830 opened vast spaces of land for settlers and the United States gave it to white Europeans for free. Shortly after the Trail of Tears and forced Cherokee removal, the state enticed settlers to move or stay in Tennessee with free land and resources.)[58] Stephan's father cofounded Grundy County in 1844, likely never knowing the horrors the displaced Cherokee were subjected to. Stephan's father became the first chief justice of the peace and his brother became the first constable. As many founding myths go, the Tipton name became sacred in the county as integral to its legitimacy over the formerly Cherokee territory.

When Carl was born, his mother was still healing from the tragedies surrounding the Civil War. She and Stephan had lost an infant just months after their wedding. They did not try for more children for years. As tensions rose in the North-South border states in the 1850s, Stephan had to decide whether to join the Union or the Confederacy. Although he lived his

Mark and David Ferrow pose for a 1939 photo in *The Daily Mirror*.

An 1895 sketch of Effie Smith. COURTESY OF THE
ST. LOUIS POST-DISPATCH.

Jos. Leonard & Son.
Boot and Shoe Makers.
Repairing a Specialty.
Shop between jewelry store and
blacksmith shop,
Lebanon, Oregon.

1889 advertisement for Ray and Joseph
Leonard's shoe store. COURTESY OF THE LEBANON
EXPRESS.

Twenty-year-old Gerda von Zobeltitz in 1913 from her *Das interessante Blatt* interview. COURTESY OF THE AUSTRIAN NATIONAL LIBRARY.

The 1930 *Die Freundin* advertisement for the cruise to the Waldhaus-Restaurant that led to the Rauchfangswerder riots. DIGITIZED BY META-KATALOG.

Restored photo of Muksamse'lapli at an unknown date. COURTESY OF THE
KLAMATH COUNTY MUSEUM.

A news clipping covering Sadie Acosta while
she was incarcerated in 1941. © THE FORT COLLINS
EXPRESS-COURIER – USA TODAY NETWORK

Josephine Robinson at an unknown date from
her 1909 exposé. COURTESY OF THE ST. LOUIS POST-
DISPATCH.

An undated photo of Elsie Marks from a 1946 article. COURTESY OF *THE LONG BEACH INDEPENDENT*.

Albín Pleva's profile from the Lety Concentration Camp, July 1942. COURTESY OF SPOLEČNOST PRO QUEER PAMĚŤ (CENTRE OF QUEER MEMORY).

WAS ONCE A JOCKEY.

A sketch of Frank Williams as a jockey featured in a 1905 article on his escapades. COURTESY OF *VALLEY SPIRIT*.

Like many other trans boys of his time, newspapers across the country sensationalized Frank Williams' story. COURTESY OF THE *ST. LOUIS POST-DISPATCH.*

Young Agustín Rodríguez in his toreador costume in the 1890s. COURTESY OF THE BIBLIOTECA NACIONAL DE ESPAÑA.

La Fiesta Nacional featured twenty-eight-year-old Agustín Rodríguez on its cover, June 1906. COURTESY OF THE BIBLIOTECA NACIONAL DE ESPAÑA.

Agustín Rodríguez smiling after a successful
bullfighting exhibition in 1912. COURTESY OF THE
BIBLIOTECA NACIONAL DE ESPAÑA.

Ahora interviewed fifty-six-year-old Agustín
in 1934 when he returned to bullfighting.
COURTESY OF THE BIBLIOTECA NACIONAL DE ESPAÑA.

Czechoslovak athletes board the train on their journey to London for the 1934 Women's World Games. Zdeněk Koubek (top, left) holds the flag while Stefan Pekar (bottom, right) poses for the camera. COURTESY OF THE NÁRODNÍ MUZEUM.

Stefan Pekar shortly after transitioning in 1937.
COURTESY OF ČESKÁ TISKOVÁ KANCELÁŘ.

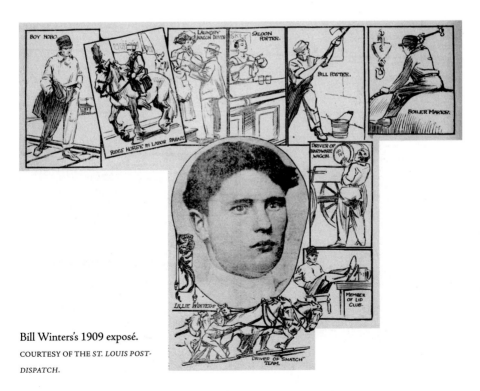

Bill Winters's 1909 exposé.
COURTESY OF THE ST. LOUIS POST-DISPATCH.

GIRL WHO WORKED IN THE FIELDS AS A BOY AND TOOK MAN'S ATTIRE WHEN SHE CAME WEST

People we may now understand as trans were so common in 1909 St. Louis that the *Post-Dispatch* declared them emerging in an "astonishing number."

"Come Out Here, Sis!" Said the Detective.

Cartoon of police arresting Bill Winters in February 1909. COURTESY OF *THE MANHATTAN MERCURY*.

Accompagné par son père, Pierre Bresoles va quitter Carcassonne pour venir subir sa deuxième opération à Paris.

Teenage Pierre Brésolles with his father in Paris around 1946 in *Qui? Detective*. COURTESY OF WILLIAM STRAW.

whole life in Tennessee, which joined the Confederacy in 1861, he enlisted with the Union Army in 1862. This meant trouble for the whole family.

Stephan earned the rank of captain and led a cavalry through his state the following year. He and his seventy-three-man unit were tasked with protecting railroads from the Confederates. The Southerners got word of his betrayal and hatched a plan to murder him in 1863. The notorious Confederate Major Hiram Bledsoe sent two men from his company to Stephan's house. They dressed in Union uniforms and shouted, "Captain, the rebels are coming!"[59] Stephan dashed outside along with Louisa and Carl's half siblings, young Amos and infant Flora. Louisa saw the Confederates shoot Stephan dead as their children watched. She never fully recovered from the sight of her husband's slaughter.

Stephan left the family some savings, but it was not enough to sustain them. He had many siblings and his family's fortune was not sufficient to keep them all comfortable. Carl, born ten years after Stephan's death, and young Amos, his half brother, toiled on a farm to support their family. Louisa also worked as a seamstress but never made enough to sustain her three children alone. With the tragedy now behind them, the four were close and supportive of one another.

Carl grew up only knowing the remnants of the Civil War. His small town gave him limited knowledge of the outside world—and of the possibility of transitioning. However, he still expressed his gender when he could. His brother-in-law gave him the nickname "Tom" in 1885 and told reporters Carl "always impressed me as a boy."[60] Carl eventually married William Bryon Leard in 1892 when he was eighteen and still perceived as a woman. They tried living together but separated fewer than two weeks later.[61]

Not long after, Carl fell deeply in love with a woman. Unfortunately, she did not return his affection. Newspapers later reported he was left in despair, attempting to end his life by shooting himself with a .38-caliber revolver.[62] Community members reportedly found him and gave him the care he needed to recover from his wound. This was not his only flirtation with death, as a housemate later told curious reporters that Carl had said he would kill himself if he was forced to wear dresses.

Carl traveled to Fort Worth, Texas, for a year in late 1899. It was the first time out of his home county for an extended period. He then returned to Grundy County and planned his transition. In August 1901 the forward-thinking trans man obtained seven letters affirming his right to live as a man. After the short reprieve back in Tennessee, Carl fell in love again and followed an unnamed schoolteacher to Waco, Texas, that summer. Journalists noted he moved into the Hodge residence, although it is unclear if one of the Hodges was the schoolteacher he trailed.[63] Shortly after arriving, he transitioned and adopted his name, Carl Goodwin Crawford.

Residents of Waco circulated rumors that Carl was a woman as he only weighed one hundred pounds, had delicate features, and spoke in a high voice. Yet Carl's persistent masculine presentation prevented any private gossip from leaking to the press. Locals would often see the young man out and about in the city of some twenty thousand, always surrounded by the Hodge family. Neighbors remembered Carl's crisp, dapper aesthetic and short, medium-brown hair finely parted down the middle.

Everything changed for Carl on August 17, 1902. Officer Bob Buchanan suspected Carl's sex and arrested him under Texas's cross-dressing laws. The twenty-seven-year-old was simply peering into a store window when Bob took notice and harassed him for his attire. Carl wore a fine linen suit with a derby hat, standing collar, and white tie. He smoked a large cigar, which was seen as socially unacceptable for women at the time. The officer began accosting him, but Carl denied being trans, returning the insults. The papers did not quote his retort, but he allegedly "used words to the officer that were not pleasant for him to listen to."[64]

Undeterred, the officer forced the young trans man to visit the city physician. Carl recanted before the exam and told the officer that he was a woman. The officer arrested and charged him with "parading in male attire." They released the dapper young man on a bond of twenty-five dollars. In court the next day, Carl argued that he had the right to dress himself as a man. City officials disagreed. The city recorder fined him one dollar with an injunction that he would not wear men's clothing again. Carl did not comply.

Carl Crawford's hearing is where his narrative becomes a breakthrough moment in transgender history. Instead of fleeing the impending punishments for transgressing gender, he decided to take up a legal fight—and he *won*. Most transgender court cases at the time ended in apologies, fines, and imprisonment. Carl, on the other hand, published three of the sworn affidavits two days after his arrest that attested to his manhood.

Carl sent the seven Tennessee letters he received in 1901 to the *Waco Times-Herald*. Each pleaded his legal right to be known and exist as a man, regardless of his assigned sex. The testimonies included two city clerks and his family doctor. While there should not have been a need to have cisgender officials prove his manhood, their steadfast support for him represents a remarkable case for trans self-determination. Carl's preamble to their testimonies (likely written in 1902 after his Waco court case) amazingly understands that being a man does not necessarily denote a body type but rather an identification:

It is in justice to myself and my adopted mother, Mrs. Hodge, that the papers below are submitted to publication. These papers were given under the official seal of the state of Tennessee and beg people of intellect who give weight to the mental, moral and spiritual man as well as the physical. It was on these and other truths Mrs. Hodge founded her belief in my right to my place as a man, and on truths high as God I knew the right was mine.

I am very respectfully,

C. G. CRAWFORD

The three published statements were each accompanied by the seal of Tennessee. First was the county clerk who worked in the courthouse that his grandfather founded:

We, the undersigned, having known Carl F. [sic] Crawford [. . .] from his birth, do solemnly declare that to the best of our knowledge and information and belief he has a perfect right to masculine attire and all the rights and privilege of an American citizen. Through mistake of his parents he has suffered for years in feminine attire calumny and blamed for their love affairs with women, finally becoming convicted of the criminality and injustice to himself and society took his place in the world and his father's name. And we as men of honor approve. This, August 29, 1901.

    JOHN SCRUGGS, County Clerk

The second letter came from Carl's family doctor, who had never examined him but was willing to provide a statement anyway. Unlike the county clerk, he misgendered Carl.

I, W. C. Barnes, wish to state that I endorse the above statement and wish to say further that I have been the family physician of the party, [Carl Crawford], who has assumed the name of Carl G. Crawford, during [his] life up to December 1, 1899, when [he] left Tennessee, and though never having made an examination believed that [he] ought to have been attired in masculine attire and grew stronger in that belief year by year as [he] grew up. This, August 29, 1901.

    W. C. BARNES, M.D.

Finally, his brother-in-law, who also worked for Grundy County, attested that he knew Carl was a boy before he even announced himself as one:

I, J. K. Howland, endorse the above statements of Mr. John Scruggs and others with the exception I have not known the party from birth but have known [him] since 1885. I married [his] sister in 1886 and have been intimately acquainted with the family ever since and the party always impressed me as being a boy and therefore always called him Tom.

    J. K. HOWLAND,

    Circuit Court Clerk

Days after Carl's arrest, the Hodges began publicly fighting in the papers over their connection with the young trans man. Jesse P. Hodge, the ex-husband of Susie Hodge, publicly shamed his former wife for her affiliation with Carl. Susie, Jesse, and Carl lived together, although no official records of their short cohabitation exist. It is possible Susie was the schoolteacher who Carl followed to Waco or was related to her.

The Hodges' public letters were purposely vague, meant to address "certain false and malicious reports" surrounding living with Carl.[65] The format of the letters points to either an implied affair with Carl or simply the matter of Susie concealing his transness. Susie Hodge felt the need to write to the *Waco Times-Herald* without directly addressing the content of the gossip. "C. G. Crawford came into our family with my [ex-]husband's full knowledge and approval [. . .] in extending the courtesy, kindness and protection to a stranger in a strange land none of us dreamed of breaking any law, social or divine," she explained. Jesse was sympathetic to his wife of nineteen years and called for "idle gossipers" to "honor and esteem her" for her transgression of supporting Carl. He apologized for shaming her, and they did not make their disputes public again.

With the fine paid and letters sent to the press, Carl left Texas to bring his fight back to Tennessee. He traveled over eight hundred miles to the court in Altamont that his grandfather founded. The case was scheduled for September 27, over a month after his initial arrest. On top of his family's historical influence, his mother also joined him in the legal struggle. She proudly testified on his behalf. The same John Scruggs who wrote him a letter of recommendation was the clerk for his case and took notes. Officially, the matter was a petition "for change of name, & to declare sex, etc."[66] The court heard his case and issued one of the first written decrees of transgender legal affirmation in the United States (note that I changed Carl's pronouns and deadname in the text below).

In the matter of the petition of Carl Crawford for the change of name and to disclose sex, etc. This cause came on to be heard on this, Sept. 27, 1902, before the worshipful R. Smart, chairman pro tem. of the county court of Grundy County, Tennessee, same being a special or adjourned term of this court, upon the petition of Carl Crawford, filed in this cause, proof, etc. And it duly appearing to the court from the petition filed and sworn by the complainant, Carl Crawford, in this cause, and also from the sworn statement of Mrs. E. L. Tipton, the mother of said Carl

Crawford, also filed as an exhibit to said petition, and also the sworn statement of Dr. W. E. Barnes, the family physician, also made and filed, and the further petition of Carl G. Crawford, alias Carl Crawford, also sworn to and filed, that a very grave error and injustice had been made and committed against the petitioner, Carl Crawford, in the disclosure of the sex of the said Carl Crawford at the time of his birth, he being a male child and his mother and friends mistaking said Carl for a female child and thus unintentionally depriving the said petitioner, Carl Crawford, of the legitimate rights of an American citizen. And it further appeared from the proof that said Carl Crawford from his childhood has been and appeared masculine in all his deportment and manners and when arriving at the age to disclose his true sex, has been rendered very unhappy since by the condition in which he has been accidentally placed by his mother and friends. From all of which it duly appears to the court from the proof which is positive and unquestionable that petitioner, Carl Crawford, is justly entitled to the redress sought. It is therefore ordered, adjudged and decreed by the court that the sex of petitioner, Carl Crawford, be and is hereby declared to be masculine; that the name of said petitioner be and the same is hereby changed from that of [deadname] to Carl G. Crawford: and that petitioner be and is hereby clothed with all the rights and privileges of a male person and a male American citizen; and in the future be recognized and known as Carl G. Crawford, and that all the rights and privileges guaranteed by law are hereby granted to the said Carl G. Crawford as an American male citizen and that said petitioner be and is hereby vested with such relief. And petitioner will pay the cost of this proceeding, for which execution may issue.

To the modern reader, the ruling may appear to imply Carl was intersex. However, the judge seemingly adopted Carl's idea that he was a "mental, moral and spiritual man," rather than a "physical man," since his birth. The court records were closed for two years before their publication in the *Nashville Banner* in 1904.[67] Snippets of the decree circulated to news outlets from St. Louis to Washington, DC, within days. Chairperson

Smart knew Carl's family well and both families were related on multiple levels. Carl's cousin John Tipton traveled with Smart earlier that year and John's daughter even married into the Smart family in 1906.[68] Carl's legal struggles ended within hours. He was lawfully Carl Goodwin Crawford from that day forward.

Following the declaration, Carl lived a rather quiet life. He remained in Tennessee and opened a store in his home county for a short time. He then moved to Florida , where he became a real estate agent and married Mary E. Coachman, twenty years his senior, in 1906.[69] The marriage only lasted a few years. Like any other man of a certain age, he was forced to sign a draft card during World War I in 1918 but never saw combat. He settled down with his final wife, Annie M. Selleck, in 1919. By 1920, he took up clerical work at a plumbing company while Annie tended the house. Carl and Annie spent the rest of their lives together on Sixteenth Street in Jacksonville, where they retired. They lived with his mother, who died at age ninety-nine in 1939. Carl was buried next to his mother and sister in Jacksonville in 1944.

THE RUNAWAY: MOLLIE WILSON

Mollie Wilson's story remained unpublished until her childhood friend, Hattie Robinson, identified her body. After being nearly lynched as a teenager, Mollie lived a life of fighting for her freedom and autonomy. Her story, as you will see, was also shrouded in layers of mystery, which may have been the result of the cover she needed to survive as a trans person in the late nineteenth century. This secondhand narrative, the central source of this chapter, helps us better understand the lives of Black and Indigenous trans people of her era.

The story of Mollie's life begins with her death from tuberculosis in 1900.[70] Hattie Robinson, a laundress, saw her childhood friend Mollie for the first time in sixteen years just three weeks before Mollie died. The two coincidentally moved near each other in Kansas City, three hundred miles from their hometown of South McAlester, Choctaw Nation. The women struck up a conversation and Mollie told Hattie her life story.

According to Hattie, Mollie was born around 1865 in rural Choctaw territory. She grew up on a farm near the edge of town. Not much is known about her childhood other than that her parents were married and "well-to-do." She was Black and Native American, only speaking Chahta Anumpa (Choctaw) until later in her life.

Around age nineteen, while Mollie was still perceived as a man, rumors circulated that she assaulted a white woman with red hair (the rumors were not clear if it was sexual or physical assault). At the time, interracial dating was wildly stigmatized, so the accusations were questionable at best. "They did not give men a trial there in those days for any devilment they had committed," Hattie would later explain. "They lynched them." Mollie knew of the danger she was in and prepared to leave the territory. She put on her mother's dress intending to use her escape to transition. However, before she had time to flee, the alleged victim's mother led a lynch mob to her house. They were prepared to murder her. Armed with only a long knife, Mollie managed to kill three men and the mother during her brave escape from the attackers.

There is little information about Mollie's life over the following years. All we know is that she began using the name Mary Taylor before adopting the name Mollie.[71] In the 1890s, she returned to her hometown with her new name. Eventually, she moved to Kansas City, Missouri. She reportedly had a large group of friends, mostly Black residents of the city. Mollie always wore a dark dress and fascinator, and with a tall and thin frame, passed with ease. Her transition allowed her to blossom into a social butterfly without the fear of lynch mobs.

In 1899, after years of staying out of trouble, police arrested Mollie for walking while Black in Leavenworth, Kansas. Leavenworth was not officially a "sundown town," a municipality with racist laws that required people of color to leave the town by sundown. However, Mollie was reportedly targeted for being outside and Black at 1:20 a.m. She claims she boarded the wrong train while returning home, but the police accused her of sex work without evidence. She sat in jail wearing a lovely calico dress for nine days before the jailer discovered she was assigned male. The police refused to call her by the correct name, and she would not give them her birth name. They renamed her "Jim" out of spite. She was fined ten dollars and released.[72]

Mollie returned to Kansas City with her husband, Will. While it is unclear if they were legally married, the two were undoubtedly close. They moved in together near the Missouri River, which flows through the center of the city. Although there is no record of them separating, Mollie later moved in with Lou Byrum, a local woman. Lou did not know Mollie was assigned male at birth, though she recounted a sharp razor on Mollie's desk after her death and questioned if it was to shave her facial hair.

Only one year after her initial arrest, Mollie was detained in Kansas City in 1900 for sex work. The police let her off with a warning and ordered her to never return to town. Despite the officers' demands, Mollie would never have a chance to permanently leave: she caught deadly tuberculosis the following March.

Hattie Robinson, who narrated Mollie's story, coincidentally rented a room above where Mollie died. Hattie became curious after hearing a woman from Choctaw territory had died a floor below her. "I wonder if it's [Mollie]?" she murmured to herself. Officials dragged the body out of the flat, and Hattie joined a large group surrounding the corpse. She was astonished to see Mollie's remains. Hattie informed onlookers of a white mark on Mollie's leg that had been there since childhood. Indeed, she had found her old friend and told a *Kansas City Times* reporter the full story as the crowd watched in amazement. It is worth noting Mollie asked Hattie not to out her to the police. Hattie respected her wishes until her passing.

Police continued to scrutinize Mollie's life even after her death. They began to suspect Mollie and Will were responsible for a series of muggings over the previous months. Officials reported she was "wanted in the Indian territory for many bad deeds." The Black couple always had money, which roused their suspicions. This claim is dubious, however, considering the notorious racism of Kansas City police at the time.

We must, of course, always take these second- and thirdhand accounts with a grain of salt. Hattie or the reporter may have decided to embellish the story, which was typical for news at the time. Mollie's death still leaves us with many mysteries. She left a trunk full of letters, all addressed to

Mollie Wilson and her previous alias, Mary Taylor. These letters showed that she had recently sold land in South McAlester, contradicting Mollie's claim to Hattie that she had never returned to their hometown.

The Kansas City police's investigation was similarly inconclusive. The investigator contacted Mollie's hometown marshal. However, the marshal could not confirm or deny details from Hattie's story. The police found a grand jury indictment against Mollie in her pocket from her hometown. Yet, even stranger, the deputy could not locate any indictment in the court records. Perhaps there was a bookkeeping issue. If not, why would Mollie have a fake indictment against herself? The question was never settled.

The deputy eventually tracked down the man who purchased Mollie's land in South McAlester. He immediately identified Mollie as Mary Taylor and claimed she had been in federal prison numerous times (I could not locate any federal prison records under any of her names). The investigator consulted a few old residents of the town about the attempted lynching and assault of the red-haired girl. None could remember the event from sixteen years prior, although it is unknown if the police or reporters were asking the correct residents in the first place. The reporter and Hattie shared a narrative largely supported by government records like death certificates and arrest notices. Perhaps Hattie or the reporter fabricated the attempted lynching to draw attention to the story. Or, perhaps it was all accurate.

Mollie's life was undoubtedly marked time and time again by moments of unlikely survival in the face of deadly violence. With more records being discovered every year, someday we may find the truth of the matter. But today, we are left with the 120-year-old mystery of Mollie Wilson.

THE HEALER: MUKSAMSE'LAPLI

Muksamse'lapli, known to Oregonians as White Cindy, was always a fighter. A member of the Klamath nation, she had to battle settlers and members of her own tribe to survive. She was born in 1845 on Klamath land, about a year before the United Kingdom transferred ownership of the region to the United States. An outspoken self-advocate who was once accused of murder, she brought conversations about gender and race to the new territory. As someone we may now call two-spirit, or transfeminine, she described herself as "half she and half he" and "female."[73] Muksamse'lapli took on numerous roles in her community. She was a shaman, basket weaver, fire-eater, whiskey smuggler, dancer, cook, rancher, medic, and fighter.[74] Muksamse'lapli's exciting story helps us better understand the complicated relationships between settlers and Indigenous trans people during the early colonization of the United States.

By all accounts, Muksamse'lapli had a good sense of humor. She gained the ironic nickname White Cindy from settlers. Her "complexion was almost black" according to a local historian. Settlers described her "as black and forbidding-looking as a thundercloud."[75] She was six feet tall and her feminine attire was complemented by her reportedly masculine bone structure, leading to the feminine name Cindy. Yet almost all settlers used she/her pronouns for Muksamse'lapli and they respected her gender. They even continued to use them after her death, when settlers discovered her genitalia. White citizens of Klamath Falls did not know what to make of her gender/sex, but that did not stop Muksamse'lapli from becoming a pillar of her community.

Both during and after her life, townspeople were in broad disagreement over Muksamse'lapli's gender. To some, she was a masculine straight cis woman. To others, she was a feminine gay cis man, a woman pretending to be a man, or a man pretending to be a woman.[76] None of these terms were correct. There were several Klamath words— such as *t'wini꞉q* (pronounced twin-eek)—for people we now may call two-spirit.[77] T'wini꞉q individuals were of either assigned sex and lived outside respectable Klamath society but were largely accepted by their communities. By 1890 Muksamse'lapli used the unique subjective pronoun *Ämmä'ri* (pronounced eh-meh-ree), roughly translating to "neatly dressed."[78] It is unclear if other Klamath people used this term, but the white ethnographer who described the creative pronoun believed it was Muksamse'lapli's own invention.

Muksamse'lapli was far from the only member of her nation who took on gender roles that transgressed Western norms. In fact, contemporaneous scholars noted a multitude of gender presentations among Klamath people. T'wini꞉q typically adopted cultural roles that transgressed both male and female around the time of puberty. They were frequently healers and shamans like Muksamse'lapli but took on a variety of positions. While there is no record of when Muksamse'lapli first expressed her identity, her gender expression was noted by her mid-twenties in the 1860s.

Muksamse'lapli fought her way through decades of colonialism following the United States' claim over Oregon as a territory in 1848. In 1864, when she was only about nineteen, the Klamath tribes ceded over twenty-three million acres to the hostile settlers. They received relative peace, land use rights, and a small compensation in return.[79] Cattle ranching and timber were promoted within the former Klamath territory, helping the tribe retain some of its power through production. Muksamse'lapli took up ranching and earned a living from her herds for years. These profitable occupations helped the tribe interact with the surrounding colonizers, meaning historians have more knowledge from nineteenth-century Klamath people than most other Indigenous Nations—albeit predominantly from settler records.

There are many other delightful—and relatively unrelated—details of Muksamse'lapli's life that were only reported long after she died. Her neighbors would fondly reminisce about Muksamse'lapli's love for bright colors, which she frequently incorporated into her wardrobe. She often sported a green-and-white striped skirt, pink belt, and bright hat with vibrant flowers. She once danced for nickels to afford colorful ribbons that she sewed into her headpiece.[80] The red, yellow, and purple ribbons poured down the brim of her sun hat like a waterfall before Muksamse'lapli tied them into bows. Klamath Falls residents fondly remembered these aspects of Muksamse'lapli's life for decades to come. Although such details may be less significant to Muksamse'lapli's story, they show how far she ventured to express herself in a rapidly changing world.

White terror

In the fall of 1870, Muksamse'lapli was forced from her home and onto a nearby reservation organized by settlers. While traveling to the new reservation, she led a group of six Klamath women who cooked for their camp. At the time, twenty-five-year-old Muksamse'lapli dated a Klamath man whom the colonizers called "Mountain Pete." One night, Muksamse'lapli took a log from the fire against Pete's wishes. She reportedly removed the timber to make it easier on the cis women who gathered the wood while the men gambled. Her small act of camaraderie with the cis women shows a sense of solidarity and empathy the white journalists failed to report in their news articles, which consistently framed Muksamse'lapli as angry and violent. But no good deed goes unpunished. Pete was not keen on her decision to cool the fire and suddenly attacked his partner with a knife. A Klamath sergeant stopped him from killing Muksamse'lapli by tripping the man.

Muksamse'lapli married at least twice. First, she married a Molala man named Tčĭ'ptcĭ. It is unclear if this was Mountain Pete's real name. Later, she married a man named Tc!o'mŏks. It is again unclear if this man was Blaine Ben Johns, born in 1849 in Oregon Territory, who was listed as one of her husbands by settlers decades later.[81] Over the following years, Muksamse'lapli described herself as a widow. There are no records of either of these men dying, but government records of the Klamath tribe were limited. Muksamse'lapli managed to evade federal documentation until the 1890s, making the dates and details of her marriages fuzzy.

As a shaman, Muksamse'lapli sometimes helped the settlers with their ailments. According to historians, the tribe and settlers alike believed Klamath shamans had spiritual powers. Muksamse'lapli treated the sick and made medicine. According to settler records, her designation was even higher than a chief (although such a hierarchy is debated among Indigenous scholars). Long after she died, residents of Klamath County remembered Muksamse'lapli for sparking widespread fear when she supposedly willed lightning to strike a nearby tree. She frequently promised to curse those who bothered her. The threats worked as she was almost universally feared by those who met her.

In 1896 a botanist for the US Department of Agriculture spent three days with Muksamse'lapli for research. As the healer of the community, she knew about all the local plants used for food and medicine. The botanist gathered information on about one hundred plants used by the tribe and published a short book, *Notes on the Plants Used by the Klamath Indians of Oregon*, the following year. The book is still in print. Thanks to Muksamse'lapli's work, many traditional Klamath plant customs were retained following colonial displacement.[82]

Despite Muksamse'lapli's famous temper, many who knew her gleefully reflected on her strong sense of humor. A local physician recalled treating a tribe member around the turn of the century. He met his patient in a room filled with Indigenous locals. As the doctor examined the patient, Muksamse'lapli sneaked behind him and shouted "boo!" at the top of her lungs.[83] He jumped up in shock. The entire room laughed, including the doctor. If the colonizers were going to terrorize Muksamse'lapli's nation, she would scare the colonizers right back.

Muksamse'lapli further intimidated and mystified settlers with her elegant attire. One observer wrote to a paper in 1886 that "her style of beauty is enhanced by a black and red nubia and a dress of black velvet, trimmed with gilt buttons."[84] She was frequently spotted in elegant dresses while selling baskets and riding horses.

Assaults

Muksamse'lapli stayed out of the spotlight for years. However, on October 23, 1904, a group of settlers found one of Muksamse'lapli's neighbors lying unconscious two miles from Klamath Falls. They brought the man, Frank Jack, back to town. Frank, well-known in the Klamath reservation, was the son of Link River Jack, the famous chief of the Link River tribe.[85] Frank claimed Muksamse'lapli hit him over the head with a rock. Muksamse'lapli denied the allegation and said she saw two white settlers attack Frank Jack. Sheriff Obenchain seized Muksamse'lapli's horse, on which he found a buckskin glove, an empty whiskey bottle, and the rock that nearly killed Frank Jack and that was still covered in his blood. He arrested Muksamse'lapli and confined her to jail. She was charged with assault with a dangerous weapon. She admitted they were fighting over a large amount of whisky the two were transporting, leading Muksamse'lapli to hit Frank over the head. The fifty-nine-year-old pleaded guilty the following month and was forced to pay a fifty-dollar fine to the government.

Muksamse'lapli kept to herself for nearly a decade. On May 31, 1914, she again made headlines for supposedly swinging Peter Philips around her head with his tie, leading to his death in a Klamath graveyard. The claims were suspect, considering Muksamse'lapli would be sixty-nine that year. To pick up a man and swing him by his necktie would take incredible strength. Tribe members, however, alleged Muksamse'lapli "has the strength of three men" and made the case for the attack's possibility.[86] Frank Jack's beating did not help her cause. The news of an elder medicine woman swinging a full-grown man by his tie circulated across the West Coast from the *Los Angeles Times* to local Oregonian papers. Without evidence, newspapers had already decided on her guilt. "White Cindy Kills Aged Klamath Indian," one headline declared.[87] It did not take even a week to discover that fifty-nine-year-old Peter actually died from a heart attack hours after Muksamse'lapli beat him. By June 6, authorities freed Muksamse'lapli when the investigators decided that his death was not related to the attack.

In memory

The colonization of Oregon complicates Muksamse'lapli's story. Most reporting on the Klamath leader came long after her passing. Unfortunately, the stories in Muksamse'lapli's narrative are predominantly recounted through the lens of settlers. But, those who were alive in her time rarely forgot her. The memory of Muksamse'lapli flourished as the young people who knew her grew older and more comfortable speaking about their experiences.

Muksamse'lapli died from "old age" in 1919.[88] Edith R. McLeod, a white Klamath Falls resident, wrote a reflective article about Muksamse'lapli in 1950. She interviewed settlers who reminisced about their experiences with the Indigenous leader and described her as a fearsome yet respected figure. "Old-timers of Klamath Falls remember her well, as do I," McLeod reflected. "I well remember that as a child I always crossed the street when I saw her coming, being afraid of her from stories that I heard." Thanks to McLeod's research on Muksamse'lapli's life, Klamath Falls residents began showing a renewed interest in White Cindy. McLeod noted people like Muksamse'lapli were "socially canalized and taunted though permitted to live as they desired."[89] McLeod's accounts, while undoubtedly exoticized, helped white and Indigenous people celebrate Muksamse'lapli's life and contributions to the community.

Over the decades, Muksamse'lapli has received a sentence or two in no fewer than a half dozen transgender and queer books. Leslie Feinberg briefly mentioned her in hir award-winning 1996 book *Transgender Warriors*. Despite this recognition, her post-1950 depictions were only elements of broader stories, never the story itself. Hopefully, this retelling will help Muksamse'lapli's colorful life shine once more.

THE PACIFIST: SADIE ACOSTA

Sadie Acosta may have delivered her most iconic line from jail: "I rather be a woman, so I am a woman." As defiant as she was confident, she was among the first trans people to publicly protest misgendering by the US draft board (an issue that continues to this day). Sadie's story features important historical breakthroughs as an early draft dissenter, a transgender teenager, and the woman who helped bring tortillas to Fort Collins.

Sadie grew up in the tiny town of Balmorhea, Texas. She was born on April 10, 1909, to Juan Acosta and Celsa Casildo, two undocumented migrants from Mexico.[90] Her grandmother, Josephine Casildo, raised Sadie after her parents died when she was an infant. Josephine presumably supported her granddaughter's gender as Sadie transitioned around the age of thirteen under her care. She only completed sixth grade before dropping out of school. Not much else is known about her teen years, and there are no records of her using the name Sadie Acosta while living in Texas.

As a girl, Sadie moved to Fort Collins in 1922 and lived peacefully for years. The young woman soon began to receive checks from the state as a widow, although it is unclear if she was ever married. She bought a colorful adobe house on a suburban street and renovated it over the years. Standing at only five foot two and weighing 134 pounds, nobody suspected she was trans. In 1937 the American Association of University Women even brought Sadie to Colorado Agricultural College to demonstrate baking what they called "Mexican bread" (tortillas).[91] At the time, tortillas were rare in Colorado, and this was likely one of the first demonstrations of the art of baking them.

Sadie's relatively normal life came to a halt in 1940. She had to undergo an operation and her doctor realized she was assigned male at birth. He reported her gender status to the sheriff, who swiftly arrested her. She objected to being thrown into the men's prison by protesting, "I'm a woman!" The officer did not listen.

At the time, it was commonplace for police to arrest trans women under cross-dressing laws. However, 1940 was a unique era that added to the scandal. On the brink of entering World War II, the US was in a moment of heightened nationalism. Registering for the draft was not only a requirement by law but also a declaration of patriotism, masculinity, and citizenship. Perhaps this is one reason why Sadie's story shocked the public. Reporters claimed she pretended to be a woman to escape military service (despite having already lived as a woman for eighteen years). Avoiding the draft was equated to siding with the enemies at the time.

The draft board physician gave Sadie a complete physical examination. "She is definitely a man," he reported.[92]

"So?" Acosta retorted. "But I rather be a woman, so I am a woman."

Newspapers around the country picked up the unusual story from Fort Collins in early 1941. The word *transsexual* was not coined for another eight years, leading to much confusion among publications. Sadie continued to wear dresses, long hair, and jewelry after being outed, removing any doubt of her gender.

The draft board officials declared the law "does not give prospective draftees the right to choose their sex." The officials forced her to sign a draft card, which was released to the public decades later. Her handwriting is pressed deep into the paper, typical signs of anger, resentment, and frustration. She refused to provide her address, marking her street simply as "General Delivery." She entered only the minimum required information before disappearing. There are no records of her following the scandal.

Today, conscription remains a controversial element of transition. US trans women between eighteen and twenty-five are still required to register for selective service, even if they have changed their legal documentation.

They may be stripped of federal student aid if caught avoiding selective service. The government can still arrest unregistered trans women during a draft. Ironically, trans women could not openly join the military until 2021 (except for 2015 to 2019 under Obama administration policy). This meant they were required to submit selective service information despite the impossibility of legal participation.[93] Contradictions like these continue to this day for trans women as the state struggles to keep up with the flourishing of gender identity and expression.

THE COMMUNITY LEADER: GEORGIA BLACK

Georgia Mae Black was a beloved mother, friend, and church volunteer. The outgoing woman traveled across the South to find love, family, and a community where she fit in. Her story is not only one of transition but also self-advocacy. The community leader's unending commitment to those around her helped her thrive in a time when prejudice against Black and trans people often turned deadly. Georgia, a teenage transitioner and pillar of her town, embodied the sort of radical kindness that can unite all people.

"By every law of society, Georgia Black should have died in disgrace and humiliation and been remembered as a sex pervert, a 'fairy' and a 'freak,'" *Ebony*'s 1951 exposé on Georgia's life began.[94] Yet residents of her town of Sanford, Florida, came to her defense when she was at her most vulnerable. She was not a typical activist who fought for broad social justice issues. Instead, she worked to improve her town with mutual aid, community organizing, and kindness. Georgia's narrative is the story of how one Black trans woman unified a city during an era of extreme segregation.

Georgia was born around 1892 and grew up in Greeleyville, South Carolina, on a rural farm.[95] The state did not have compulsory education and she remained in school only until the third grade. She reportedly ran away at age fifteen because she despised the harsh manual labor her family forced on her. After departing from her hometown, Georgia first moved to Charleston and began working for a gay man who owned a mansion. He decided he wanted to date her after the two bonded. She happily obliged. She began to dress in clothing designed for women and they lived together for a short time. The older man soon broke off their relationship. Without the ability to read or write, Georgia traveled to Florida and became a laundress. At sixteen, she lived openly as a woman in Sanford.

Georgia's relatives soon grew to accept her. They respected her gender and never spoke of her transition. She kept in touch with her family after moving and updated them on her life. The whole family grew closer through her transition as they learned to support her. She even had a younger brother and sister who claimed not to know she was assigned male at birth until after her death.[96]

Georgia met Alonzo Sabb during her travels. Alonzo became violently ill and Georgia nursed him back to health. The two held a strong bond and married on January 14, 1912.[97] Despite being openly trans, Georgia found a judge who would allow her to marry Alonzo, and she legally became Georgia Sabb. She entered a masculine name on the record, although it is unclear if it was her birth name. They permanently moved to the city of Sanford, with a population of around four thousand. The city is about thirty miles north of Orlando but had a more conservative outlook on social issues. Sanford was heavily segregated, and job opportunities were limited. The young woman rented out and maintained an extra room in her home for income.

Sanford is a historical city for all the wrong reasons. It's most well-known for ejecting baseball legend Jackie Robinson from an exhibition league game in 1946 after Ku Klux Klan protests. Later, the city would regain fame for being the site of Trayvon Martin's slaying. It incidentally helped launch the Black Lives Matter movement. There is no record of why Georgia moved to such a fiercely segregated town. However, she would find ways to thrive among her neighbors for the rest of her life.

Georgia and Alonzo adopted a baby, Willie, in 1913.[98] Willie was the biological son of Georgia's cousin and was born in her hometown. Willie's mother died when he was only three weeks old, leaving him with the Sabbs. His adoption gifted her with a cherished son. Unfortunately, Willie barely had a chance to know his adoptive father. Alonzo was killed in 1917 in a nearby town.

Outgoing and personable, Georgia quickly met another man, Muster Black. Muster worked on engines in a railroad and lived his entire life in

Sanford.[99] The two courted and married in early 1918 when she was about twenty-five. "When I got married the second time, I was dressed all in white chiffon. Those days are still fresh to me," she would reminisce later in life.[100] They were wed at the home of a respected elementary school principal. A prominent minister officiated the ceremony. Georgia, Muster, and Willie moved into a four-room frame house in a white neighborhood. They reported being content and comfortable there, with no significant issues.

Five months later, the government drafted Muster into the army to fight in World War I.[101] He enlisted as a private but was honorably discharged just six months later. He never saw combat. The couple spent seven happy years together in Sanford before he died of hepatitis in 1925. Georgia collected forty-five dollars of monthly pension as his widow for the rest of her life. She used the extra space to turn her home into a boardinghouse.

Everyone who knew Georgia attested that she was a loving mother. Her son did not know she was transgender—nor did he care. The two lived together for decades and they adored one another. Like his mother, Willie received only an elementary education and took up manual labor for the rest of his life. Willie was large and tall. At six foot two, he towered over most around him and was recruited for various manual jobs. He worked at a box factory for twelve years for $1.50 per day.[102] Later, in 1930, he took up work at Shinholster Mill in Sanford while his mother stayed home. By 1940, he took up labor on a freight line. Willie would often send his extra income, along with gifts, to his beloved mother.

Following the Great Depression, Georgia became a cook for a local family. She labored through intense forty-two-hour weeks for eighty dollars a month. Georgia allegedly became famous for her recipes and "was one of the best, if not the best, cake maker in town."[103] Always modest, she would call her talent "just a gift God gave me." She also became a servant to a nearby family.[104] Even while working full-time, she always dedicated her extra moments to her church group at her local St. James AME (African Methodist Episcopal) Church. They raised funds and reached out to the community, helping Georgia gain the adoration of all those around her, Black and white.

Illness and outing

Georgia became extremely ill in 1950. She vehemently refused medical treatment until she was no longer able to. "Don't want to go to no hospital," she repeated to her son.[105] Eventually, Willie's wife Henrietta drove her to Dr. Orville Barks. The doctor examined her and instantly realized she was assigned male at birth. "Do you see what I saw?" Orville asked Henrietta.[106] The doctor claimed that she was "a man" and the pair drove back home in silence. Her physicians then tested her for intersex traits but found none. Orville reported her condition to the police. Chief Roy Williams swiftly probed her background but decided not to prosecute her upon discovering she had no criminal history. The news of Georgia's terminal cancer was only secondary to her gender.

Georgia may not have been legally prosecuted, but her trial was just beginning. The local *Sanford Herald* picked up her story and she became the talk of the town. A radio station aired an episode on her curious case. The Associated Press then circulated it nationally. After hearing of her incredible life, *Ebony* decided to interview Georgia and others in the town. Unlike most other papers reporting on Black trans women, it took a neutral stance on her transition and decided to let her speak for herself.

Her two siblings and son had never seen her in the nude and had no idea she was transgender. In fact, no living person in Sanford appeared to have known her sex before she was outed. "I never did nuthin wrong in my life," she explained.[107] She referred to her genitalia merely as "growths" and demanded to be called a woman, even after being outed.

Her town felt similarly. They not only defended her but also took action against those reporting on her case. Locals rebuked Dr. Barks for outing Georgia, and he admitted his regret in being involved. The town's reverend later called the newspaper to complain about the reporting on her. The editor apologized and ceased all writing on her. Her church held prayers for her recovery.

During her hospital stay, the *Ebony* reporter traveled through town and interviewed locals about Georgia's trans status. They described the town as divided into two camps: "Those who didn't believe Black had deceived them and those who didn't care." The journalist noted the typical sentiment among her neighbors was, "as far as I'm concerned, her life is her business." One of Georgia's employers added, "I don't care what Georgia Black was. She nursed members of our family through birth, sickness and death. She was one of the best citizens in town."

Others simply didn't believe the stories. "It's just impossible. We've known Georgia for years. Why, we think the world of her. We've been to see her and taken her food and gifts. If she was a man, she really fooled us. It's impossible," a white couple explained.

Georgia remained close with Muster Black's sister, Lugenia, after his death. Lugenia took care of Georgia during the final months on her deathbed. *Ebony* photographed the pair as Lugenia combed Georgia's hair. Georgia gazed into a mirror, hands frail from her illness. Shortly before her death, she reflected, "My husbands and me had a peaceful, lovely life." Her close family, friends, and church each demonstrated just how lovely it was. Willie and Henrietta also helped tend to Georgia's needs. One day, Henrietta found the foam Georgia used to enlarge her breasts. She did not think much of them at the time and did not even ask Georgia about them.

Over her final weeks, Georgia sent Willie a letter expressing her love for him. "You've been a wonderful son to me," she wrote. Willie, now living in Philadelphia, prepared a speech to tell her when he arrived at her deathbed in Sanford: "Mom I know there has been an awful lot of talk [. . .] about you, and a lot of people have talked to me about you and a lot of people have been spreading some pretty strange stories. But I want you to know I don't believe a word of it. You're still my Mom and I love you. You were a wonderful mother to me."[108] He never had the chance to tell her directly before her death but stated his feelings to the whole the world through his writing, instead.

Willie penned a long-form *Ebony* article defending his mother in June 1953. "My mother was a man, but I'm not at all ashamed of it," he explained.[109] He wrote the essay to correct the "many mistakes in these accounts of her life" because "my love for her is too strong even after death, to permit her story to be twisted and distorted." He fondly remembered her cooking, particularly the "chicken, pork chops and fish dishes" she would make him.[110] "Mother was a man all right. But to me she was the most wonderful mother a man could want. [. . .] Some say she lived a lie, I don't. Georgia Black raised me to manhood and gave me tenderness and affection. I loved her with all my heart and shall cherish her memory as long as I live. She will always be Mom to me."[111]

Georgia passed in Sanford a few weeks after her 1951 interview appeared in *Ebony*. Despite the media circus around Georgia's gender, the town came together to mourn her death. Her neighbors refused to condemn her transness, and there were no public complaints of "deception." Her funeral cortege slowly meandered the streets of Sanford while Black and white neighbors came together to pay their respects. Whites brushed elbows with Black residents and they shared memories of Georgia with one another. Her family buried her in the clothing of her choice.

Cultural theorist C. Riley Snorton's 2017 monograph *Black on Both Sides: A Racial History of Trans Identity* is one of the only texts to discuss Georgia since she died. The short section in his book reviews the *Ebony* article and points to a certain irony. "Black's death did what for many black and blackened peoples felt unattainable," he writes.[112] Georgia's passing imbued her with life in the eyes of the public. She found innovative means to obtain empathy in the highly segregated era. Snorton suggests the *Ebony* article disrupts the presumed history of progress in the trans community. That is, cultural attitudes toward transition do not simply improve with time. Anti-trans sentiments have always fluctuated and are ultimately inseparable from race.

Ebony printed the article on Georgia seven months after she died. The commentary may provide one of the earliest accounts of a whole town coming together to celebrate and defend a trans person. Hopefully, Georgia's story will inspire others to do the same.

THE GUARDIAN: OKIYO

Okiyo was born in 1916 in Osaka, Japan. Her history represents several key events in both Japanese and US trans history. She witnessed a rapidly transforming nation in her lifetime, working under disparate treatment in Imperial Japan and the US occupation that followed. In 1948, she incited a forgotten trans and sex worker–led riot against police that helped dele-gitimize the Japanese force across the country. Okiyo's story helps us better understand the complex legal and sociocultural dynamics between trans people in the US and Japan.

To call Okiyo "trans" is not entirely accurate. There were specific (al-though still transgressive) gender roles for women like her. She is most often described as a dansho: a sex worker who was assigned male at birth and worked—and generally lived—wearing clothing typically associated with women.[113] Nevertheless, Okiyo certainly fits all the qualifications of who we would describe as a trans person today. She also lived most of her life as a self-described woman. Her narrative provides us with vital, underreported context into how trans people lived and resisted under US and Japanese rule.

Osaka and World War II

Little is known about Okiyo's background before she entered work on stage as an *oyama*. The common Kabuki theater role parallels drag in the US.[114] As a young woman, Okiyo realized she was queer and began her oyama career in Osaka. She transitioned during this period, sometime before early 1946.

Life in Osaka was not easy during the 1940s. Okiyo survived the US military killing of over ten thousand people, including her friends and neighbors, throughout the city. On March 13, 1945, one of the largest air-craft deployed during World War II dropped 1,733 tons of bombs on the metropolis, beginning a siege that would last until the final days of the war in August.[115] This day was among the deadliest for the city, razing a greater area than the nuclear bomb dropped on Hiroshima. Craters marked the ground like paint splattering on canvas. The US followed with additional mass bombings in the summer. On August 9, 1945, the United States dropped the "Fat Man" bomb on Nagasaki. The Japanese government offered to end the war if Emperor Hirohito could remain in power. The US refused and the attacks on Japan continued over the next five days. The military bombed Osaka on August 15, and within hours Japan announced its surrender. The final air raid infamously killed over seven hundred civilians sheltering in a train station.[116] The conclusion of World War II was only the beginning of a new conflict for Okiyo: US occupation.

Following the Japanese surrender, General Douglas MacArthur took command of the nation and its territories in 1945. The notoriously conservative veteran exercised supreme power over the archipelago. Among his first orders was cracking down on sex work and non-Western sexual expression. The occupation forces established what historian Mark McLelland calls a "censorship regime."[117] The attempt at westernizing Japan meant strict control over discourse. All publications had to be sent to the new Civil Censorship Detachment for review before release. The unit only allowed materials aligned with the US and its subjective values. This meant severe limits on discussions of gender and sexuality.

Sex work was regulated and partially legal before the end of World War II. Japan had strict guidelines, but it was ultimately lawful to sell sex under the correct legal circumstances. However, when General MacArthur began administering occupied Japan, the government outlawed almost all forms of sex trade.[118] These new laws led to additional challenges for dansho, who often struggled to find work. In May 1948, the official maximum punishment was two years of hard labor and a fine of ten thousand yen (several months' salary for most sex workers). Conversely, the occupiers increased the demand for sex work and paid higher rates. In one district, women reported Westerners paying them around twice as much for the same services.[119] Wedged between strict punishment and increasing rewards, the colonial government sent dansho sex workers conflicting messages.

Tokyo

With 65 percent of Tokyo's homes destroyed and new laws against selling sex, World War II pushed sex work into public spaces.[120] Ueno Park in Tokyo became Japan's most significant site of the transgender sex trade in the 1940s. The 133-acre park had many escape routes, hiding spaces, bush cover, and transportation options. City planners accidentally built an ideal space for the underground economy.[121]

Okiyo moved to Tokyo between late 1945 and 1946.[122] With the war over, dansho began working in large groups together for the first time. Although many were left desolate and homeless, they found solace in Ueno Park, where they could find clients and other gender-transgressive people.

The group of danshō called one another *go-ren-san* (someone together) and protected each other from the police.[123] At the beginning of this wave of collaboration came Okiyo. The other danshō called her *o-nē-san* (older sister). She was considered the group leader and took on a guardian-like role. Instead of taking a commanding position like Western trans leaders, she nurtured and protected the group as more of a steward than a boss. The twenty-nine-year-old was among the first danshō working out of Ueno, although smaller groups operated in the park before the war.

Ueno Park featured a spatialized hierarchy of workers. Young cis women (predominantly teenage girls called *panpan*) were among the most popular workers at the park. The *yama no pan* panpan subgroup would operate in the highest hills of the park. They wore more traditional clothing and were considered among the "lowest" in social status. The *shita no pan* subgroup operated near the park's south exit by the train station in more modern attire. Danshō would congregate near a famous 1898 bronze statue of Saigō Takamori. The renowned samurai orchestrated a rebellion against the Meiji government, unintentionally serving as a symbol of subversion for the workers operating under him. The queer and trans individuals comprised around 10 percent of sex workers in the park in 1946, increasing to 50 percent by 1952.[124] Japanese ethnographer Ōtani Susumu estimated that 1,500 to 2,000 sex workers occupied the park each night in 1948, depending on the season. Shortly before the riot, another researcher noted that danshō as young as sixteen operated from the parks. Other trans people sold drugs and ran gangs in the park. A well-known transmasculine (*dansō*) gang leader known as the "Elder Sister of the Mountain" also operated out of Ueno.[125] Trans sellers of methamphetamine were common after the Japanese government overproduced the drug, which it had distributed to boost the energy of pilots and soldiers during the war. The cast of queer figures touched every corner of the park, each avoiding authorities with their own distinct strategies.

The Tokyo Metropolitan Police were aware of the illegal activities in Ueno Park. The district police later boasted they produced a list of 610 danshō with pictures, which they used to arrest offenders.[126] The sex workers of the park were equally aware of being surveilled as the police often came to them with photos of suspects and missing persons. Although Tokyo police claimed they had a benign relationship with danshō, the sex workers described being unhappy with the scrutiny, knowing it would be used against them under the new government.

Police chief Eiichi Tanaka was at the center of the conquest against sex work, drug dealing, and protesting during Okiyo's years in Ueno Park. The large, outspoken forty-seven-year-old man was appointed superintendent general of the Tokyo Metropolitan Government in 1947.[127] He would later represent Tokyo in the National Diet (Japan's legislative branch) for the conservative nationalist Liberal Democratic Party (LDP). Tanaka and his political party were notorious for suppressing leftist causes and those already targeted by police like danshō. According to critics of the LDP and the Japanese conservative movement, politicians who harassed these groups would be rewarded with promotions, respect, and favorable attention. Tanaka's grandfather coincidentally died while fighting for Saigō Takamori during the Satsuma Rebellion. One could only imagine how he felt seeing danshō operating under Takamori's statue. We cannot know Tanaka's internal motivations for targeting the sex workers of Ueno Park, although there were clear material benefits to his campaign against them.[128]

The Ueno Park Riots

Police Chief Tanaka led a large group of officers and government officials directly to the danshō on November 22, 1948. Dozens of the feminine sex workers waited around the Saigō Takamori statue during the cool, hazy fall evening, not aware of the imminent danger. Police, officials, and reporters marched into Ueno Park like soldiers as the fog thickened around the fall foliage. Various reports note there were between thirty and sixty officials at the scene and thirty to thirty-five danshō. Verbal harassment quickly ensued between the groups. A physical scuffle then began when the police group's photographer attempted to capture photos of the sex workers. Frustrated with the surveillance, Okiyo approached Tanaka and hit him in his round, close-shaven face.[129]

"I was so angry that I punched the one who looked the biggest," Okiyo later explained to a journalist.[130] The riot ensued. Many of the danshō were former soldiers, meaning they had combat training. The whole group had a wide array of experience (in combat and employment) and ranged in age from twenty to fifty.[131] Some took on more physical means of defense than others. One in Okiyo's group, Akiko, proudly hit a detective with her purse to break free of his tight clutch on her wrist.[132] While police beat the danshō near the statue, some reports mention other sex workers joining as the melee escalated.[133] Police also harassed the various groups of panpan. The Ueno Park riots served as a rare opportunity to collectively resist. We have few details of exactly how the sex workers beat the police, but reporters noted there were injuries on both sides.

Although over thirty danshō participated in the riot, the police arrested only five of them, including Okiyo. She was eventually released from jail as a hero of the people. The police were deeply unpopular in occupied Japan. There was "considerable dread of the police" and "the average Japanese was just plain scared of them, and wanted nothing to do with them" according to one government-funded report in 1947.[134] When photos came out of the danshō attacking the police while wearing highly feminine kimono and handbags, much of the public believed it was an inspiring moment of rebellion. The authorities were humiliated, and the potential for resistance suddenly emerged from the police's own naivety. Following the incident, Okiyo gained the nickname "Okiyo of the Iron Fist" from those who recognized her bravery. Cis or trans, underground or formal worker, locals valorized Okiyo. Her punch and the ensuing collective action empowered the workers of Ueno Park for years to come.

The following month police cracked down on sex workers again. Residents destroyed the shanties built by unhoused people throughout the neighborhood, many of whom were trans sex workers. They closed Ueno after dark until six in the morning.[135] However, it was too late for the authorities to maintain their reputation for diligence. The media already took up the danshō's struggle and began conducting sympathetic recorded discussions (*zandankai*) for the group. Many of the danshō involved in the Ueno Park riots recounted their experiences of triumph, struggle, and solidarity during the 1940s and 1950s roundtables, which provide us with much of what we know about the small uprising today.

The government would make dozens of additional attempts to curb sex work in Ueno Park. Not one of their efforts ever succeeded in eliminating it. In 1950 police closed Ueno Hill, a wooded area overlooking the large Shinobazu Pond, after dark. A danshō named Machi was one of the early victims of the new lockdown. An officer accosted her for breaking the Ueno Hill curfew while she walked down the hilltop around 3 a.m. A longtime practitioner of judo, Machi flipped the officer onto his back, ripping his uniform in the process. Various danshō cited Okiyo as their inspiration for fighting back like this. If police successfully drove sex workers from one area of the park, they would simply move into a different one. Ueno Park continues to be a significant site for Japanese sex work to this day.

By 1952, there were seven major areas around Tokyo where male and trans women sex workers congregated. However, Ueno Park remained the only site where more than a dozen of them would congregate at once, with around sixty regular workers.[136] Danshō were so entrenched in the local culture that some of the veteran sex workers established schools so others could learn the trade. Okiyo, on the other hand, retired. That year, she opened a bar, also named Okiyo, in the red-light district of Yoshiwara. The bar became widely popular and frequented by celebrities like novelist Junnosuke Yoshiyuki and actress Ava Gardner. Okiyo hired another trans woman, Tokiyo, for various services in her establishment. Tokiyo received the nickname "Okiyo's Doll" for her intense beauty and unexpressive demeanor.[137] The two were often confused for one another due to their similar names and working relationship.

While the public viewed Police Chief Eiichi Tanaka's attack as a humiliating defeat for him, he continued to gain prominence. He became increasingly fixated on law and order, citing inspiration from the United States. He penned a book, *American Places*, describing his travels throughout the US for the International Association of Chiefs of Police in 1953.[138] Tanaka met with J. Edgar Hoover, the director of the FBI, while in the States. Like Tanaka, Hoover portrayed himself as the adversary to various social movements, believing he could stop them through shame, scrutiny, and sabotage. Tanaka strongly believed in the FBI director's surveillance tactics, and the two promised to stay in touch. However, the police chief quit his job in protest of Japan's 1954 police reform bill, which established a more centralized police command and enacted a basic accountability system. The law explicitly banned activities such as police sexual abuse and forms of brutality not otherwise subject to oversight.[139] Tanaka then joined two Japanese prime ministers' cabinets in succession as deputy chief cabinet secretary through 1958. Voters subsequently elected him to represent the 1st district of Tokyo in the National Diet for the right-wing Liberal Democratic Party for six terms. He retired in 1976 and died in 1980.

Okiyo's life also improved after facing Tanaka. Well-known Japanese journalist Keiichi Hirooka's interview of Okiyo in 1955 is among the most detailed accounts of her struggle. It was later published in Hirooka's book *Sengo fūzoku taikei: Waga megami-tachi* (*A survey of entertainment after the war: My goddesses*). Included among the book's photos is a portrait of Okiyo.[140] She posed with a half smile while holding a tabby cat. She stared slightly away from Hirooka's camera into the background with her full face of foundation and lipstick. Although there is no color in the photo, the woman's kimono breaks up the otherwise neutral palate of the scene. Hirooka wrote fondly of Okiyo's resistance, "Because of this heroic episode, Okiyo was regarded as a hero by danshō all over the country." There are few records of Okiyo after this time, but her legend lives on among the queer and trans community of Japan.

THE PROFESSOR: MAUDE MILBOURNE

Maude Milbourne is one of the few subjects in this book who was eager to tell the story of her gender to the entire nation. "I am physically a man, yet spiritually and intellectually I am neither a man nor a woman," she wrote for outlets around the country in 1905.[141] "While I feel that in form and spirit I incline more to effeminacy and am gradually taking on more of the nature of womanhood." Maude's story radically shifts the timeline of trans activism through her work as an outspoken advocate from the 1880s to

1900s. A talented musician and writer, she also became what we may now describe as the first openly transgender elected official in 1885. This chapter recounts her exciting life, from the Civil War to her national organizing, including long-lost autobiographical statements and a 1904 proposal to manufacture a device that could change one's sex.

Born in Fayette County, Ohio, on August 15, 1843, Maude was gender-nonconforming for as long as she could remember.[142] She was the child of a twenty-one-year-old mother, Almira C. Waugh, and father, Isaac Milbourne. Isaac died when she was a baby. Almira remarried in 1846 to a schoolteacher named William DeVoss, who died when Maude and her younger brother, Austin, were ten and five respectively. Almira, widowed twice, began raising her two children on her own. It was shortly before William's death that Maude started to express her gender-nonconforming behavior. Young people of all genders would wear dresses until they came of age during the nineteenth century. However, Maude "screamed and jumped" when her mother tried to force her into pantaloons. Instead of rejecting her child as most parents did at the time, her mother supported her desire and let her wear what she wanted while in the home.

Maude joined the Union Army soon after the start of the Civil War.[143] She enlisted in 1861, a month after her eighteenth birthday, while still a student. She spent the next two years as a private in the Eighty-first Regiment of the Ohio Infantry. The famous unit was commonly known as Morton's Independent Rifle Regiment for its use of high-quality Enfield rifles. The regiment saw extensive combat, including the battles of Shiloh, Corinth, and Iuka in Tennessee and Mississippi from 1862 to 1863. Maude lost the tip of her finger and experienced severe scarring from combat. She also had edema of her legs and groin (which is coincidentally now cured with the same medication trans people take to suppress testosterone). Maude transferred to the Veteran Reserve Corps due to her injuries on December 15, 1863. However, the scrawny five-foot-nine twenty-year-old was determined to fulfil her three-year term. As a talented musician, she was appointed as a drum major, leading a Union military band in battle. Drummers, typically teenage boys, still played an essential role in fighting. Union bands learned dozens of patterns to relay information across battlefields.[144] Maude later received an impressive monthly pension of twenty-four dollars after her 1864 discharge as an injured veteran.

Maude became a wagon painter in Concord, Ohio, after the war. She soon started playing the cornet as a hobby.[145] The instrument, similar to a trumpet, developed into her new passion. By the 1880s, Maude contemplated becoming a professional. She also began spending more time in her county's big city, Washington Court House (population 3,798 in 1880). In March 1883, a local paper reported on Maude's first public escapade in a dress. She appeared on the street "*a la* Oscar Wilde—knee-breetches [sic], silk stockings and low cut shoes."[146] The reporter noted she was quite the talk among boys.

In November 1884, age forty-one, she posted in her local newspaper about considering leaving for Warren, Ohio, to study at Dana's Musical Institute (the institute, a well-known music school, still operates through Youngstown State University). It did not take Maude long to decide. She enrolled and was taking courses by the spring. She soon began teaching as a music professor. She continued to study over the following years and could reportedly perform on nearly any instrument by the 1900s. The drums of the Civil War led to the music industry flourishing in the States, much to Maude's benefit.

Along with her activism, teaching skills, and musical talents, Maude was also involved in local politics. On October 13, 1885, she was elected as the magistrate of Concord Township in Fayette County, about five miles from Washington Court House.[147] If voters were aware of her gender, it would make her the first openly queer or trans elected official in the United States, long before Harvey Milk (elected to the San Francisco Board of Supervisors in 1977) or trans woman Joanne Conte (elected to Arvada, Colorado's city council in 1991). It appears likely the town would know of Maude's gender nonconformity, considering that her 1883 tromp around the county in a dress became public information. The level of awareness of the county about her 1880s gender transgressions was never reported on by the media, however. As a magistrate, she managed court dockets, presided over trials, and aided in hearings. Magistrates in small towns at the time had a variety of tasks, filling in where other court officials could not. Terms typically lasted several years.

Maude's journey as a musician took her around her state. In 1888 she taught at a music school in London, Ohio.[148] With her earnings, she and her mother purchased a downtown building in April 1890 to open her own studio. By the end of the year, she had a strong cohort of students to whom she provided voice lessons.

In 1895 Maude started to dress in skirts and dresses again. She was constantly wearing a corset at this point in her life, significantly shrinking her frame. The aging woman was not arrested or bothered by officials and lived relatively peacefully for years. Maude married Louisa Eberly, two years her senior, in February 1897. Their wedding was followed by around one hundred children "belling." The old practice, also known as a *shivaree*, involved a large number of children playing "horns, bells, tin pans and horse fiddles" to celebrate the newlyweds.[149] Maude later serenaded them and gave them cigars and candy before they went home. The professor was relatively private about her love life, with many friends and neighbors only learning about the marriage from the belling. The two did not live together, and Louisa wrote that she was a widow by 1900.[150]

In May of 1900, Maude's mother died, leaving her with a modest estate of $1,500.[151] She stayed out of the spotlight for two years following the death while she perfected her theatrical act. Maude, now in her late fifties, entered the most publicly visible phase of her life. She began working in "high class parlor entertainment" as an actor and musician in Akron, Ohio.[152] There, she officially adopted the name Maude. She listed herself as an "imitator, impersonator and musician endorsed by leading society people everywhere." Reporters described her as a highly talented artist with piercing green eyes and a flare for the theatrical. She often performed in dresses. The famous show producer Al G. Field offered Maude $300 per week ($3,500 in 2024) to perform in dresses at his events. Field gained fame and fortune from his minstrel shows, eventually amassing over $150,000 by 1921.[153] Another company offered Maude one hundred dollars a day to work at a show in New York City in 1902, but Maude preferred to stay in Ohio and refused the generous offers.

From 1902 to 1904, she drew impressive crowds from Dayton to Columbus as a multi-talented entertainer. Billed as Maude, she played "male characters," in which she took on more theatrical qualities, and performed "as a burlesque college professor."[154] When she returned to Washington Court House, she went by Maude Milbourne in her daily life, with most of the town knowing her birth name and choosing to respect her chosen title.

Maude became more comfortable in her gender by 1904. She began advertising her services beyond mere performance with an innovative idea: technology that could physically transform its users. The machine, she claimed, could make the old young again and change the user's sex. She called it "Prof. Milbourne's 20th Century Vitalizer and Automatic Transformation Device."[155] It is unclear if the proposal was hypothetical, satirical, fraudulent, or a call for investors. She wrote to the local newspaper:

To whom it may concern:
    New Thought Practically Utilized
    A Wonderful Piece of Mechanism
    Any young lady or gentleman dissatisfied with their personality or sex,
can experience an immediate transformation by a small remuneration.
This machine, by a reserve attachment, can be so utilized that by
placing old decrepit people into the front part they emerge from the
other end young people. The utility of this wonderful piece of mechanism
is so simple in construction that, by pressing the button, the work
is consummated. We guarantee satisfaction in every ease or money
cheerfully refunded [. . .].
    PROF. MILBOURNE,
    Originator and Patentee

She ended her letter with "A live agent wanted. Address: Hades, Death. etc. All rights reserved," indicating a satirical tone to the advertisement. Rampant fraudulent devices and remedies were advertised in papers around the country in 1904. The United States did not regulate drug safety or effectiveness until 1906. Scam artists sold snake oil (in the literal and figurative sense) across the country with ease. Maude's idea, even if in jest, is notable as it proposes a nonsurgical method for transition, something that would not be available until years later via hormone therapy. Some of the first gender-affirming genital surgeries took place in Berlin around the same time as Maude's machine proposal, but it is unlikely she would have heard of these rare procedures.

At age sixty-one, Maude's trans activism again entered the national spotlight. Like so many consequential events, it all began in the most mundane of situations. Maude sat down to eat in a restaurant in Washington Court House on the night of April 1, 1905.[156] She expected to have an uneventful dinner, but her black skirt, plush cape, and light waist shirt quickly caught the attention of local police. The officers grabbed her and took the well-dressed woman directly to the mayor. Her clothing was no April Fools' prank. She explained her legal rationale for her dress to the officials: she was advertising her business, which required she wear feminine attire. The mayor of the small town was more sympathetic than most others during the early twentieth century. He let her go with a warning not to do it again. The mayor threatened to send her to the men's workhouse for forced labor if Maude went out in her clothing of choice once more.

Maude strongly believed she had every right to dress how she wanted. She wrote a letter to petition Ohio attorney general Wade H. Ellis to allow her—and other gender-nonconforming people—to wear their clothing of choice on city streets.[157]

Attorney General Ellis, Columbus:

DEAR SIR—Kindly inform me if there is a state or municipal law prohibiting a man from wearing the attire of a woman or any part thereof, or vice versa, on the streets of American cities? I carry a state soldier's license, and by profession I am a female impersonator. Inclosed [sic] find a newspaper clipping which explains itself.

Hoping to hear from you at your earliest convenience, I wait with pleasure your decision.

"Yours in F. C. and L."

"R. F. MILBOURNE."

In response, Ellis denied he had the authority to advise officials on dress reform. In doing so, the attorney general declined to pass any legal opinion, driving Professor Milbourne to write Dr. Mary E. Walker of New York. Walker was one of the first public advocates of what was called the "dress reform movement."[158] She fought to abolish cross-dressing laws across the country and was among the most well-known gender-defiant people of her time. Walker was well respected as a Civil War medical veteran and the first woman to win the Medal of Honor. She even openly wore her hallmark suit in public. Yet because she was so renowned, she rarely found trouble through her sense of fashion. Walker made headlines earlier that year while corresponding with Frank Williams, a young trans man in Ohio (featured in the chapter "The Boy-of-All-Work"). Maude realized Walker may be able to help.

"I have always regarded my arrest at that time as an injustice," Maude reflected. "I could not understand why it was that Dr. Mary Walker, of Oswego, N. Y. should be allowed to go to and fro throughout the country and not run counter to the law, while I was arrested and dragged into The Police Court for doing nothing more than is being done by the famous New York lady, who masquerades in public in full male attire–silk hat, Prince Albert coat, pantaloons and all."[159]

Maude's statements were some of the first to name the phenomenon of transmisogyny, the distinct subjugation faced by trans people who were assigned male at birth. For the time, this was a remarkable sentiment both linking, comparing, and contrasting the struggles of trans people assigned male and female at birth. During the early 1900s, this connection was not quite as clear, yet Maude saw these issues as intuitively connected. Mary Walker quickly wrote her back with practical advice.

Professor Milbourne—

Sir: Yours has been received. If you wear a beard on your face and a badge, with your full name on the same, you are not "dressed in disguise." It is the attempt to disguise the sex that the law has to deal with. Catholic priests wear lady robes and are not arrested.

Mary enclosed a picture of herself in a suit. After receiving the letter, Maude quickly had a silver plate engraved with her birth name and "I am a man." While the effort sounds humiliating, it certainly worked. "Since I have been wearing the identification badge I have never been arrested or molested by the police," Maude later announced to a reporter.[160] She disobeyed the mayor and continued to dress how she wanted to.

Milbourne was then a professor in both the literal and occupational senses. She professed her gender to those around her at great length while also teaching. Maude turned to the Bible to explain her gender: "As a man thinketh so is he" (Proverbs 23:7). One may be a man (or not) by believing oneself as such. The saying was a fitting adage for a trans woman living in the highly religious state of Ohio.

Over time, Milbourne found more detailed language to describe her gender expression at length. She made her case in the *Cincinnati Enquirer*, later published in the widely circulated *Boston Globe*.

It has been my intention for a long time to discard man's clothes and dress only in female garb. For years I have worn ladies' garments about my home, and I feel much better than when dressed as a man.

There is today too much attention paid to the kind of clothing a person wears. In the New Testament times[,] men and women dressed alike, in long, flowing robes, and now I am arrested for wearing garments in vogue in those days. Why should I be arrested for wearing clothing of my choice when I am doing it because I think it is my duty to do so?

Dr Mary Walker, a woman, of Washington, DC, chose to wear men's clothing because she thought it better suited to her profession, holding that the sick room men's clothing does not stir up the dust of the floors as women's skirts do, and hence should be worn by her. Dr Mary Walker was arrested for wearing men's clothing. She pleaded her own case and won in the courts.

If Dr Walker can lawfully wear men's clothing upon the streets of American cities why should not I be allowed to wear woman's garments if I prefer to do so?

Another thing: My form is better suited for female dress than for male attire, and I never feel comfortable in male attire, while I am at perfect ease while I dressed as a woman. For 10 years I have worn a woman's corset, and I could scarcely live without it. I have four dresses.

If authorities insist upon preventing me from wearing the attire of a woman in public it is my intention to petition the Ohio legislature at its forthcoming session for special privilege to wear female attire.

Some people do not understand me and call me eccentric, but I am not so "queer" as they may think I am. I do not desire to violate the law, but as I have been wearing a woman's attire for no improper purpose I should not be interfered with in so doing. The people should become educated and accustomed to persons wearing any decent garb they may choose, so long as it is done with good intentions.[161]

By May 1905, Maude made headlines that could have come out of a newspaper a full century later. "Is there such a thing as the transformation of sex?" the *Austin American-Statesman* asked.[162] "That is, can a male become a female or vice versa?" The paper asserted Maude "expects soon to become a full-fledged woman" and sought legal recognition. Due to these same questions, Maude reported not being able to vote. During a court discussion over a contested election, Maude explained that poll workers told her that her vote would be challenged if cast. Ohio was at the forefront of women's voting rights, but suffrage did not exist anywhere in the state until white women gained municipal voting power in 1916 Cleveland.[163] The dilemma was never solved, and Maude continued to abstain from voting.

Letters began to flood Maude's home following the wave of media attention. She spent hours reading and responding to "voluminous" correspondences every day.[164] Maude's dress brought about a small revolution, with more people realizing the expansive possibilities of attire due to her publicity. A. J. Reimer, from the small city of Keokuk, Iowa, reached out to Maude in 1905 with nearly every word misspelled. "I am One [of] your Folowers as I have ben Wering Female atier and will ware it as Long as I

Live," they explained. "But I have Only Ware it at home I have ben Wering it Far the Last ten years and I Find it Ever so mutch mare Comfertable then male garments. I hope you Will Be successful and Be Premited to Ware Female atier as I am Very mutch interested in you and would like to farespond With You."[165] Clearly, Maude impacted other people who were dissatisfied with the gendered status quo.

Another article on Maude circulated in London, leading Harold J. James to find her. The two exchanged letters and quickly became "more than fast friends."[166] Harold was assigned male, claimed to have been raised as a woman, and wanted to continue living a life of gender nonconformity with Maude. They sought to live with Maude as their "sweetheart." It is unclear if the two ever moved in together.

In 1906 Maude had the idea to hold a dress reform convention in Washington Court House, bringing in Mary Walker from New York. They planned for advocates from across the states to attend. If the event occurred, it went without notice in local papers. Although I could not find any records left from the event, the time seemed to mark a shift in the treatment of trans people in Washington Court House. The city's elected officials gave no pushback and newspapers treated the possibility of the event with respect.[167] Maude then disappeared from the press for four years as her health deteriorated.

The next documentation from Maude's life was her admission to a retirement home in 1909. The aging trans woman had an array of health problems, which made living alone no longer possible. She died on January 30, 1910, from kidney disease. The sixty-six-year-old was buried in the Washington Court House cemetery.

Despite Maude's many achievements, her story never received more than a few sentences of attention until now. Perhaps her rural location and nondescript gender identity resulted in less interest in her narrative. She also married a woman, meaning she did not make it into historical texts on sexuality that might have misgendered her as cisgender and gay (which was the case of those like Effie Smith and Bill Winters). As a relatively powerful and educated white woman, her self-expression was not as much of a scandal as those without her racial, educational, and economic background. Her work still influenced more famous figures like Mary Walker, who overshadowed Maude's contributions to trans history. But we cannot overlook the professor's creative, innovative, and clever means of expressing herself during her later life.

THE WORKERS

When I was growing up, no one even acknowledged that the system was stacked against women. But the women's liberation movement laid bare the built-in machinery of oppression in this society that's keeping us down. It's not your lipstick that's oppressing me, or your tie, or whether you change your sex, or how you express yourself. An economic system oppresses us in this society, and keeps us fighting each other, instead of looking at the real source of this subjugation.

—LESLIE FEINBERG[1]

Sylvia Rivera, one of the most accomplished transgender activists in history, could not find a steady job for most of her life. After returning to New York City in the early 1990s, she lived in an outdoor encampment near the Christopher Street Piers. Sylvia founded one of the first transgender advocacy groups and rose to prominence in the 1970s at the forefront of what was then called the gay movement. Despite these achievements, she could not find work in the formal economy as she was deemed unfit for hire by employers. She sold sex and drugs to strangers and spent most of her final years in tents and shelters. Sylvia's friend and collaborator, Marsha P. Johnson, faced similar challenges. "Darling, I don't have a job. I'm on welfare," she told a reporter in 1973. "I have no intention of getting a job as long as this country discriminates against homosexuals."[2] Historical (and many current) trans workers—no matter how famous—were subjected to similar treatment for their gender. Work was a struggle—a hardship that led to the romantic, infuriating, and occasionally heartwarming stories of survival you will read over the following chapters.

Work in the 1850–1950 period was divided by gender. There was "women's work" and "men's work." The two rarely overlapped. However, for the seven trans individuals of this section, each found a way to make work *work*. From the confines of the gender binary, trans workers navigated the economy through creative means.

It is often assumed that trans people's gender identity makes it more difficult to find work. However, several narratives you will read explain how some trans people creatively used their genders to survive. Elsie Marks, for example, was a stealth trans woman who became a bearded lady for the circus and the eccentric "Cobra Woman" of Long Beach, California. She used her work so others would not question her transness and used her transness so others would not question her work. On the other hand, Josephine Robinson was ostracized from domestic work after her employer outed her. The individuals in this chapter either used their trans status to obtain employment or were fired after being outed.

In the United States, where most of these stories take place, employers still have the upper hand. They can fire you for any reason as long as they are not breaking a contract or law (this is called at-will employment). The hierarchical structure of the workplace under capitalism means that bosses have the authority to dismiss trans employees for simply being trans so long as it is not explicitly the given reason for their firing. To this day, it is nearly impossible to prove discriminatory intent, even with policy "antidiscrimination" protections in place. As trans legal scholar Dean Spade explains, "Courts have made it very hard to prevail in cases attempting to enforce anti-discrimination laws, and discrimination on the basis of race, disability, and sex, for example, is still commonplace despite being officially illegal."[3] Antidiscrimination laws assume individual bad actors and, even in the rare cases of legal wins, companies seldom follow course to support their trans employees. The laws do not change the structure of capitalism, which benefits those at the top to the disempowerment of everyone else. It is then up to the workers to foster healthier relationships around gender identity so unfair treatment does not happen in the first place.

Frank Williams's story shows how outing made finding employment an endless task. No matter how hard Frank worked—no matter how much more productive he was than those around him—he still could not maintain a job due to the bosses power to fire him. Frank's bosses laid him off at least four times for being trans between 1901 and 1903. These bosses could still find non-trans reasons for his removal even if there were antidiscrimination laws at the time. As you will read in his chapter, the moral of his story demonstrates that it is not simply discrimination that trans people must fight. Instead, we must question how hierarchies in the labor force grant bosses undue authority over workers.

To this day, working conditions are among the main concerns of the trans movement. Capitalism is not entirely different today than it was from 1850 to 1950. Trans people are three times as likely to live in poverty and twice as likely to be unemployed.[4] While more openly trans people are employed than at any other time in history, workers are proportionately paid less than in the 1950s (despite being more productive). On a broader scale, the workweek is now longer than in 1930. The pay gap between Black and white workers has not significantly shrunk in the past seventy-five years, and trans women are paid sixty cents for every dollar earned by the average non-trans person (with even lower wages for trans women of color).[5] The fight for trans workers is the fight for all workers. The struggle for economic justice impacts everyone.

Trans labor history

Between 1850 and 1950, trans people adopted as impressive a range of work as any other community. The following chapters review the stories of workers from everyday jobs like bartending to unusual professions such as snake charming. Everyone in this section worked at least two different jobs, with some working more than a dozen over their lifetime. Underreported trans narratives also give us new information about how labor intersects with gender. These histories do not only describe an increased difficulty finding work but also the creative ways in which trans people used their identity to access employment.

Long before *transgender* entered popular vocabulary, work came to define the trans movement. News articles around the world featured young trans men who found it easier to live as men if they wanted to be employed. Who could blame them? Men today still receive better pay in the same jobs as women. These workers used their labor as an explanation for dressing how they wanted. Frank Williams, for example, told reporters, "I'm going to wear men's clothes. [. . .] It's no use for me to try to do women's work. I just can't."[6] The press accepted his decision and did not insult him for his choice to transition. Josephine Robinson similarly explained that she was sick and could not do manual labor. As a Black person, she had few options while presenting as a cis man. As a woman, she immediately received a position as a maid. These stories made it easier for the public to understand gender identity while helping trans people find employment.

We need to continue reflecting on how today's economic system diminishes trans people's opportunities. Trans freedoms—regarding healthcare, community, housing, and personal identification documents—are still contingent upon income. What would it mean for trans people to collectively share in the fruits of their labor? What would it mean for our wealth not to limit our ability to determine our own lives? We have much to learn from these trans workers who navigated life, love, and labor long before gender.

THE MAID: JOSEPHINE ROBINSON

High society never had a chance. Living as a young Black trans woman in the early 1900s was onerous, yet Josephine Robinson made it work for six years. Josephine, also known as "Jeanette" or "Josie," landed in the lap of luxury as a maid before her fall from grace. In 1909 her gender led to much media speculation that plateaued in a long-form interview in which she provided unique insights into her philosophies of dedication, service, and transition—which she undertook "in order to keep body and soul together."[7]

Josephine's early life went relatively unreported. She was born around 1888 in Alabama.[8] She told the *St. Louis Post-Dispatch* that her father was a wealthy Western rancher. However, she was not suited for farming. "I couldn't stand the monotonous life of the plains and ran away from home when I was 15 years old," she explained. She traveled to Chicago without friends or much money. The teenager began a factory job but quickly became too sick to work. She spent time in a hospital and started wearing dresses after her discharge.

At least six houses hired Josie in the first decade of the 1900s. She started her first cleaning job in 1903 at the home of two French girls, Marie and Anne. She became close with the pair and cared for them like a nanny. They studied fine china painting while Josephine tended to their home. There, she realized she loved the work and began to consider herself "a first-class ladies' maid." She had no trouble finding positions thereafter. Her strength returned after her illness, and it was only when she could partake in traditional men's work again that she realized she was not a man at all. She decided she could not bring herself to wear masculine clothes once more.

Josephine continued to work for several houses in the area. Each belonged to some of Chicago's most well-known society wives, all wealthy and white. She also worked in a hotel on Chicago's West Side and as the maid to the wife of a famous minister. None had a clue she was trans.

In May 1909, Josie responded to an advertisement for a maid position at A. H. Marsten's house. Mrs. Marsten was impressed with her references and confidence. However, she doubted Josie was a cis woman. The applicant provided glowing recommendations and Mrs. Marsten decided to give them a call.

"Yes, Josie is an excellent maid," Mrs. Marsten's friend told her over the phone without hesitation. Yet Marsten's suspicion grew as she closely observed the woman. "Josie, if you're not a man you ought to be!" Mrs. Marsten told her soon after she was hired. Josie continued to insist she was a woman. The society woman was still not convinced. "I don't think you have any right to be wearing a woman's clothes," she scolded. However, she relented and kept Josie on her staff.

On her second day on the job, Josie took over for Mrs. Marsten's sick cook. The employer remembers Josie "cooked everything [s]he could find in the house and nothing of it was fit to eat." She asserted Josie's lack of cooking knowledge was evidence of her manhood.

Josie did not have much money at the time. Mrs. Marsten noticed a "funny looking dusting cap" on her head and inquired about it out of curiosity. Josie explained that her hairdresser had forcibly removed the extensions she couldn't pay for. With them went clumps of her own hair. Mrs. Marsten sympathized and advanced her pay to replace her headdress. The next day, she arrived in much more fashionable attire, which she continued to wear even after she was outed.

Josephine's work ended abruptly when she fell over a rug, only four weeks after A. H. Marsten hired her. The terrible tumble came right in front of Mrs. Marsten, who observed Josie's short hair and "man head" under her cap. She concluded Josephine was assigned male at birth. Black cisgender women frequently wore short hair at the time due to racism against their hair texture. However, Marsten insisted Josie's short hair was proof of her manhood. She threatened to have Josie arrested but the young maid left before the difficult society woman had the chance.

Josie was forced to sell books on the street over the following days. On June 7, 1909, plainclothes officers approached and questioned her. Although she was not harming anyone, they began to suspect she was assigned male at birth. Wearing feminine clothing at the time was a criminal offense for any trans woman. "I think 'she' is a man," one detective told his partner. They circled back to charge Josie under Chicago's harsh cross-dressing laws and locked her up. She was set to appear in court the next morning.

Josie arrived at her hearing in a gorgeous black satin belt, gray skirt, high heels, and black wig. She explained to the court that she was forced to wear women's clothes "in order to keep body and soul together." She had no intention of detransitioning. She also explained that her birth name "is not her name" and she would only be referred to it for legal reasons. While she enthusiastically worked as a servant for those who paid her, she was certainly not servile to the court that was determined to charge her for simply being herself.

After she was outed, Josie's story circulated throughout high society. Reporters and the court called the six homes of the past employers, but all were either "busy" or "just stepped out." They did not want to be caught up in the scandal. None would testify against Josie, and none would respond to calls in the following weeks. A short conference of previous employers gathered to discuss the matter. They were not amused. "I shall die of mortification!" one exclaimed. "Horrors!" shouted another. One explained her discomfort with a trans maid: "I wouldn't let my own husband see me until I had my hair dressed." The women worried about Josie revealing their secrets, but she promised to never tell them as a professional maid. The women's shame around their proximity to Josie's transness helped the maid in the end: none of her former employers would testify against her.

Josephine made several excuses for her dress. She claimed she preferred less physical labor, which was rarely available to Black men at the time. She wore dresses so she "wouldn't have to be a strap hanger," she explained to a reporter.[9] Another journalist claimed she testified that she wore dresses "to be sure of a seat in the street cars."[10] The writer questioned if "perhaps hundreds of men are going around in female clothes to play on [riders'] unsuspecting innocence and get their seats." Bolstering the moral panic, the reporter added, "Now that there appears even a slight ground for the suspicion that a large per cent of the women in cars are merely disguised men, it may be said to have received a blow from which it will probably never recover."

At the end of the short trial, a municipal court judge fined Josie eighty-five dollars (equivalent to around $3,000 today). Unable to afford such a hefty penalty, the twenty-one-year-old was sent to the infamous Chicago House of Corrections (popularly known as the Bridewell; later replaced with the Cook County Jail) to pay off the debt from the fine with hard labor. She left the following year to work in a Black-friendly hotel near the city center.

Josie mused about writing a book about her experiences, although it does not appear one ever came to fruition. She spoke truthfully with the court and even admitted to having a boyfriend. The only thing she did not reveal was his name, which would have put him in danger with the law. Josie's legacy is one of determination to be the best woman she could be.

THE COBRA WOMAN: ELSIE MARKS

Elsie Marie Marks used every objection society had about her body as an opportunity. Weighing 295 pounds, she worked in the circus as a six-foot-three "monkey man."[11] A trans woman with facial hair, she continued her show as a "bearded lady" and "half man, half woman." An Indian immigrant, she later used South Asian stereotypes to sell her independent snake show to the world. A large woman with an even larger personality, Elsie led a life of love and performance, between three husbands and several continents.

Elsie Nadir was born in Agra, Uttar Pradesh, India, in 1888 to A. Nadir and Isabella McCaul.[12] Her family had British citizenship and immigrated to the United States when she was about two years old. She reportedly began living as a girl at age four, around 1892. Conflicting narratives claim she either never went back to wearing masculine attire or would switch her gender during performances while regularly living as a woman in public. She changed her name to Elsia Marie Nadir in her early years, so her birth name is lost to history.

Elsie's documented life begins in July 1923, eight miles outside Topeka, Kansas, during the infamous Hagenbeck-Wallace Circus train wreck. The speeding circus train hit a tractor, leaving several people injured and thousands of dollars in damages. A truck carrying elephants fell off the track and tore up a nearby road. A giant Siberian tiger named Lenine escaped and had to be hunted down.[13] The crash destroyed Elsie's personal records, leaving us without much information on her early life.

The surviving documents show that Elsie married a man, only known by his last name, Celigne, between the mid-1900s and early 1920s. The two divorced and she met Charles Gilbert Baker, another performer. They married on June 8, 1923.[14] Charles was a full decade younger than Elsie and lived in Kentucky. The two performers traveled together over the following year. However, the marriage did not last long. Charles had recently separated from a Polish woman, Josephine, with whom he had a child only six months before his marriage to Elsie.[15] Charles and Josephine renewed their love and Elsie left for California.

It is unknown exactly when Elsie picked up snake charming, only that she claimed around thirty years of experience in 1946.[16] The profession was clearly her passion, with her community frequently commenting on her love for pets. Her friends later described her as "extremely kind hearted and fond of animals and reptiles." She had a knack for handling snakes and would not let anything stop her from pursuing her dream of becoming a widely recognized snake charmer. Her pets bit her numerous times over the decades, but that never stopped her from caring for them.

Elsie married her third and final husband, newspaperman Alexander Francis Marks, in November 1927 in San Francisco.[17] He was twelve years younger than her and was a tall, handsome man with blond hair and piercing gray eyes. The two got along splendidly. The couple traveled to faraway vacation spots like Sydney and Honolulu.[18] Elsie, then thirty-nine, still had incredible energy and excitement for shows. The couple moved to Union Street in San Francisco near the famous Marina during the early 1930s. Alex reportedly did not know Elsie was trans until later. He explained, "I didn't know Elsie was a man until after we were married, and then there wasn't much to be done. And besides, she was such a nice wife to me that it didn't really make much difference."[19] The two became so close that he left the news industry to become his wife's manager.

Eventually, Elsie realized Southern California was the perfect place for her solo show. Elsie and Alex purchased their first home in Long Beach around 1938. They later moved into a comfortable, bright, renovated bungalow on East 15th Street, where Elsie spent the rest of her life. They collected souvenirs from around the world, which decorated their home. Elsie eventually adopted a bear that she kept in her backyard but had to send it to a Los Angeles zoo after neighbors began protesting.

Elsie's work thrived in Long Beach, and she had the confidence to match. She regularly garnered hundreds of attendees at her outdoor performances. Unlike many other trainers, she never removed the venom sacs from her snakes, using the risk to heighten her performance. She was certain she could live through any snake attack. But unfortunately, this confidence would be her downfall.

On a warm April day in 1946, Elsie went to the nearby Long Beach Pike waterfront, where hundreds of spectators gathered around to watch her handle a new specimen: a deadly seven-foot Texas diamondback rattlesnake. The massive reptile was untrained and meant to shock the onlookers.

Elsie casually draped the rattlesnake around her neck like a scarf, as she had before with so many other snakes. The wild reptile, however, was not used to being handled and immediately became agitated. It lashed out and bit Elsie three times on her right hand. At first, the audience scoffed at the attack, believing it was all part of the act. However, she quickly fell victim to the venom and spectators began to scream in horror.

The experienced snake charmer's pets had bitten her many times before. Yet this was an unusually severe attack. The local herpetologist explained it was "one of the most vicious" she had ever seen. The manager of a nearby concession stand rushed over to place cups on her wounds. He applied a tourniquet to her swollen arm while they waited for an ambulance. Police called Grace Olive Wiley, a renowned local herpetologist, who could not help (she similarly died in Long Beach from an Indian cobra bite two years later). Elsie's usual luck had finally run out.

Officers called the fire department but struggled to find crew members strong enough to lift Elsie into the ambulance. While en route to the hospital, she declared she was "going to die this time."[20] Elsie arrived at the nearby Seaside Hospital and immediately received the city's entire supply of antivenom. The five doses they gave her were not enough due to her size. Elsie's doctor pleaded for the police to assist them, and a motorcycle officer sped to the Los Angeles County Hospital to grab five more ampules. She survived for eighteen hours while the bite shut down her organs. She died before the officer had a chance to return with more antivenom, becoming a victim not only of the snakebite but also of medical bias against heavier people like her (in this case, assuming five doses would be enough to neutralize the venom).

The coroner quickly found out she was transgender after her body was moved to the morgue. Her trans status actually garnered even more media interest than her dramatic snakebite death. A media spectacle ensued and reporters plastered her name in papers across the United States. Importantly, even after she was outed, most outlets continued to use she/her pronouns for her. They interviewed her husband, the only person who seemed to know her closely. He passionately defended her, remembering the woman only as his caring, loving wife of eighteen years. He buried her in the clothes of her choice, respecting her final wishes to be remembered as a woman.

THE DANCER: ALBÍN PLEVA

Albín Pleva was a trans woman so bold she solicited Nazi officers for sex, returned to sites where she had been arrested, and showed up to court in feminine attire during an era when wearing her clothing was considered a crime. Often adorned in her characteristic red silk headscarf, her escapades became so famous in Moravia (in today's eastern Czech Republic) that her name would reach papers across the globe. Her life story offers a rare glimpse into the experiences of a trans woman who died in the Porajmos, the Romani Holocaust. Very few early twentieth-century trans Romani narratives remain after the Nazi regime, but Albín's penchant for mischief left us a detailed trail of her adventures. The traces of her story were more than enough to weave together her path from escaping the police to being interned at a concentration camp.

Born on January 20, 1912, in Marcheggu, rural Austria-Hungary, Albín moved to Brno, Czechoslovakia (now the Czech Republic) by the age of eleven. The dancer first appeared in newspapers in 1937. That year, she traveled around Czechoslovakia with another transfeminine person, Čeněk Vodák. The pair faced intense scrutiny from law enforcement and citizens alike. Police arrested Albín and Čeněk for their attire in the small Czech city of Jihlava shortly after Albín's twenty-fifth birthday. Papers described them as "two conspicuously dressed and painted ladies."[21] A group of men stricken by their beauty invited the pair to their table, believing they were cis women. At some point, they discovered Albín and Čeněk's assigned sex. The men were so shocked that they called the police. Local papers reported, "In the end, even the police were surprised. It turned out that the 'ladies' they had taken were men." We do not know exactly how the two identified, but Albín was counted among women until at least 1943. The pair paid a fine and were released. Undeterred by the police, they returned to the same café, causing a similar sensation.

One week later, Albín drew more attention in the northern Czech city of Liberec.[22] She was interrogated by a plainclothes officer and asked to identify herself. In lieu of providing her papers, she bolted off into the city streets. After running for thirty minutes, the officer finally caught and arrested her. At the station, she gave her name as Albine von Dračkova and stated she was a professional dancer. As the police harassment escalated, she took off her blonde wig and lamented, "Leave it, I'm a man." Reporters provided no reason for her confession, but historically, trans women would make this admission to tamper down the questioning and end the interrogation. The police arrested nearby Čeněk shortly after. Law enforcement found German and Czech newspaper clippings of the pair, which documented their escapades and arrests in various cities throughout the region.

Albín was arrested again about two weeks later. An officer noticed her and a man on the street. Curious about her gender, the officer detained Albín while the unknown man fled. At this point, the popular newspaper *Lidové noviny* took notice of Albín's frequent arrest record and jokingly called her "a good friend of the Brno police."[23]

In 1938 Germany annexed Czechoslovakia. Hitler claimed he would not enact the Reich's authoritarian laws over the nation but soon rescinded his pledge and launched a complete occupation the following year.[24] The Nazi regime used propaganda against people like Albín to justify their invasion. They promised to "protect" Czechoslovakia from other ethnic groups, including Roma. Czechoslovakia became the Protectorate of Bohemia and Moravia, which was little more than a German puppet state. The country adopted Germany's ethnonationalist laws. Brno itself had a large ethnic German population and support for the Nazis was high among its residents. As the soldier population in the city increased, so did the demand for sex work. Albín reportedly sought out clients from the influx of men. However, with more potential sex buyers also came greater risk. Nazi foot soldiers were permitted to stop whoever they liked and were notoriously violent toward queer, trans, and Roma people in the former Czechoslovakia.

On May 23, 1940, Albín found herself in trouble again. She approached three Nazi police officers on a cold evening in Brno's main train station. Draped in her trademark red silk headscarf and fine shoes, she did not go unnoticed. The Nazi soldiers claimed she offered them sex in exchange for money. The officers detained her and handed her off to a local guard, who drove her to the police station. She was imprisoned for five days under cross-dressing laws and had to appear in court for "indecency" charges. She arrived before the judge in the same red scarf and feminine attire to plead her case. Czech reporters wrote, "She explained again that she had done nothing wrong, asking why she should wear pants if she felt like a woman." The paper speculated another sex worker falsely reported her, seeing the beautiful young woman as competition. The Nazi police did not show up at the court hearing, so the case was dismissed due to the lack of evidence. Most Roma communities were not immediately sent to concentration camps following the Nazi occupation, so she initially escaped persecution.

Czech historian Jan Seidl is one of the few scholars to study the complicated dual system of anti-queer persecution in occupied Czechoslovakia.[25] Ethnic Germans were subject to the Reich's laws, while most other citizens were subject to laws dating back to when the nation was part of Austria-Hungary before 1919. At first, this worked in Albín's favor as Czech punishments for sex work and "homosexuality" were not as frequent or severe as in the Third Reich. However, in 1942, Germany began to intensify the Holocaust. Members of the Czech government eagerly collaborated with the Nazis. There were few places for queer and trans Roma people to escape to.

The next records of Albín date to 1942. Officials forced the young woman into the infamous Lety concentration camp over one hundred miles from Brno.[26] The Czechoslovak government established the compound two weeks before Nazi occupation as a slave camp for citizens without jobs. Nazis rebuilt the site into a concentration camp for Roma in July 1942. Only designed for 600 prisoners, it officially held over 1,100 people by the following month (with survivors reporting much higher numbers). Conditions in the camp were gruesome. Jan Vrba, who was born in the camp, described the horror of the site:

> I know from my parents that it was a place of cruelty; that starving children were eating raw cabbage from the fields, and that the townspeople from Lety paid no attention to them. Small children were dying on piles of—I don't want to say it—piles of excrement. My parents managed to protect me and my brother, so that we survived. But I lost my sister here and my grandfather.[27]

The records do not acknowledge how Albín arrived at Lety. Most victims entered the camp by train after being rounded up by police. Others came by their own wagons, not knowing the terror that awaited them. Only two men were recorded arriving on foot, desperately searching for their captive families.

Upon entering Lety, Albín was met by a wooden fence enclosing rows of small plywood trailers. Eight-by-ten-foot cabins encircled two larger modules.[28] Albín's new lodging resembled a wheelless skeleton of a vardo wagon (traditional Romani caravan). Lacking decoration or basic utilities, each structure was designed to accommodate only four to six Roma. Some were stuffed with more than ten.

After detainees entered the camp, guards seized all their possessions. They washed the prisoners and disinfected their clothes with steam. Women were allowed to keep their clothing while most men were forced into official work attire. Cabin blocks were divided between men, women, and children. Albín's gender was not listed on the few remaining camp records, although she was later listed as a woman in 1943–1944.[29]

The camp officially existed "to exclude gypsies and gypsy miscegenates from society and to educate them to work, order, and discipline."[30] In reality, no one was legally eligible for release from the camp after its first month. Their supposed "work education" was slavery. A few families escaped using bribes (allegedly the equivalent of around $16,800 today). Most did not have the funds to leave. Prisoners were rented out to private businesses and government institutions for hard labor like farming and forestry. By the end of 1942, the enslaved Roma officially generated the equivalent of $380,000 in cash for their captors.[31] Officers did not allow for even the smallest grains of freedom while overworking the detainees. For instance, on paper, the Roma were provided with haircuts of their choice (including traditional Romani hairstyles). However, most hair was cut short against the captives' will. Nazi and Czechoslovak regulation over the prisoners was all-encompassing.

Lety had strict rules regarding punishments and rewards. Ignoring commands, speaking past the fence, or begging for food could lead to beatings or death. Obedience could mean correspondence with the outside world and smoking privileges. There were scant disciplinary records from the camp, but with Albín's pattern of rule-breaking, we can only imagine how she was treated.

Albín was among the first of Lety's detainees, admitted in July 1942 when the camp initially opened. Lety did not retain records of her condition other than her departure on July 31, 1942, to the criminal police in Prague.[32] The reason for her departure also went unnoted. Lety's director reported she was not sick while in camp. However, she was admitted to a hospital in Brno three weeks later for phlegmon (soft tissue inflammation often related to the infections caused by a lack of sanitation). It is likely she returned to Lety after her treatment. The hospital administrator sent her medical admission form directly to the camp and listed the camp as her employer.

Killings of Roma escalated during the 1939–1945 period, particularly in the final years of the Nazi regime. When Lety closed in August 1943, the remaining prisoners were sent by train to Birkenau, Auschwitz's notorious extermination camp, where the Reich killed many new arrivals.[33] The Nazis destroyed Lety following the final transport, leaving us with unanswerable questions about its captives.

At first, Albín managed to evade the death camp after Lety's closure. The performer was listed as a dancer for a Nazi-administered theater in the 1944 edition of the *Deutsches Bühnen-Jahrbuch* (German Stage Yearbook).[34] Nazis often used Roma for entertainment, which aligns with their penchant for what they called "degenerate art." The book listed her, twelve other women, and one man as being members of a theater troupe immediately after officials dismantled Lety. Assuming the book is correct, she danced in the famous North Bohemian Opera and Ballet Theatre at some point between September 1943 and August 1944. The grand neobaroque theater, built in 1909, had a capacity of nearly nine hundred, towering stories above Adolf Hitler Street in Ústí nad Labem, a small city fifty miles north of Prague. Based on the yearbook's notes, we know Albín likely died after her final dance tour at the theater between September 1943 and the liberation of Auschwitz on January 27, 1945. In total, over twenty-one thousand Roma died in Auschwitz alone.[35] There are no records of Albín's death outside the mass extermination of other Roma and subsequent cover-up by German and Czech officials.

Roma, Jewish, and leftist trans people were generally marked for killing during the Holocaust. However, the Nazis showed favoritism toward certain trans individuals and saved them from the fate of the rest of the trans population. Certain well-respected white trans men—such as famed athletes Zdeněk Koubek (an intersex Czech trans man from Brno) and his friend Stefan Pekar (a Slovak trans man with a chapter in "The Athletes" section)—were not killed during the Holocaust, despite being openly trans in Nazi-occupied territory. Pekar was openly trans while in Prague medical school only a year before Albín's arrest by Nazis. This is not to claim Albín's transness was inconsequential to her killing. Rather, the Czech and Nazi governments targeted the intersections of her experiences (transness, Romani heritage, and sex work) that certain transgender ethnic Czechs and Slovaks could escape.

Despite the overwhelming evidence, there is still widespread denial of queer, trans, and Romani persecution during World War II. One of the most common forms of Holocaust denialism is refuting the fact that queer and trans people were targeted by the Nazi regime (or suggesting that the Nazis, themselves, were all gay). Similarly, there is still denial that the Nazi and Czech regimes killed hundreds of thousands of Roma. Far-right groups continue to claim that Roma people are "dirty" and thus caused their own deaths from disease during their internment in the hundreds of camps throughout Czechoslovakia.[36] Others attest that the camps were for necessary labor training that coincidentally overlapped with disease outbreaks.

In the 1970s, Czechoslovakia erected a massive pig farm over Lety's camp ruins. According to the Brno-based Museum of Romani Culture, "The pig farm became a symbol for the disregard of historical events, a reminder of the lack of respect for the people who suffered and died in the camp."[37] Silos replaced the demolished wooden shanties. Rows of gray concrete and metal pig barns lined the land where soldiers held Albín captive.

In the 1990s, Roma activist and writer Paul Polansky discovered over forty thousand documents related to Lety in Czech archives. He donated them to the United States Holocaust Memorial Museum in Washington, DC. Thanks to his work, we know much more about Albín's conditions during her final years. Polansky called the Czech government's response to Lety a "cover-up."[38] It was not until 1995, when Czech president Václav Havel finally unveiled a small monument to the victims, that officials would begin to recognize the genocide. Still, the state did not dismantle the pig farm, which survivors considered insulting. The farm's manager, Jan Cech, was a Porajmos denier himself. He dragged his feet when it came to selling the land. "Nothing extraordinary happened at Lety. It was a labor camp. There were 220 such camps here during the war. And some people unfortunately died of typhus," he told the *Washington Post*.[39] While there were indeed hundreds of labor camps, very few received such widespread denialism as Lety. People in the camp died not only from typhus, which the Czech government claimed for decades was the primary cause of death, but also from the brutal conditions of internment. Nor are there prescribed limits on the number of memorials for Holocaust victims (memorials could exist at all camp sites).

Protests against the pig farm escalated in the 2010s. Roma activists from across the continent worked with the European Grassroots Antiracist Movement to shut down the farm. They blockaded the main gate for a full week in 2014. With mounting pressure, the Czech Republic ultimately bought the land. The pig farms of Lety finally closed in 2017.[40] AGPI, a Czech farming corporation, agreed to sell the farm only after the government offered them 450 million Czech koruna ($21 million). The nation approved an additional $5 million to excavate the land and demolish the farm. The Czech government relinquished control of the land to the Museum of Romani Culture in 2018 after decades of international pressure.

The farm purchase helped us understand Albín's conditions at Lety. Archaeologists almost immediately began uncovering hidden Roma graves. This not only illuminated the history of Lety but also provided direct evidence of the systematic killing of Roma during the Holocaust. The discovery of the Lety gravesite—containing a mother and newborn, among many others—marks the first time that Roma victims of the Nazi genocide were found in Europe.[41] Most graves up to that point were mass burials and most bodies went unidentified. Čeněk Růžička, the chair of the Committee for the Redress of the Roma Holocaust, seized on the moment to end any disagreement over the genocide: "During this occasion, I would like all xenophobes and racists in this country to stop saying people did not die on this location, that victims in this camp died for other reasons, etc. I ask that they stop doubting the hard facts and the evidence. They will look truly ridiculous if they do not." Along with the graves, archaeologists also found a trove of documents related to the Lety prisoners. With more time and discovery, we may finally learn what happened to Albín.

Anti-Romani ideology, or antiziganism, is still prevalent around the world.[42] It is only through multifaceted, multigenerational campaigns that the brutality endured by the Roma of Lety and many other regions may finally be stamped out.

THE FLORIST: JOHN BERGER

John Berger was a dapper young trans man with a heart that betrayed him. His life was like something out of a modern rom-com: he was caught in a classic love triangle between an old girlfriend pretending to be his sister and a new lover with a jealous father. It was his passion for women that eventually led to his downfall.

John was born on December 26, 1863, in the Sellerhausen neighborhood of Leipzig, Saxony (today's Germany). He was the son of a gardener and spent his early years looking up to his father. The young trans man began working as a typesetter for the newspaper *Bazar* at age seventeen. At the time, he wore clothing designed for women during work and switched to men's clothing at the end of the day. He transitioned to live as a man full-time at age twenty-one, around 1885. The *Bazar* did not fire him, and he continued to work there for a total of thirteen years. The young trans man tested different names, such as Hans and Carl Burger, before setting on anglicized John.[43]

John's life radically changed when he met Hetwig Lutze in 1891 in Leipzig. He reminisced, "It was almost a case of love at first sight."[44] The two could not bear to be apart and spent all their time together. The couple immigrated to St. Louis in September 1893 to escape anti-trans harassment. St. Louis was a blossoming queer metropolis in the 1890s, with numerous queer and trans spaces popping up throughout the city. It was, for many trans people, a safe haven compared to their hometowns (Effie Smith's chapter also discusses trans life in St. Louis in 1893).

After walking past a sign seeking tenants, John and Hetwig found lodging in Swiss jeweler Ferdinand Gammater's house. John introduced Hetwig as his half sister or stepsister to avoid suspicion about their constant companionship. John then found work arranging printing blocks for St. Louis's popular German newspaper, the *St. Louis Tribune*. His income was enough to support the couple and they lived peacefully for two years.

Trouble first struck in 1895 when John began sleeping with Martha Gammater, his landlord's daughter. He promised Martha he would marry her "if [he] could." All the while, Hetwig was still in the house, leading to an awkward love triangle. John still had affection for Hetwig and it became obvious they were in love. As one reporter explained, John "made the mistake of not getting off with the old love before [he] got on with the new, and [his] attentions to [his] supposed half-sister, caused Mr. Gammater first to wonder, then suspect." Both Martha and Ferdinand felt something was off. They cast the couple from their house.

The *Tribune* fired John for unknown reasons shortly after he lost his home. The industrious thirty-year-old started working the boilers at a florist's nursery. John moved into the nursery while Hetwig became a servant at a nearby residence. John again lost his job and moved closer to downtown to work as a florist at another nursery, C. Young & Sons. With his father's gardening experience, he felt qualified for the position at the distinguished business. Hetwig followed him and began working nearby as a servant for Charles E. Barney, a well-known businessman. The pair would meet two or three times a week to go on dates.

All this time, no one in St. Louis suspected John's assigned sex. He reportedly carried himself with confidence, assertiveness, and style. He even slept in a room with three other men, sharing a bed with one of them. John's boss's brother-in-law, Dr. Helwig, also lived with him by the nursery. One day, he noticed John's chest while the trans man bent down. "Say, boys, I'll be hanged if John hasn't a breast like a woman," he joked to the room.[45] John laughed along without any indication of the anxiety over his outing. Another one of the men added, "Say, boys, we'll have to find out for sure if John ain't a woman after what Dr. Helwig said." John showed no apparent discomfort but moved to another nearby house the next day.

John's fault ultimately rested in his heart. One day, he called Martha and tried to gain entry to her house. Ferdinand would not let his former tenant in. He figured out John was dating Hetwig, whom he still believed was his half sister. Frustrated, he wrote to John's former employer in Saxony to inquire about his history. While waiting to hear back, John came by the house several more times, allegedly to have sex with Ferdinand's daughter. The old jeweler heard back from John's employer a month later. The letter revealed John's birth name and assigned sex. His Saxon employer also believed Hetwig was his half sister instead of his lover. Yet he was not surprised John dressed in clothes designed for men "because [he] has shown such a desire here."

A St. Louis police detective named Frese set out to arrest John on June 7, 1895, after Ferdinand tipped him off. He found the man casually trimming roses, fully clad in a fine gardener's suit. When the officer commanded him to follow, he asked to finish his work. The officer denied his request but allowed John to change his clothes. Frese believed he would change into women's garments as he was outed. However, the stylish man came out in a different light-brown suit with a chic bow tie and fedora.

The police sent John to the courthouse and made him undergo a physical examination. The doctor declared him a woman and he was locked in a holding cell. The doctor expressed a particular interest in the case because John was not intersex. He was amazed that John strongly believed there was nothing wrong with his gender transgression. The physician regarded John's case as "one of the most peculiar in the medical annals." Of course, trans people in St. Louis were actually quite common at the time.

John spoke freely with the *St. Louis Post-Dispatch* soon after his arrest. The reporter noted he had a command of the English language after less than two years in the country. John was eager to share his side of the story.

I came to America about two years ago, in September, 1893, with Hetwig Lutze. She is about my age, and my very best friend. I love her as my wife. Ever since I can remember I have always preferred the love of women. When I went to school I used to love to engage in the sports of the boys and ran after the girls. When any one who did not know would speak to me they would call me "Johnny," and not address me as a girl. The first time I put on man's clothes was when I was 21 years old. I fell in love with a girl. I wanted then to come to America and got as far as Hamburg, but had no passport for a man and so had to go back to Leipsic. The reason I came here at last was that I fell in love with another girl, Elizabeth Kejel, in Leipsic, and everybody taunted me and said I was neither man nor woman. I was working at type-setting and had saved some money, and so came to America, bringing with me Hetwig Lutze, because we could not bear to be parted. She loves me just as I love her. Miss Kejel got married a short while ago.

As John went on, he became increasingly anxious about his life as a man. "I hope they will not compel me to put on women's clothes," he added. "I want to keep these. I can't stand woman's clothes." He asked if there was anything he could do for Hetwig before the courts made any decisions.

Like John, Hetwig was also upset. She had a different theory to John's outing: "Old man [Ferdinand Gammater's] second son is responsible for it all. He wanted me to marry him and I wouldn't do it. Then he exposed [John] for spite work." The scheme appeared to have worked as newspapers attempted to publicly shame both Hetwig and John.

The *Post-Dispatch* also called Ferdinand. He had moved from Berne, Switzerland, to the US in 1888 and struggled with English. He communicated that he was pleased that John was arrested but exclaimed, "My daughter is very sick," when the affair came into the conversation. Martha refused to speak of their relationship.

The *Post-Dispatch* reporter tracked down Hetwig last. Hetwig claimed she had nothing to do with calling the police on John. Overhearing the conversation, her employer remarked, "Well, well. Bless my soul! What does this mean, Hetwig? Is that chunky little fellow who's been coming to see you every Sunday as your brother a woman?" Hetwig nearly burst into tears at the rude remark. He reassured her she wouldn't be fired if she did nothing wrong. She told the reporter and her employer the full story, actively refusing to use "she" pronouns for John. "He was always telling me he believed he ought to do this because he wasn't certain whether he was a man or a woman. I don't believe he's a woman," she said. Despite Hetwig's efforts to protect John, police took the trans man to the same holding cell that trans woman Effie Smith had been in three months earlier (as discussed in "The Kids"). At least one newspaper drew comparisons between the two, although media was much more sympathetic to John.[46]

A day after being placed in the holding cell, John retained seasoned lawyer Victor Sarner to defend him. The trans man showed up in court in a full suit, knowing that he did nothing wrong. Sarner decided to take a medical route to defend John, noting that his condition may be a medical or psychological anomaly. At the same time, John proposed a compromise to the chief of detectives, suggesting he would be willing to wear bloomers in lieu of pants or a dress. The detective refused.

"If I get out," John proclaimed, "I shall try to get my old place back at the nursery. If I succeed, I'll try to persuade them to let me continue wearing man's clothes. If I don't get my job back, I don't know what I shall do. If they won't let me wear man's clothes I'll try to get them to let me wear bloomers."[47] John was confident he could win his case.

Following the media frenzy of the trial, a rural farmer from Washington mailed a marriage proposal to John. Unsurprisingly, he did not respond. John's whereabouts by the end of the month were unknown, and there were no reports of him thereafter. His final punishment was a twenty-dollar fine and exile from St. Louis.[48]

THE BUTLER: ALFRED GROUARD

Referencing a butler conjures a particular image. Often, it involves an English accent and a tuxedo jacket. Perhaps Alfred Pennyworth from Batman. However, this is the story of an entirely different Alfred, predating the original Batman comic by two years. The butler's story became an international 1930s mystery as investigators struggled to track down his missing fortune and motivation for living as a man for fourteen years.

Alfred's early life is unclear and contradictory. His coworkers claimed he was born between 1882 and 1888 in France to a Jewish father and a French mother before immigrating to Pennsylvania at age four.[49] However, on a census record, he stated he was born in 1868 in Pennsylvania (and that his mother was from France). Nothing quite explains the twenty-year discrepancy between his coworkers' claims and the census record. But the two stories agree that he grew up as an orphan in Carlisle, Pennsylvania, before Rebecca F. Cornelius adopted him in the 1880s. He ran away around 1897 but occasionally wrote to his adopted mother over the following years. She never responded and they lost contact for decades.[50]

After leaving the Cornelius household, Alfred transitioned and moved to Brooklyn. He became a chef in an unnamed New York hotel until his forties when he decided to make a dramatic career change that would soon come to define him.

Retired millionaire publisher Joseph Hamblen Sears put out a newspaper ad looking for a male butler in 1923. Alfred responded and met all the qualifications. He made it obvious he was up to the job. Joseph's wife, Anna Wentworth Caldwell Sears, inspected him and he quickly won her approval. She drove to Brooklyn and retrieved Alfred for his new life on their Oyster Bay, Long Island, estate. He had shoddy clothing and few belongings. Yet because he was tall and weighed 180 pounds, neither the family nor the staff suspected his assigned sex. "He came to me with grand references as a chef. I took him on and, by gosh, he certainly could cook," Joseph explained to the *Daily Mirror*. "True, he was also a trifle queer, but, after all, a man doesn't inquire into the private life of his domestics, and I just put him down as a sort of eccentric."[51] Joseph housed Alfred in a cottage with the other servants on his estate.

Sears was the retired president of D. Appleton & Company, famous for publishing the works of Charles Darwin and books like *The Red Badge of Courage*. He retired years earlier to live off his vast fortune. He paid Alfred one hundred dollars a month for his labor. The butler was the "perfect servant" according to all who knew him.[52] Alfred was reportedly an out-standing chef, good company, and incredibly reliable. He eventually became the majordomo of the estate, organizing sixteen other workers in the house.

Everything came to an end when Alfred fainted on the job in September 1937. The Searses offered him hospital care, but he refused. Newspapers speculated he rejected care to avoid being outed. At the end of the month, Joseph's wife, Anna, died, throwing the house into disarray. Alfred took no time off and continued to help Joseph, wearing him down through hard labor and tireless chores.

On November 13, Alfred lapsed into a diabetic coma. He died a day later and the home's residents quickly discovered he was assigned female at birth. The doctors reviewing his case contended they could have easily saved him with insulin if he had accepted treatment. Word made way to reporters, and his story quickly became an international mystery. Police had no clue of his birth name or identity. They had limited information about his history and ultimately did not know how to treat his case.

Investigators were stumped as to how to figure out Alfred's upbringing. They made a death mask and took photos of it to distribute to police stations. However, the effort was to no avail. It was not until they found a returned letter that they received their first clue. Alfred sent the note to Rebecca Cornelius and his adopted sister on November 4, 1937.[53]

> You may be surprised to hear from your old servant, [Alfred]. I have been very sick, am getting old, and have no money. I wonder if you could let me have a little. Address me as Alfred Grouard, as that is the way I am known. It is the only way I can keep decent.

Alfred's frequent requests for healthcare funds led to another unsolved mystery. In the man's fourteen years at the Sears estate, he had never taken a day off and rarely left the house. He only ever had one visitor, a Catholic priest. With his food, lodging, and clothing costs covered, he had few op-portunities to spend the $15,000 (equivalent to over $300,000 in 2024) he would have amassed. Where did the fortune go? His coworkers and boss had no idea how he would have "bought anything that would take even a small part of the $15,000."[54]

It took a nationwide search before Alfred's niece, Laura Clarke, confirmed his identity. Alfred had sent another letter back to his adopted brother-in-law in Carlisle, making a similar plea for medical funds. Unfortunately, Alfred did not know his relative died three weeks before he sent the letter. Laura received the letter and heard the news story. She revealed the truth about Alfred, although she only knew him when she was a child. She claimed he was "obsessed" with being a man.

Joseph Sears exclaimed the discovery was an "amazing surprise," expressing ambivalence about the case as a whole. He repeatedly told reporters how excellent Alfred was as a "perfect servant." "Naturally I wouldn't believe it at first," he explained to a reporter. "[He] was probably trying to protect [him]self from the advances of men. Though why [he] should want to do that when [he] was about sixty years old I can't understand. Besides [he] looked like a man and talked like one. Perhaps [he] had been doing it so long that [he] became like a man in the end."[55]

The mystery of the missing $15,000 was never solved. The police did not recover a cent from his estate and they never discovered where his money went or why he requested funds for healthcare despite his high pay. Alfred was buried in Carlisle on November 20, 1937. The state respected his chosen name and paid for his coffin and headstone.

THE CRAFTSWOMAN: ANN STORCY

Anna Storcy, or "Peg Leg Ann" as her neighbors called her, was undoubtedly a tough woman. She resided in the rural Michigan forest and lived a life of radical solitude. It was not until her death that her neighbors learned she was assigned male at birth. Born in 1823, the disabled Potawatomi trans woman built her world between displaced Indigenous groups and intrusive settlers. Her remarkably autonomous way of living was a spectacle for decades and caught the attention of national reporters from the 1880s until her death in 1904.

Ann was a woman of two stories. The first story, one of fascinating mystery and questionable Potawatomi tropes, seemed to originate from the convergence of sincere belief and local tall tales. The second story is told by a close friend who claimed Ann shared her narrative with him shortly before her death. It similarly features an account of Ann's life from her upbringing to her lucrative penchant for homesteading.

All accounts of Ann agree she transitioned at some point before 1862. She was not from Michigan but began moving through several rural cities in the southwest of the state in the mid-1800s. She finally moved near the tiny towns of Watervliet and Covert in 1862 with an older woman who claimed to be Ann's mother. The supposed mother "mysteriously disappeared" according to one of Ann's neighbors, who questioned their true relationship.[56] Ann claimed her "mother went visiting" less than a year after they moved to their new home. She was never heard from again.

Industrious, Ann Storcy quickly became famous in the region for her strong hard cider, excellent crafting skills, and penchant for privacy. One newspaper noted it was her attitude that truly set her apart. "[She] hasn't an angelic disposition, and does not hesitate to use brickbats, pitchforks or shotguns if interfered with," one reporter commented. It makes sense why she moved near a town named Covert to hide her assigned sex.

Ann, although not an amputee, strapped a wooden plank to her leg so she could more easily walk after she became disabled from a childhood illness. Reporters speculated that those unfamiliar with her may have assumed she had a wooden leg due to the visible wood. This resulted in her nickname, "Peg Leg Ann."

Ann's legend became well-known in Michigan in the 1880s. Among the earliest news articles about her was one published in the *St. Joseph Herald*. "Near Rush Lake, just north of Watervliet, lives a female wonder," the feature began.[57] "She is a carpenter by trade and built her own barn also is a blacksmith and wagon maker, and can set a tire on a wheel in first-class style. She may be found any day at her forge. She drives to town with her own rig, owns a farm and with the help of one hired man farms it in first-class manner, minds her own business and compels intruders to do the same."

It was never clear how she came to own the land in the first place, but she developed it far beyond what the townspeople expected.

Much of the information we know about Ann Storcy comes from the Stoddard family. The family gathered in 1961, almost six decades after Ann's death, and a reporter interviewed them about her for a local newspaper. The Stoddards explained Ann was exceptionally close with them, saying she was like family. The older generation lived near her for much of their younger lives. The Stoddards had thirteen siblings, some of whom worked with Ann directly. The patriarch of the family, Stanley, also helped Ann learn to read and write (she was illiterate until meeting the Stoddards). Two of the siblings, Mary Ann and Laura Ann, were even named after the elder trans woman.

Ann's short temper was famous in the region and often led to armed conflict. She warded off trespassers with her six-foot barrel shotgun named "Long John." This violence was everyday behavior in rural Michigan in the nineteenth century when shotguns like Long John were not nearly as deadly as those of today. Ann once shot Ed Stoddard when he climbed on her haystack. "It smarted a bit," he later recalled. When Ed's brother Daniel stole some cider from her, she physically picked him up by the nape of his neck and tossed him into the air—so the story goes. She also shot the brother of the local Potawatomi chief after he took too much of her hard cider.

Ann was quite proud of her cider. Like with many businesses, the first hit was always free. She gave two cups to one of the Stoddard children, seven-year-old Harry Camp. Harry became so drunk that he could barely walk home. Decades after her death, the Stoddards still remembered Ann fondly despite her temper.

Ann's friends and neighbors did not publicly debate her gender. While there were some contentions over Ann's womanhood throughout the years, everyone reportedly respected her pronouns until her death. After her genitalia was discovered, newspapers and speakers mixed her pronouns depending on the individual. The matriarch of the Stoddards, Cornelia, was once offered fifty dollars to "tell whether Annie was a man or a woman." She refused the small fortune to respect Ann's wishes.

Over the decades, Ann always wore a calico sunbonnet, which hid her hairline. She smoked an old clay pipe and shaved every day for a smooth face. Her distinctive sense of fashion made her neighbors question her lifestyle, but no one would interfere with her solitary way of life.

One day, a local farmer asked Ann to marry him. Ann became so enraged at the thought that she yelled at him, "By golly, get out of here! I'm not going to marry you or anyone else!" There were no other reports of love interests, although she made it clear she was uninterested in telling media about her personal life. This is where the stories diverge, contradicting one another. One romanticizes her Indigenous history, while the other presents her life in a respectful but adventurous manner.

The goddess

Regardless of accuracy, it is helpful to report on how others understood Ann Storcy's narrative. Her story as a goddess circulated throughout the US and was how most people at the time knew her. Whether true or not, it gives an idea of how others perceived her legend.

Upon Ann's death, media outlets around the country reported her uncommon lifestyle. Publications recounted her exceptional story as one of extraordinary independence and respect. According to these reports, she arrived in Watervliet in 1862 with a group of Neshnabék (Potawatomi) tribe members who worshipped her like a goddess. She was a member of their tribe, who "regarded her as a supernatural being and for years she led the band as a chieftain until death and desertion broke up the [Indigenous] village."[58] "Peg Leg Ann" was supposedly the translation of her Potawatomi language name.

It was not uncommon for some Native American cultures to treat members that transgressed Western gender roles as spiritual figures (also see the chapter on Muksamse'lapli for more information on those we may now call *two-spirit*). Potawatomi use the term *m'netokwe* to describe people assigned male at birth who took on feminine roles.[59] The word comes from a portmanteau of *m'neto* (supernatural being) and *eθkwe·wa* (young woman). There is no exact known origin of the term, but it was used among the Prairie Band Potawatomi (in today's Kansas) since at least the early twentieth century.

M'netokwe does not directly mean trans but signifies a specific social function among Potawatomi people for those assigned male at birth. White anthropologists like Ruth Landes noted Potawatomi people in the prairie region treated people like Ann as "someone endowed with supernatural power."[60] Her descriptions were remarkably similar to the reporting of how Michigan Potawatomi regarded Ann Storcy. However, we must still take these descriptions with some skepticism. White anthropologists at the time habitually misrepresented and embellished their stories.

Ann Storcy spent the remainder of her life in the forest south of the town. One paper claimed that during this time, "She ruled the band as a chieftain."[61] White farmers would come to hear her stories but were disappointed when Ann turned them away. She valued her privacy more than sharing her awe-inspiring narrative. Despite her solitary lifestyle, she reportedly received no fewer than ten marriage proposals over the years. The man closest to becoming her fiancé left the country before the marriage could be formally arranged.

The traveler

Several newspapers reporting on Ann had a divergent yet similarly embellished tale that was explained only through an anonymous source. According to the local *Dowagiac Republican*, Ann told the unknown informant that she was born in early 1823 in Alsace, France.[62] She was orphaned at age two and adopted by a family that immigrated to Ohio. She had a fever that same year. The terrible illness left her legs without muscle control. She tied a board to one leg to help her walk thereafter.

At age three, another Frenchman adopted her. He promised he knew her mother. The man, Nicholas Villard, was not who he seemed. He carried her away on horseback after tearing pieces off her clothing to imitate a wild animal attack. Another man eventually saved her and brought the young girl to Milan, Ohio, where Villard's sister lived. Ann stayed there until her early teens. She moved to Cincinnati in 1847 to labor at a mill. She later became a caretaker for her boss's sick family. Unfortunately, germ theory was not yet widespread, and Ann became ill. Her boss appreciated her work and staked a hefty long-term investment for her in Dayton (which we will return to later).

Ann finally saved enough money to leave. She transitioned after departing Ohio around 1848. She then traveled down the Ohio and Mississippi Rivers to California. The twenty-five-year-old joined the Gold Rush while helping prospectors with washing, horseshoeing, blacksmithing, and repairing wagons. Traveling through the Isthmus of Panama appeared to have cultivated her love for travel. She went from the West Coast of the US to Cuba, Cuba to Europe, and Europe back to Ohio, taking three years to complete her journey. The woman "returned to the states with a sack of golddust," according to the anonymous source.

Upon her return, she bought a farm in Madison County, Ohio. Yet she sought a new adventure and moved to Michigan, where she quickly built a new farm in Hamilton. And the papers meant "built" in the literal sense. She cleared the property and erected multiple buildings by herself before selling the land and moving to Covert, near Watervliet, Michigan, in 1872. She lived near the local Catholic church, to which she belonged. She constructed another farm there, including a house, barn, and two mills on 120 acres. She added blacksmithing to her repertoire and truly became a woman of all crafts.

According to the *Dowagiac Republican*, her boss from the Cincinnati mill died during these years and his investment turned into several thousand dollars (over $100,000 today). He gifted her the money, which she used to live the rest of her days at ease. In 1893 she transferred her property to another couple in Covert, who cared for her in her old age.

The rumors of her leadership among Potawatomi were discounted by the reports claiming she was French. These stories contended that the tribe members were simply her neighbors. One paper confidently claimed her birth name was Monsieur D'Arcey, without providing a source. It is unclear if the writer knew that *monsieur* is not a personal name but the French word for "mister." Regardless, it is almost certain that Monsieur D'Arcey was not her name.

The final years

The two stories of Ann's life—one of the goddess and the other of the traveler—converge during Ann's later life. A local newspaper interviewed the Stoddard family in 1961 during a large picnic family reunion, and the elder Stoddards reminisced over their interactions with Ann in a full-page exposé. This is where the two stories meet the myths and truths of her narrative.

"A secret life [she] no doubt lived, a queer character [she] truly was, but in my memory [she] will ever remain, a nice old lady, who once called me 'a sweet little girl,'" recalled Bertha Hoffman, a friend of the Stoddards.[63] Ann Storcy spent her final years with her caretakers. She was unhappy that she had to live with other people and still preferred that others leave her alone. However, she was too frail to take care of herself and had to adjust.

In 1904 Ann died, age eighty-three, and the many reports on her death led to her outing. Some townspeople suspected her trans status, but there were no investigations of her transgression before her death. The Watervliet undertaker, Francis M. Keasey, was the first to discover Ann's assigned sex. However, she respected Ann's gender and did not broadcast the finding. Keasey told a few people close to Ann and the story was eventually leaked to the press. Her narrative became a romantic tale of autonomy and mystery in the community. Despite being outed in such a sensational way, her town still respected her. Watervliet even named a small street after her, "Peg Leg Annie Road." Ann left her 120-acre estate to her caretakers. Farmers still use the land she cleared 160 years ago for their crops.

THE BOY-OF-ALL-WORK: FRANK WILLIAMS

Frank Williams told a nurse his life story on his deathbed. The young trans man succumbed to paralysis in 1905 at just twenty years old. Yet his tale had enough adventure to last several lifetimes. His story became a legend before he died, with each tale told a dozen different ways in a hundred different papers. While dying, Frank was cast by the media as a noble adventurer who had no choice but to give up dresses. A jockey, newsboy, nurse, bartender, seminarian, bellboy, bookseller, barber, and porter, Frank was dubbed by journalists around the country as the "boy-of-all-work."[64]

Frank Williams told reporters he was born in Limoges, France, in 1885. He was the son of two entertainers with big personalities. His father was a comedian and his mother a Parisian dancer and singer. The young boy began to wear clothes designed for men when he was just five years old. Shortly after, the family immigrated to Chicago, where no one knew he was transgender.

His mother, Carrie Lamouche, reportedly danced and sang in famous Chicago vaudeville theaters. She often brought little Frank to attend. There, she encouraged him to continue dressing in boys' clothing. "Remember, little one, you will be left alone in the world some day and you will find it much easier to make your way as a boy than a girl," she allegedly told him.[65] Of course, Frank's blaming his mother for his gender transgression served to lessen possible punishment later in life. The claim must be taken with a grain of salt. A reporter sympathetically summarized Frank's lifelong troubles, "[He] has a man's brain and a woman's frail body—a man's indomitable energy and a woman's lack of power to carry out her schemes." Womanhood had little to offer Frank and he renounced it ever since he was a child.

Tragedy struck when Frank's father was accidentally killed in a Chicago saloon gunfight. He and his mother later returned to France when he was nine, around 1894. There, Frank claimed they visited a racetrack in Paris. The pair overheard two men mocking him.

"There is a likely little fellow. I'd like to see him on Fly-away."

"Show me Fly-away and I'll ride him!" Frank retorted.

"Can you stay on?" he snipped back.

"Try me. I've sat on the wildest horses in America's west and I'm sure I can manage anything over here."

The man chuckled and told him he would pay him fifty dollars to ride Fly-away whether he won or not. All Frank had to do to prove himself was ride around the track four times. Frank then not only rode around the track but also won matches. One paper reported he worked as a jockey for several months after a French noble became his sponsor. He took the name Frank Lamouche and amazed the spectators. He eventually gave it up and moved back to Illinois.

"[W]hen I saw how it frightened my mother I would not do it again, even though they begged me to and offered me more money. She did not forbid me to do it, but she said, 'My little son, I can make money enough to care for you, so don't feel bad about that part of it.'" It is dubious that much—if any—of his horseracing career is factual. Yet it provided a compelling enough story to be reported as fact around the country.

Carrie brought Frank to a boys' school in Keokuk, Iowa, where he was one of the top athletes. He reportedly loved tennis, baseball, and skating. However, his sex was eventually revealed and he was forced to leave. He later attended a Catholic boys' school near Columbus, Ohio, but ran away. He completed high school shortly thereafter.[66]

Frank wandered from city to city following Carrie's death around 1901. He slept in barns, halls, and anywhere he could rest. The young man received his first adult job as a newsboy in Chicago. He later picked up bookkeeping in the same city. At age sixteen, he went to a Catholic monastery and requested to become a priest. He trained for a year before he was revealed to be assigned female and was compelled to leave.[67]

Struggling after his religious departure, he went to the Convent of the Good Shepherd in Columbus. He confessed that he was assigned female at birth and begged for admission. They allowed him to join for a year or two. However, he could not tolerate pretending to be a woman. He quickly left to wander again, preferring to be unhoused over being misgendered. "I had promised the sisters to wear the girls' clothes, but I often wanted to throw them in the river and get some real clothes," he explained.[68]

Of all the incredible details of Frank's biography, there is only one aspect that almost no newspapers could agree on: his college life. One journalist reported he studied at a small men's college in Iowa and had to leave after his assigned sex was discovered.[69] Another paper reported he attended a college in Columbus, where he earned his bachelor's degree.[70] The *St. Louis Post-Dispatch*, on the other hand, asserted he went to the University of Iowa and was one of the most popular students.[71] He did not complete his education there, but the reporter claimed that men all over the state wished to give him financial aid after hearing his story in the papers.

Frank reported that his mother's love helped him enter college. He frequently ruminated on their experiences together and told journalists he looked up to his mother more than anyone. She inspired him to strive in and beyond higher education. They spent the warm months on an Iowan lake. "Those lovely summers," he reminisced, "how beautiful they were, with the leaves blowing softly, and the breezes bringing fresh roses into her cheeks, which had grown thin and pale during the winter of hard work."[72] Frank credited Carrie Lamouche's unwavering support for him as his motivation for obtaining education, work, and friendships.

Frank drifted to Cincinnati, Ohio, in 1904. There, he rotated jobs on a near-weekly basis. He began living at the Adams Hotel with only the feminine clothing from the convent in his closet. With just three dollars in his pocket, he first took up work and board at the hotel kitchen. He also played piano and sang. He soon met another hotel resident who hired him as a nurse for his family. Earning twenty dollars a month, Frank was delighted at the offer. However, he only had the feminine outfit from the convent to wear. He told his new employer about his "longing to wear boys' clothes," perhaps seeking to obtain some. The man quickly fired him.

Realizing he would need to transition to survive, Frank went to a secondhand store and bought a suit, giving up on his final, failed attempt to detransition. He would never return to women's clothing. The young man continued to live at the Adams Hotel, with around a dozen people promising to hold his secret. Frank soon began work at another nearby hotel as a bar porter, a position he held for a short time until he began working as a hotel barber. His employers never knew of his assigned sex. "I got the job as a barber. The men in the hotel [. . .] never dreamed I ever wore skirts." He worked cutting hair for three weeks.

The new hotel paid him twenty dollars a month plus room and board. He left his previous quarters at the Adams Hotel as his employer's wife refused to let him into the parlor dressed in pants. He lamented that she called him "Miss" Williams. He then moved into the Grand Hotel, one of the largest hotels in the world at the time. His final vocation was bartending for the upscale establishment. It was there he fell ill with paralysis and went to the hospital in January of 1905. It is unclear exactly what caused the paralysis or how long it had affected him. By February, doctors believed he had a brain tumor.[73]

Frank, about to turn twenty, initially joined the men's ward but confessed his assigned sex to a nurse, who would have undoubtedly figured it out during examination. He shared his life story with staff and reporters while slowly losing mobility. One reporter from Davenport, Iowa, commented, he "never utters a word of complaint" and "lived gallantly as [he] suffers gallantly."[74]

Frank reached out to Dr. Mary Edwards Walker, the first female surgeon in the US Army. Dr. Walker was the most well-known advocate for abolishing cross-dressing laws during Frank's lifetime (she is also featured in Maude Milbourne's chapter). She was famous for her dapper suits and organizing for gender-nonconforming people throughout the States. Dr. Walker invited Frank to live with her and even offered to pay his fare from Iowa to New York. At the time, Walker planned to establish something resembling a clinic for trans people on her large farm. Her gentle words were some of Frank's only comforts during his final weeks.

> Come right to me as soon as you can. I have patients in the summer and you can stay here and dress as you please.
> Until you are able to do boy's work it will not cost you anything.
> Yours ever,
> Dr. Mary Walker

Frank wrote a response that the newspapers could not locate. He quickly received another message from Dr. Walker.

> You need not be afraid to wear boys' clothing here. We dress to suit our inclinations, and the fact that you have discarded the horribly conventional clothing of women shows you to be a [man] of more than ordinary intelligence, and consequently worthy of companionship.

Other letters poured in containing job offers, sympathy cards, and several marriage proposals. Frank was adamant about recovery for the following weeks. People from around the country were compassionate about the young trans man's struggle. A businessman from North Carolina offered to take Frank in as one of his family. A traveling salesman from Texas offered the young trans man a job taking care of his wife while he was away. Frank grew more confident. He told reporters, "I'm going to wear men's clothes if I ever get out of this. It's no use for me to try to do women's work. I just can't."[75] Unfortunately, Frank never had the opportunity. Doctors determined he suffered from "a fatal form of paralysis," and he died in late February without the opportunity to leave the hospital.

There are many contradictions and misstatements in the countless articles on Frank published between February and April 1905. Some were minor, such as confusion about whether Frank was twenty or twenty-one. Others would drastically change the story. Was Frank orphaned at fifteen, as most newspapers claimed, or nineteen, as he told one reporter? How did he complete college at such a young age? What exactly killed him? We cannot know all the details of his life, but his reputation as a boy-of-all-work has survived all the gossip.

The discussion on transitioning only flourished after Frank's death. The famous suffragist Nixola Greenley-Smith wrote about Frank's struggles with great empathy just a few days after his passing. She described Frank's situation as a rather common occurrence in her article "Girls Will Be Boys."[76]

It is only when the little girls grow up that they discover that the little boys' most desirable asset is freedom and the little boys realize that the little girls' most enviable perquisite is ease. And still the only thing that reconciles the most fortunate girl to her fate is the superior loveliness of feminine clothes. But there is seldom a man so abject, so broken on fortune's ever-turning wheel, as to wish himself a woman. Whether it is better to be man or woman depends altogether on whether it is better to be free at one's own expense or comfortable at another's.

If the great desire of one's soul is for independence the advantages of being a man are too obvious to need pointing out. But if we belong to the large class who believe in comfort even at the expense of free-dom we ought certainly to be content to be women. For it is surely more comfortable to be worked for than to work, to be protected than to protect, to be loved than to love, and that, after all, is what being a woman means.

Nixola Greenley-Smith empathized with Frank's desire to be understood as a man. Why *should* he be forced into feminine attire? If gender stereotypes persisted, why not allow trans men to live their lives as men? Nixola continued fighting to abolish cross-dressing laws for the rest of her life.

Frank's story received scant attention after 1905. Yet his legacy lives on in the footnotes. He was an inspiration for Dr. Walker to continue struggling against cross-dressing laws. His narrative also helped shape Magnus Hirschfeld's *Die Transvestiten*, published five years after Frank's death. Hirschfeld established the world's first transgender clinic, using Frank's story as an example of trans people in need.

THE ATHLETES

*Because they don't want me to run, I have to run harder. I want to go
to nationals in order to prove them wrong, to be like, You guys don't
want me to run?* But look, I qualified for nationals.

—ANDRAYA YEARWOOD, trans high school runner[1]

*Every person should dedicate themselves to what they feel predilection
and enthusiasm for: to work, to study, to learn, to excel, to be something;
and when you begin to be something—you are already everything.*

—AGUSTÍN RODRÍGUEZ, transgender matador, 1905[2]

Media often represents transgender people in sports as a new issue. Yet the stories in this section, some from before the first modern Olympics, beg to differ. Trans athletes were frequently at the forefront of sports media, notable for their exceptional achievements and determination to play. Despite their fame, officials and writers erased the stories of each of the six athletes from this section after their trans status became public.

Arguments surrounding trans participation in sports hit a peak in 1977, when Renée Richards won her suit against the United States Tennis Association to play with other women in the US Open.[3] She believed she had the right to participate, but debates broke out over gender and fairness in sports—unseen again until the 2020s moral panic over queer and trans people. Is every individual with XY chromosomes inherently more athletic than everyone with XX chromosomes (see: sexism)? Despite all the controversy, Renée only ever reached twentieth place in 1979.

The debates over trans athletics, riddled with the most boring forms of misogyny, also miss a significant historical component: trans people have competed in the correct gender categories for centuries. Recent books like

Michael Waters's *The Other Olympians* track how trans people were actually at the *center* of sports discourse during periods like the 1930s. Whether playing on the team with one's gender or not, trans athleticism is nothing new.

Everything changed for trans athletes when rudimentary sex testing in sports began in the 1930s, most notably in the 1936 Olympics.[4] Although exceedingly rare cases of "sex fraud" (cis men pretending to be women) did exist, scrutinizing players' genitalia tended to exclude trans athletes rather than level the playing field. Trans and intersex people worried about being outed, which led to several of the athletes highlighted in this section exiting from sports at the height of their careers. Physical inspections turned into chromosomal examinations in 1958 with the Barr body test (indicating XX chromosomes). These tools of exclusion, however, shifted again in the 1990s and 2000s when major athletic events like the Olympics changed policies and began allowing trans athletes to participate in the sport of their gender. Severe restrictions on trans people still exist, reducing athletes to their chromosomes and hormone regimens.

As trans athletes like to point out, Michael Phelps, the most medaled Olympian of all time, produces half the lactic acid as the typical athlete. This means he does not experience as much fatigue as other people. His larger-than-average wingspan also facilitated his record-breaking feats. In women's sports, Simone Biles's short stature (of course amplified by her hard work and ability to push boundaries) helped her win more medals than any other gymnast in history. Natural differences exist between all people. Why should trans people be treated any differently for their biology?

Sex testing in sports continues to this day. Many leagues still require athletes to live within specific ranges of testosterone. A new wave of protests against mandatory hormone levels arrived after the World Athletics association demanded Black intersex cis woman Caster Semenya suppress her testosterone levels or face disqualification. Organizations like Human Rights Watch found that runners from the Global South like Caster are disproportionately targeted under these sex testing laws.[5] Several groups have contested the ruling and the fight continues.

On the other side of sports are men's teams. Dozens of trans men have won medals in professional men's sporting events over the past years and, as you may have guessed, this is nothing new. Charles Winslow Hall, a trans man who died in 1901, competed in rifle competitions in the United States and Italy in the 1890s. Charles also played different forms of ball games with other men. The thirty-something was best known for his watercolor paintings, which outshined his athletic abilities.[6] The idea that trans men are incapable of winning against cis men is one based on little more than sexist fantasies.

Each of the athletes featured in this section won medals, broke records, and became household names in their home countries. The women's 400-meter dash and Czech shot-put records were achieved in the 1930s by two trans men (Pierre Brésolles and Stefan Pekar). Trans woman Frances Anderson was widely considered the greatest female billiards player of the 1910s and 1920s. Two trans men, Stefan Pekar and his friend Zdeněk Koubek, broke the world record for the women's 75-meter relay together in 1934. Another two trans men broke the French relay record in 1946 (Léon Caurla and Pierre Brésolles). Each had their records contested due to anti-trans and sexist beliefs. Officials can remove trans athletes' records from the books, but they cannot permanently silence their stories.

THE BILLIARDIST: FRANCES ANDERSON

According to newspapers across the US and Europe, Frances Anderson was "the recognized, undisputed lady [billiards] champion of the world."[7] The outgoing trans woman commanded audiences of thousands to watch her talented cue skills. Born in Iowa in 1871, Frances lived a life of adventure from a young age. Although she earned fame and fortune from her work, officials erased her records and celebrity after she was outed in 1928.

Frances received much local news attention in her teenage years. She grew up in the small town of Newton, Kansas, with her father, auctioneer and store manager John Dickson Anderson, and her stay-at-home mother, Mary Electra Bissell. As the middle child of ten siblings, Frances distinguished herself with an extremely outgoing demeanor. She "has never been known to allow the grass to grow under [her] feet" a local reporter attested.[8] She participated in gun clubs in the 1880s, which appear to be her first foray into sports. Soon after, her father taught her how to play pool in their home. She had a knack for the game. When her family scolded her for playing too much pool, she had a habit of running away from home in protest.

Frances knew how to use her outgoing demeanor to her benefit. She hosted a fifteenth birthday party so large that it made local news. She frequently traveled around the country, making friends wherever she went. In 1887, at age sixteen, Frances followed in her father's retail footsteps and opened a new clothing store. The local newspaper called her "the youngest merchant in Newton."[9] She used her extroversion to encourage clientele to buy her wares.

In her late teens, Frances became a successful reporter. She traveled across the West and was promoted to full-fledged journalist by her early twenties, an impressive feat for the era. Frances's thirst for adventure overwhelmed her. She ran away from home again in 1890 and did not return for years, only occasionally contacting her family by mail. "You will never see me again, and when I die you won't know anything about it," she once told her sister in a letter.[10]

In 1893 her interest in bar games became part of the public conversation when she was arrested for playing in a rigged card competition.[11] It was her first documented arrest—and many were to follow. She married her first wife, Minnie Lane, a few months later. They quickly had a child, leading to much stress and dispute between them. Around this time, a doctor diagnosed her with rheumatism (inflammation) and prescribed her morphine and cocaine. Frances and Minnie split up shortly after her diagnosis. The young trans woman's habits intensified over the following months and she became addicted to the drugs. She took 1,300 milligrams of morphine and 650 to 1,300 milligrams of cocaine every single day.[12] Such quantities of either drug are easily lethal to the untrained body. In 1896 she went to Wellington, Kansas, to seek medical treatment for her addiction. However, she was run out of town for dating married women. Soon after, she moved to Galveston, Texas, and dropped out of public life for two years.

In 1898 Frances had a new partner, Babe Tamsey. The two ran a speakeasy near Hunnewell, Kansas. The bar quickly earned a reputation for drunken brawls.[13] Kansas prohibition lasted from 1881 to 1948 and, upon discovery, the local Good Citizens' Council convened to determine they would arrest Frances and Babe. On April 14, locals broke down the door and smashed any liquor they could find. Babe fled to Oklahoma while Frances signed a sworn statement of guilt in exchange for a lower penalty. She paid $7.65 and promised to never return to the county. The court provided her with a one-way train ticket out of town. However, Frances returned on April 30 to collect money owed to her. The sheriff immediately spotted her at the train station, and she attempted to flee. The officer caught up to the outlaw before she made her escape. The only item in her possession was a nearly empty whiskey bottle. She returned to the county no fewer than four additional times that year attempting to collect more money owed to her.

On February 10, 1899, Frances traveled to East St. Louis and sold her last pair of underwear for more drugs, which led police to arrest her and send her to a hospital. "Oh, I haven't the nerve to kill myself, or I would have been dead long ago," she told a reporter.[14]

Frances joined the world of professional billiards around the turn of the century. She played with her chosen name when she started her transition that decade. However, she was still only presenting as a woman part-time. She skillfully hid her assigned sex while playing smaller exhibitions. She went to the games in dresses at night while searching for work in clothing designed for men during the day. She eventually found a steady job selling newspapers before becoming a professional trader. During this time, she met one of the wealthiest women in the Choctaw Nation. She credited the woman for saving her from addiction and the two married in 1907.[15] They avoided Missouri's strict anti-miscegenation policies because they only applied to Black and Asian spouses.

Frances quit morphine and developed a new addiction: billiards. She spent years honing her skills and attracted notoriety for her talents throughout the 1910s. Her exhibitions began to draw crowds of hundreds. She started presenting as a woman full-time after earning enough money from her billiards career around 1915. Immediately drawn in by the fame and fortune, she toured all over the US and Europe. She moved throughout the States, from Chicago to Virginia to Los Angeles, showing off her skills.

In 1919 Frances picked up extra work as a nurse during the Spanish Flu epidemic. "I was in Richmond, Va.," she explained. "The city was full of 'flu' and the reports from other cities that I intended to visit were no better. The city was in need of nurses. I offered my services."[16] She worked in a hospital catering to elderly women for three months before resuming her full-time career as a billiardist. In anticipation of her highly publicized journey, newspapers began running articles on her talents. "Miss Anderson is said to exhibit a skill that has never before been equaled by any woman billiard player," a reporter said. "She lays claim to the world's championship and issues challenges to the best in the game." She traveled from Richmond to Macon, Georgia, to play against the best cue artist in the city. "Her opponents should ask the Gods of Fortune to have mercy on their souls," a reporter contended.[17] "As a lady player, she is a real champion and stands in a class by herself," another professional billiardist remarked. Frances would continue to tour for the rest of her life.

Since her earliest years, Frances was never one for subtlety. She wore elegant makeup and fine dresses while beating her competitors. She advertised her exhibitions in the newspaper so everyone would know her name: "Lady Billiardist, Frances Anderson."

During the height of her fame, she encouraged other women to get involved in the sport. She took out newspaper ads noting reserved seats just for women. Her name became associated with the game and, as several newspapers argued, she was the most well-known billiardist in the world by the early 1920s.[18] She even exchanged letters with Willie Hoppe, who is still considered one of the greatest billiards players of all time.

Frances offered $5,000 (equivalent to $80,000 in 2024) to any woman who could defeat her. While many women took her up on the offer, she claimed to have remained unbeaten for twenty-five years. During all this time, nobody suspected her sex assigned at birth. Ads for her matches were always gendered correctly and typically noted she was the "champion woman" of the world. Frances then shocked the public when her story came to an abrupt halt at the height of her career.

The billiardist ended her own life on March 29, 1928, in Sapula, Oklahoma.[19] The police found her body in her hotel room and quickly discovered her assigned sex. Officials sought to find her true identity, intrigued by her decision to live openly as a woman. A nationwide search and media spectacle ensued with much curiosity surrounding her mysterious upbringing. Eventually, Frances's sister recognized the deceased billiardist and claimed her body. The family buried her in a golden silk dress trimmed with brown fur. She was laid to rest in her hometown by two of her siblings.

THE MATADOR: AGUSTÍN RODRÍGUEZ

Agustín Rodríguez was already one of the world's most well-known bullfighters when he first joined the ring as a man in 1909. He dazzled audiences across Europe and the Americas, soaking up the attention like a sponge. A confident trans man who shined in the spotlight, Agustín saw every hurdle as an opportunity. When he was skewered by a bull, he used his injuries for publicity. When the Spanish government declared a ban on women's bullfighting, he used it as his opportunity to transition. When he was deemed too old to be a matador, he used his age to surprise and entertain audiences. Taking on the ring name "La Reverte," or occasionally "El Reverte" (the Reverse), he was celebrated as one of the most successful matadors of his era.

Bullfighting is largely recognized as a cruel sport today. However, in the early 1900s, it was central to Spanish culture. Matadors like Agustín became national celebrities for their skills. Elders in Spain may still recognize La Reverte's name as he made Spanish headlines for decades and surprised the country when he continued to live as a man after he left the ring.

Officials and reporters sanitized Agustín's life story, typically removing references to the trans aspects of his existence. The media molded him into a picaresque hero worthy of empathy for an early twentieth-century audience that may not have fully understood trans people.[20] Today's reflections on his legacy continue to mistake his identity for fraud and often incorrectly report he was a trans woman. This chapter weaves together dozens of articles and documents on his life to give a more complete picture.

The young matador

Agustín was born in Senés, Spain, in 1878. He was the son of Juan Rodríguez Vedio and María Tripiana Ejea, respectively a miner and caretaker.
He expressed his interest in becoming a matador at a remarkably young
age. Like many trans men of his time, his masculine demeanor earned him
the childhood nickname La Marimacho (The Tomboy).[21]

Agustín alternated jobs intended for men and women during his early
years. He reported working in the mines for his parents in his childhood,
a shockingly common practice at the time. Everything changed when he
attended a bullfighting match in his town square. This was not any ordi-
nary exhibition but one featuring Dolores Sánchez, known as La Fragosa.
Sánchez was famous for wearing matador attire designed for men, making
gender transgression relatively popular among women in the sport. She was
one of the most respected fighters in the country throughout the 1880s.
Agustín decided to become a matador like her.[22]

The trans boy then began his career in 1888 when he was just nine
years old. Even as a child, he was so successful at the sport that he was presented with the ears of the bull, a symbol of excellence. His junior practice
was not enough. He continued to fight alongside increasingly prominent
matadors and became one of the most well-known bullfighters by the turn
of the century.

One of the first notable women-led *cuadrillas* (matador teams) formed
in 1895. The group became so popular that Agustín knew he had to join
the sport. Bullfighting reporters celebrated La Reverte's exploits almost
immediately. "La Reverte has shown great courage in the death of [his]
bulls, and as a colleague from the court says, [he] has shown us that [he]
is a woman with a full beard," one 1899 paper read.[23] "May [he] always
dominate the monster with the two horns, and may the weapon of the
beast never cause the blood to flow from [his] flesh," read another.[24] Many
of these newsletters would go into gruesome details of the killings (which
I will not repeat here!).

Despite the widespread praise, some more conservative mainstream
reporters were not happy with gender-nonconforming matadors in the ring.
One critic from *El Enano* complained, "La Reverte was very brave, but I am

not for feminism in bullfighting."[25] A reporter from *La Correspondencia de España* described Agustín as only adequate in the ring: "[He] is very brave and very dark. [He] dodges, stabs, kills and jumps the fence like a man. [He] has a lot of determination, but nothing more."[26]

Twenty-five-year-old Agustín famously fought in Lisbon on June 24, 1904, sixteen years after his first match. Scouts for the sport used the coveted competition to court future leaders of Portuguese bullfighting. Needless to say, Agustín's presentation was so impressive that he signed contracts to fight in rings around the country that same day. Following his international tournament, Agustín became a folk hero across the Iberian Peninsula. Every business in the city of Cádiz and neighboring towns reportedly had a portrait of Agustín.[27]

With increasing success came increased frustration. Agustín grew upset at being forced to compete against women. "Why," he pleaded, "there is no question at all of any competition between us. There is no case for a competition, and the fact that I have to fight full-grown bulls, and that these girls will only dare to fight mere calves bears me out. [. . .] It is me whom the bullfighting spectators carry on their shoulders after a fight from the bullring to my house." He believed he was greater than any other man, and his assigned sex had little to do with his ability.

La Reverte continued to push himself harder as he toured across the country. His masculine swagger only brought more crowds to his arenas as he impressed audiences with his moves. In 1905 the popular *El País* periodical questioned why Agustín was so dedicated to bullfighting. He explained that bullfighting was his art, his niche. "Every person should dedicate themselves to what they feel predilection and enthusiasm for; to work, to study, to learn, to excel, be something; and when you begin to be something—you are already everything."[28] The journalist compared him to philosopher Arthur Schopenhauer, also noting their similar aversion to women.

On August 5, 1907, he again stirred national controversy when he refused to kill an *utrero*, a bull between three and four years old. The governor had to force Agustín to kill the animal.[29] A bull also gored La Reverte in northern Spain later that year. Medical experts said he would never recover, but he went on to consult a doctor who specialized in bullfighting wounds.

Within months, Agustín was as good as new and ready to fight once more. Reporters celebrated his return to the ring and his wounds made him more popular than ever. However, his greatest trial was just about to begin.

Transitioning in the arena

In July 1908, the Interior Minister of Spain, Juan de la Cierva, outlawed women from bullfighting. He was notoriously conservative and believed it was too dangerous for women to participate. He believed their sport was "a spectacle that is not proper and so opposed to culture and any delicate sentiment that in no case should the government authorities permit this offense to morality and good customs to take place."[30] La Reverte was at the center of the scandal, the most famous bullfighter the public believed to be a woman. *El País* considered his ban an "unspeakable outrage" and spectators complained of the new rule.[31] Agustín, however, saw this as an opportunity. He publicly protested and filed an appeal. "May Mr. de la Cierva give me a man's credentials and I will continue fighting as men can because I am as capable as anyone else."[32] Agustín hired two lawyers to fight the new law while also using the policy to transition.

Agustín suddenly changed his story. He publicly claimed he had a penis and was a cis man. He found a sympathetic doctor to sign a note saying he was a man, leading to guesswork over whether he was trans or intersex in the coming decades. Within just a few months, he returned to the ring. He finally changed his name to Agustín Rodríguez, which he was known as thereafter.

At first, viewers thought Agustín's male identity was merely an act to bypass the ban on women bullfighters. However, he kept his name and pronouns for the rest of his life, even in private. Journalists were confused as to his gender and would alternate pronouns. Some used "El Reverte" while others kept the feminine "La." A few would even use "Lo Reverte" as a gender-neutral title.[33] He began bullfighting again by that September.

Agustín's decision to publicly transition turned out to be a blessing. He received his first male contract in Madrid in 1909. To fight in the capital was an honor. The city was the center of bullfighting globally. He performed remarkably, as per usual. The following morning, a Madrid newspaper declared, "Of all the bullfighters that had appeared the previous day in the Madrid bullring, the best was the female."[34]

The matador regained his status with his transition. In 1911 a series of exposés featured discussions and interviews with Agustín. He was the talk of the country. His transition was "an event and completely filled [every] square" according to one 1911 paper.[35] Another commented that "he was made a man by divine grace." He applied new artistry to his sport and was immediately hired for more shows. With the profound awe of the nation, he also changed his legal documentation that September.

Agustín finally began to slow down in 1912. He declared, "If I don't win, it will be my last exhibition."[36] Eventually, he decided to retire at age thirty-four. He stayed quiet and lived rurally the following decade. In fact, there is no record of newspapers interviewing him for twenty years. He moved back near his hometown and began working at a mine in 1923. He stayed there for eleven years until he began to long for the ring once more. During this entire time, he exclusively went by *él* (he) pronouns and the name Agustín. He never wore clothing designed for women again. One reporter noted he was "always dressed as a man, with pants, chaps and girdles, and a shotgun in hand."[37]

A failed retirement

Newspapers finally caught up with the aging man in 1934. At that time, he worked guarding a copper mine in Vilches, Spain. At age fifty-six, he was ready to return to the ring. He signed an exclusive contract with Juan J. de Lara, the owner of several Portuguese rings.

"I am returning to the ring because, despite the time that has elapsed since I retired, I still miss the applause of people," he explained. "I have been 24 years without hearing any public clapping in my honour, and I really cannot live without public applause" (it was actually twenty-two years).[38] He told reporters he wanted to start at the top, where he left off. "But whatever I do, I shall make it a point to fight in the Madrid bull ring," he explained.

The older man only played a few games before permanently retiring, never to return to the ring again. The matches were not well-reported. After Agustín died in 1945, rumors of his gender became murky.[39] In 1963 the

Miami Herald falsely reported that he was actually assigned male at birth and that he masqueraded as a woman to join women's groups. Reporter Christopher Arnold wrote, "When the Spanish government decreed that it was illegal and immoral for women to fight bulls, 'La Reverte' removed her brunette wig and fought under his real name, Agustin Rodriguez."[40] Ironically, Agustín was indeed his real name and how he should be remembered.

Another slate of US newspapers in the 1970s again incorrectly stated Agustín dressed as a woman to join women's bullfighting. They also erroneously translated *La Reverte* to "The Transvestite" and implied he was a fraud. These myths continue to this day. Articles as recent as 2020 again claimed he was a cisgender man masquerading as a woman to cheat in the sport.

The truth about Agustín's life becomes more straightforward when we look at the original articles from the Spanish National Archives. He would have most likely been considered a trans man today. A stubborn, dedicated, and perhaps egotistical trans man, but a trans man nonetheless. While the sport of bullfighting fades from public sympathy, the story of Agustín Rodríguez should become clearer than ever.

THE PENTATHLETE: STEFAN PEKAR

Stefan Pekar was an all-around athlete. Born on February 2, 1913, in rural Rajec, Austria-Hungary, he became a champion sportsman in his early twenties. His story offers a rare insight into friendship and rivalry between trans men in the 1930s. Once ranked among the greatest "female" athletes globally, Stefan remains almost unheard of in the English-speaking world.[41]

Stefan grew up in a remote, tiny town twelve miles south of the small, ancient city of Žilina in today's Slovakia. The trans man initially moved to Prague in 1932 to pursue a degree in medicine. He quickly became popular among his classmates as a multitalented student with a penchant for music, academics, and athletics. Stefan tried out for several sports while in college. The teams immediately accepted him. After only minimal practice, he won gold in javelin and silver in distance running in the Czechoslovak Women's Track Championships in July 1933. He also set the nation's shot-put record at 12.82 meters (42.1 feet) that same year. He won several medals in the same competition the following year. For decades, commentators would reminisce on his athletic versatility.[42] But his national rankings were only the beginning of his story.

Stefan first met Zdeněk Koubek, an intersex trans man also playing for Czechoslovakia, in late 1932.[43] We know much about Stefan's life thanks to his friendship with Zdeněk, who was more famous—and documented—than Stefan (both before and after the two transitioned). The pair were friends, rivals, and teammates determined to win with—and against—one another. Zdeněk recounted Stefan nearly missing their first match together in his embellished 1936 memoir. After leaving for Lviv, the team waited to pick up Stefan in Bohumín, around 175 miles east of Prague. He recounted a dramatic scene among his teammates.[44]

All the girls, together with Mr. Vodička, the leader of the crew whose hair was quickly greying from worry, leaned out the window. The newbie was nowhere to be seen. The stationmaster, with the cap of a general and the beard of a sexton, already had his whistle at his mouth when a desperately waving umbrella appeared in the distance.

The girls let out a war cry: "Pekar[,] quickly, Pekar[,] quickly!" And in response, the newbie picked up the pace to racing speed with two lush braids trailing. A parcel under one arm and umbrella in the other hand hindered [his] style but even an amateur would have to notice the signs of athletic talent in the newbie. Now [he] shifted the box into [his] right hand and threw it through the open window like a discus and then, the umbrella followed it with the speed of a master of the javelin throw. Next, the newbie "threw" [him]self agilely into the coupe just as the stationmaster went "toot-toot" on his whistle and the train departed.

Stefan not only made it onto the train but delighted his new team. Zdeněk "found considerable strength for the stomach from the contents of the newbie's box. Inside was an excellent, golden baked goose. After a while, there was only a pile of clean bones left from it, and the only other trace of it could be found on the greasy lips of the runners." The team encountered more trouble at the border when an inspector refused to see Zdeněk as a woman due to his growing moustache. The administrator thought the team was attempting to smuggle a man into Poland. However, thanks to his persuasive teammates, the guards let Zdeněk go. The team proceeded to play in the Pogoń stadium, where Stefan and Zdeněk impressed the twelve thousand onlookers. Stefan won his first game 63–43, and Zdeněk returned to the border guard with their trophy. Zdeněk boasted, "See, I didn't lie to you. Here you have real documents that I am indeed Koubková and not some man who wants to be smuggled across the border." Stefan returned to Prague while Zdeněk traveled on to Brno.

The Women's World Games

Excitement built in 1934 as Stefan was close to beating multiple world records. The stylish young man was at the forefront of European sports and attracted much fanfare from around the continent. That year, he entered the Women's World Games (also known as the Women's Olympiad) in London. The event was an Olympic-level competition designed to provide a broad range of track-and-field sports for women.[45] Seventeen countries had representatives at the competition. The games were also marked by a large assemblage of trans and intersex people. Stanisława Walasiewicz, also known as Stella Walsh (an intersex cis woman playing for Poland), and Zdeněk Koubek were two of the most recognized names in sports at the time and planned to compete. The event was perfect for Stefan as it was the first to include the pentathlon, his specialty.

Embodying fame, conviction, and enthusiasm, Zdeněk was confident he would "return with as much glory as the footballers from Italy" from the 1934 games.[46] Czech press favored Zdeněk to win before he even traveled to London. Stefan joined him in the national tryouts held by the Czechoslovak Amateur Athletic Union (CSAAU; the official governing body for Czechoslovak sports). At first, the talented trans men were the only two athletes to qualify for the 1934 games in their country. Several cisgender women later joined them at subsequent tryouts. But qualifying was only their first step. They would need to find the means to travel there.[47]

The Czechoslovak team initially struggled to fundraise to go to the event. The CSAAU had to appeal to fans by posting stories in newspapers.

It was only after international film star Anny Ondra learned of Stefan and Zdeněk's struggle and donated around $3,600 to their cause did they know they would be able to attend. Anny's husband, Max Schmeling, was the world heavyweight champion from 1930 to 1932, so she had many athletic connections.[48]

Lída Merlínová, a queer Czech literary celebrity, detailed Zdeněk and Stefan's journey to London. She wrote an embellished biography on Zdeněk in 1935, *[Zdeněk's] World Record*.[49] Merlínová described Stefan as the leader of Czechoslovakia's team. She portrayed him as popular among the athletes and fans. There is no reason to doubt her characterization—he was beloved among the team members. Stefan brought a saxophone with him while traveling to the event and the group took turns with it, mildly annoying Zdeněk but amusing the others.[50] Neither Stefan nor Zdeněk could play the saxophone, but they tried anyway. The team sang along. The tight-knit group would change sports history over the following days.

Stefan and Zdeněk's team began their journey at Prague's pristine Art Nouveau rail station on the morning of August 6.[51] Twenty-five other Czechoslovaks joined Stefan. The train's wheels slowly began to roll as the balmy Prague air flowed through the open windows, while dozens of onlookers shouted and waved at the group. Zdeněk took out his copy of *One Thousand Words in English* to prepare for his travels while buildings and fields passed by.[52] The trip was supposed to be fast. However, they had an unexpected stop through Cologne, leaving Stefan and Zdeněk without a wink of sleep in their third-class cabin. Nazi officials also made the group turn over any literature not approved by the Reich. The following morning, the group boarded a boat in Belgium, the last leg of their trip to England. It was Zdeněk's first time seeing the ocean.

After disembarking in Dover, the crew took a well-maintained train to London's scenic Victoria Station. The group was amazed, not used to such luxury. After arriving at the arena, they changed into tracksuits and prepared for the opening celebration. Zdeněk led his team in the ceremony, with Stefan close behind. They paraded through White Stadium, the largest in the world, in their Czechoslovak uniforms. In Merlínová's telling, the event was highly patriotic. She reminisced about Zdeněk carrying the Czech flag for the procession on the warm August 9 afternoon. He marched around the racetrack "like a film gladiator" with his teammates.[53] The fifteen thousand onlookers cheered in amusement.

The press did not hesitate to publicize the international event. Global papers widely circulated a photo of Stefan and Zdeněk at the games after Zdeněk transitioned in 1935. The two appear close. Zdeněk held his arm around Stefan's shoulder while Stefan rested his hand on Zdeněk's hip. Zdeněk's fingers were tightly clasped around Stefan's. The pair stood in uniform with toothy grins.

After shaking hands with their competitors, Stefan and Zdeněk discussed their strategy. Stefan encouraged Zdeněk to focus on the relay and rest during the long jump and sprint.

"What do you think of Mauermeyer and Wajsówna?" asked Stefan.[54]

"I haven't seen them." Zdeněk shrugged.

"[Zdeněk], the relay is our best and perhaps only hope," Stefan explained.

"Sure, but I excel in both long jump and sprint [as well]."

"I have it on good authority that Walasiewicz will not be competing in the long jump either. It's for the same reason."

"But I will!" Zdeněk retorted.

"No, you won't!" Stefan pleaded. "The long jump is just before the eight-hundred-meter race. We can't afford for you to exhaust yourself, get injured, or be demoralized if your jump doesn't go well. [Gladys] Lunn knows your time. She's prepared for it. Besides, there are whispers about that Swedish girl, [Märtha] Wretman; she's said to be a big upset in the relay."

"I can't and won't put everything on one card."

"It's the only way you have a chance of winning. Better one win than ten problematic starts," Stefan contended. Zdeněk denounced the demands and competed in the events anyway. He won first place in the 800-meter dash, setting his most well-known world record. At two minutes and 12.4 seconds, he beat the past record holder by over four seconds. He earned the (perhaps ironic) title "recordwoman" from athletes and journalists alike. Stefan and the rest of the Czech team burst into cheers as soon as the announcer declared Zdeněk the winner. The Czech national anthem played over the loudspeaker and his victory became international news. He also earned bronze in the long jump, although his world record outshined any other successes of the competition. Stefan and Zdeněk then set the world relay record together, completing 75 meters in 37.4 seconds.[55] The two trans men helped Czechoslovakia emerge as one of the top nations for athletes in the 1930s.

Stefan performed as well as his teammate, despite Zdeněk having more recognition for his sportsmanship. The lesser-known trans man ranked among the top athletes at the 1934 games. His versatility helped him excel during an event featuring many different sports. Along with the relay, he earned a bronze medal for shot put and another bronze for the pentathlon, which included a 60-meter sprint, 300-meter sprint, high jump, two-handed javelin throw, and two-handed shot put.[56] He emerged victorious with only a small leg injury.[57]

Stefan and Zdeněk returned to their hotel and celebrated the win. However, Zdeněk contemplated his right to hold the winning title of "the fastest girl in the world."[58] He mused about shouting to the stadium, "Keep your golden reward, I don't want it! It doesn't belong to me! It is intended for the winner of a women's contest. And I [. . .] I'm not a girl at all!" After forgetting his razor blade, he stole his coach's razor and shaved to prepare for the afterparty. He felt like he could not ask for one due to anxiety over his gender, but the coach never found out. In his cheap, green suit, Zdeněk avoided the fanfare by escaping with his girlfriend to a London café.

Following an afterparty to celebrate the successful games, the Czechoslovak team finally departed England. They marveled at their praises in newspapers while traveling to Brussels for more interviews and festivities.

The 1934 Women's World Games were Stefan's largest—but not final—competition. He ran in a smaller match in Prague against Japan the following month and continued his training.[59] The 1935 track championships were even more successful for him. He won six titles—one each in the 100-meter dash, 100-meter relay, 200-meter dash, long jump, shot put, and javelin throw.[60] That same year he also won first place in the Czechoslovak Women's Pentathlon Championship and in the javelin throw at the International University Games. The CSAAU affirmed that Stefan "is in a league of [his] own," unmatched by any rival.[61] Although the CSAAU expected Stefan to join the Olympic team in 1936, he did not attend for unknown reasons. Stefan's final official competition came in July 1937, when he won the national titles for distance running, shot put, and javelin.

"What! Another!"

Stefan's history is unique in that he was cast as Zdeněk's shadow following the latter's rise to international fame in 1934. Zdeněk was a tall, blonde Czech and earlier to publicly transition in November 1935. He attracted immediate media interest. Stefan, on the other hand, was dark, shorter, and Slovak and later to publicly transition. Three more intersex trans men, Belgian cyclist Willy De Bruyn, Polish champion thrower and runner Witold Smętek, and British champion thrower Mark Weston also transitioned publicly in 1936.[62] Stefan was, perhaps for the first time in his life, slow to the game. His transition attracted much less media attention than most trans athletes of his era. Unlike the other famous trans sportsmen of 1936, Stefan was also a rare case in which we can ascertain that he was not intersex. He was inspected by athletic officials in 1935 and (quite incorrectly) declared a woman.[63]

Stefan quietly transitioned in May 1936, age twenty-three, before continuing to study medicine in Prague. When asked what his plans were after medically transitioning, he told reporters, "I'll play soccer at home with the boys. It will be fun."[64]

The presence of another Czech trans male athlete profoundly affected women's athletics in Eastern Europe. Mothers were reportedly worried their daughters would transition if they played sports. In May 1937, a newspaper headline puzzled, "Can Every Woman Be Changed into a Man?"[65] The popular Czech newspaper *Polední list* named Stefan "Koubek No. 2."[66] Surprisingly, rather than mocking Stefan or Zdeněk, Czech outlets were relatively respectful of the two young men. Several pointed to the amazing new science of hormones as something to celebrate when discussing their transitions.[67]

English-language media did not report Stefan's transition until 1937. Stefan was old news after Zdeněk's highly visible tour in Europe and the United States in 1936–1937. The *Montreal Star* simply exclaimed, "What!

Another!" when referencing Stefan's transition.[68] Following this media attention, Stefan had surgery in Prague on March 12, 1938. He returned home to Rajec for recovery. Like Zdeněk, most of his records were erased by sports authorities soon after he transitioned.[69] We may never recover the full extent to which the pentathlete competed. However, Czech sports journalist Alfred Janecký noted that his transition did not interfere with his social life. In fact, other students liked the already-popular young man *even more* after he came out.[70]

Everything changed for Stefan when Germany invaded Czechoslovakia in 1938 and news turned to the impending war. Nazis annexed the nation as a puppet state in September and the first Slovak Republic splintered from the Protectorate of Bohemia and Moravia in 1939. The split meant Stefan now lived a nation away from most of his teammates and the social centers of what is now the Czech Republic. Between the active destruction of queer and trans information and the fragmenting of European states, there are no definitive records of Stefan during or after the World War II era. Both Stefan and Zdeněk's fame dissipated as renewed cisgender, masculinized norms emerged.[71] During this period, queer and trans people throughout Europe were persecuted like never before. Studies on gender and sexuality were suspended among the Allies and many intellectuals, queer people, and leftists had to flee Axis nations. The devastation eradicated crucial information about queer and trans people of the era, likely including the remainder of Stefan's story.

Nazis stormed the University of Prague, where Stefan attended, in 1939. The Reich shuttered all Czech universities on November 17 of that year until the end of the war.[72] Over 1,200 students, including Stefan's classmates, were sent to the Sachsenhausen concentration camp through 1943. It is unclear if Stefan was ever able to complete his medical degree or if he was among those detained.

Stefan Pekar is not a rare name in Eastern Europe, making it difficult to determine if references are to the athlete or another Stefan entirely. A Slovak private named Stefan Pekar fought alongside the Red Army against the Axis during World War II.[73] Slovak soldiers like Stefan were erased from the discussion as an ethnic minority in Czechoslovakia, meaning it is difficult to obtain any details on their individual histories. A Štefan Pekár died in 1983, but again, there are no details if this is the same person.[74] Even if much of his history was permanently lost to the war, Stefan Pekar's narrative is a powerful testament to trans participation in sports. His story shows that athletics are not only about winning, but also the friends you make along the way.

THE WRESTLER: BILL WINTERS

Boys envied him. Girls fawned over him. William Winters, a trans boy reportedly so handsome he had a long list of admirers, lived freely as a man for nine years. Like many trans narratives in the early 1900s, there are conflicting reports about his life, each more scandalous than the last. With big brown eyes and lofty hair, Bill used his charm to find jobs, girls, and friends who would defend him. As tough as he was charming, his athleticism and penchant for wrestling saved him from prison after his dramatic outing.

Bill's story garnered much national attention after he was outed in 1909 at age twenty-two. What makes his case remarkable is the overflowing gush of romance that the media channeled into his story. Major outlets were so impressed with Bill's abilities that they openly praised his gender defiance. "[Bill] Winters was a man among men, in garments, with a career more picturesque than ever novelist plotted," the St. Louis Post-Dispatch applauded.[75] "[He] did a man's work as a man does it and [he] pursued masculine pursuits among them without the slightest detection." A man like no other, Bill's life deserves reconsideration through a gender-affirming lens.

William Winters was born in 1887 in Galveston, Texas.[76] It was not until September 1900, however, that his life truly began. The Great Galveston hurricane struck the island city with destruction never before seen by its people. Gusts thrashed 145 miles per hour over the region and destroyed thousands of buildings beyond repair. Boats floated through the flooded streets as though the roads were rivers. Over a quarter of the city's population was left without homes. Twenty-eight-year-old Richard "Dick" Steren saved Bill from the flood. He found the thirteen-year-old floating on a pile of clothing he used as his life raft.[77] After surviving the neck-breaking wind, the two searched for Bill's missing parents together. They were never seen again. Bill's family was among the approximately eight thousand fatalities of the hurricane, the deadliest natural disaster in US history. Dick convinced the young trans boy to flee with him to safety. Before leaving the city, Dick fashioned Bill his first clothing designed for men out of an old pair of overalls.[78] He cut the teen's hair with a pocketknife and they left Galveston together.

The two first moved to a home near Upton, Texas. Dick found work as a quarryman while Bill worked as the quarry's water boy. They then traveled the Mojave Desert before heading to Quincy, Illinois, where the trans teen posted bills for two years. Dick respected Bill's gender and closely guarded his secret. "I never told a single soul of the fact from the day that I took the [boy] out of the waters of the Galveston flood half drowned. [He] preferred to be a boy, and had not others found it out through discovery or from [his] own lips I should have never told any one of it. And I will say the little 'chap' was straight, regular in habits and well-behaved," Dick would later explain.[79]

Dick held the young man in deep regard and reported that he took him in as his child. "As long as [he] wanted to be a boy I did not have any objections, as it was the best way in which I could take care of [him] in the position that I was. [. . .] I told everyone here that [he] was my son and [he] called me 'dad.' If any one ever suspicioned [him] as being a girl I don't know it." Bill recalled the relationship quite differently. Rather than familial, it was romantic—before turning abusive.

"Of course I was nothing but a youngster then, or I would never have listened to the words of a 28-year-old man who professed that he was madly in love with me and suggested the idea of my masquerading," Bill complained. "Things went well with us for a short time, but I couldn't stand the abuse which this man heaped on me, and in Dallas, Texas, I deserted him." Dick claimed Bill told him he was sixteen at the time of his rescue. Bill stated he was only thirteen.

If what Bill said was true, he would be an abuse victim. Dick, however, denied that Bill ran away or was his lover/victim. Both had a strong motivation to lie about their circumstances—Bill to avoid "cross-dressing" charges and Dick to avoid shame. Their divergent stories came together when both reported Bill went to live with John Howard in Quincy, Illinois, later in 1900. Dick departed for Texas after leaving Bill with ninety-seven dollars. He did not hear back from Bill for years. The Howard family did not know the teen's assigned sex and simply treated him as any other adopted son. Many admirers flocked to the charming young man during his stint in the Prairie State. "He is said to have taken girls to the various high-priced shows at the Empire theater on many occasions and seated them in the best rows," a local paper reported. In 1902 the Howard family moved to Kirkwood, Missouri, near St. Louis, around where Bill lived for the rest of his life.

St. Louis

Bill reported that no one in St. Louis knew his trans status for years after his arrival. He bound his chest with bandages and told anyone who spotted them that he needed the bindings for fractured ribs that were never properly set. "I have lived here all this time as a man and not one person has suspected that I was otherwise," he later told a journalist. During this period of his life, he worked a remarkable array of jobs. The young man started working in a basket factory, earning just three dollars a week (around one hundred dollars in 2024). He also worked in a hardware store, iron foundry, stable, and plow factory over the years. Bill later entered a boilermaker's apprenticeship, where he "worked at driving hot rivets into boiler iron and wielded a hammer and lifted blocks and sheets of iron with any of them." He joined a local boilermakers' union and was even elected secretary of the group.[80] "I wasn't cut out for a clerk or a salesman," he told the *St. Louis Post-Dispatch*. "I usually picked out the hardest work there was. I liked that kind the best." He was so charming that he quickly worked his way up in the all-male boilermaker guild as one of their key members. The young man's tenacity for labor and amiable personality made him beloved among those around him.

Bill began dating Mabel Kendrick of St. Genevieve, Missouri, in 1905. The deeply infatuated couple met on the Mississippi River south of St. Louis. Bill was her assistant for an event catering job and she believed he had a natural talent for cooking. "He was very attentive to me," she said. "At that time I don't think I regarded him as a sweetheart, but rather as a good man—the best man I had ever seen. [. . .] I can't say that he ever exactly made love, but he was very attentive and seemed to think a great deal of me."[81]

Mabel's kind words were also shared in letters later obtained by news outlets. In 1905 she wrote him: "Oh, Willie, if you are sweet as that, I don't blame the girls for wanting you." She mused, "What pretty hair you have! I would give my pet cat for such hair as that. When you have it cut save me one of your curls, and as soon as I have my picture taken again you will get one in the first mail." She ended her letter with "x x x x x x x," which was "believed at the police station to represent kisses," according to a press report.

In another letter, Mabel expressed a hint of jealousy at the number of girls gushing over Bill. "I don't blame the girls for falling in love with you," she wrote. "You are almost too pretty to be a boy."

"I often wish I were a girl," Bill wrote back. "A fellow has to work so much harder to earn a living than a girl does." Bill reported that they were engaged for three years. Mabel gave more ambiguous responses as to the nature of their relationship.

The young trans man became even more outgoing over time. He sang at the famous Happy Knights Club in St. Louis, where his favorite song was reportedly Byron G. Harlan's 1907 hit "Tying the Leaves." His voice passed with a huskiness from smoking so much tobacco. In 1908 he became the marshal of a Labor Day parade division as a union leader. The young man gracefully rode a large black horse through the streets and obtained the attention of many girls watching from the sidewalks.

After Mabel, Bill began dating Alma Simmons, a carpenter. She moved in with Bill in downtown St. Louis around May 1908. The two planned to marry and she claimed that she was not aware the young man was trans. She considered him "as good a fellow as you would want to see."[82] He took her out often and Alma reflected that he "was just as jolly and pleasant as could be." Bill even introduced her to the Howards (his adopted family) and called her his wife.

Bill also joined several sports teams during his time in St. Louis. He reportedly loved baseball, sprinting, and football. He joined a wrestling club and would frequently win matches. Butch White, a bartender who knew Bill, did not believe he was assigned female at birth when reports about the young man came out. "You can't tell me that guy is a woman," Butch exclaimed. "Why, I wrestled with him too often and he threw me every time. He's as strong as a bull. You can't make me believe that husky fellow's a girl."[83]

The spectacle of William Winters

Bill was finally outed on February 14, 1909.[84] A Valentine's Day police raid on a speakeasy finally led to his downfall. It is appropriate that such a charming man would have his life overturned on a day of charm. Bill went to a downtown clandestine apartment bar to lend money to a friend. Police, upon noticing a known criminal entering the bar, conducted a full raid on the premises while Bill was inside. The young trans man wound up incarcerated in a St. Louis jail with the other patrons.[85] He could not afford the hundred-dollar bond (equivalent to $3,400 today) and was sent to the Central District Police Station. The arrest would lead Bill to a longer series of trials, more personal than legal.

Detectives Roach and McLaughlin took a stroll through the holding area later in the day. They spoke with Bill and "noticed that his hands and feet were unusually small." The two were not particularly suspicious but jokingly commented, "say, kid, we'll have to search you. You look like a woman."[86] At that point, Bill stated that he *was* a woman (likely to avoid additional trouble). Ironically, it was only then that the police actually grew suspicious of him. He thought he was protecting himself while, in reality, he was laying bare his story to public scrutiny. It took further persuasion to convince the detectives that he was telling the truth. They sent the young trans man to the examination room and confirmed his narrative. Bill continued to speak to the police about his experience. He was so persuasive that the St. Louis chief of detectives decided Bill "was an object of pity rather than censure."[87] He put Bill into women's clothes that were left at the station. In an unlikely moment of sympathy, the police worked together to remit the charges and Bill was released.

As newspaper reports came out, Alma told reporters she was furious at Bill for not disclosing his assigned sex to her. It is possible she expressed anger to exculpate herself from knowing Bill's secret. Whatever her motivation for expressing such fury at her ex-fiancé, she was never prosecuted for her love of Bill. The woman planned on sending him bail money but told a journalist if he "was shrewd enough to deceive her in that manner [he] certainly could get out of Jail by [him]self."[88] Alma's only clue to Bill's sex was his tiny hands. She once found a youth-sized ring and brought it home to give to a child she knew. Instead, Bill put it on. Alma believed the ring was still on Bill's finger when he was arrested.

Mabel, on the other hand, conveyed her shock and sympathy at the discovery of Bill's assigned sex: "I never had thought it possible for a man to be as handsome as he was," Mabel told reporters. "He took me to dances and visited me often. His good looks caused lots of people to talk about him. Some said he was pretty enough to be a woman, but I never suspected that he really was." After the discovery, Mabel appeared accepting, offering to travel sixty miles to St. Louis to support him. "If he is in trouble there may be something I can do for him or, I suppose, I should call him her now, shouldn't I?" she asked.[89]

The remarkable narrative drew an impressive flow of attention from international outlets. The Associated Press released a few paragraphs about his history on February 15, 1909. His story even made the front page of the *New York Times*.[90] The *St. Louis Post-Dispatch*, one of the largest newspapers in the country, gave Bill its entire cover page on February 21. It included several photos and drawings of his various occupations. The paper was shockingly respectful for its time, inspired by his story and adventures. The author deemed him a "man in all but sex."[91] The press excavated his life story, prodding even his casual acquaintances for answers on how he lived so freely as a man for nine years.

The papers featured several divergent stories about Bill's origins, some of which do not match historical events. What they did have in common, however, was praise for Bill's charm. A reporter from the *Evansville Journal* was impressed that the young man "made no prying enemies among men or women who might have made realities of the shispicious [sic]."[92] Bill was kept safe as his "ready, good-natured way of directing the shafts of suspicion from [him] saved [him], for there were many who recognized the feminine (not effeminate quality) of [him] and remarked it, but investigation went no further." Some of Bill's friends noticed his youthful appearance, but none doubted his manhood.

The young trans man could have been in much more trouble had he decided to defend his gender. Taking his case to court would have been a daunting task. He instead capitulated to the cisgender officials' legal and economic demands. The boilermakers' union also accused him of embezzling $249 because the bylaws excluded women from participating.[93] Despite working as a secretary for the group, the brotherhood wanted their money back. The assistant circuit attorney declined to issue a warrant for Bill, who agreed to repay the amount in five-dollar weekly installments. Police finally offered Bill an ultimatum: detransition or face prosecution. He chose the former. They released the young man on February 25, 1909. He was reportedly fined one hundred dollars on "idling" charges.[94]

The citizens of St. Louis were shocked at the revelation of Bill's identity. The young man often frequented Bob Hannon's downtown saloon before his outing. He would also occasionally work as a bartender and busboy there. Hannon told papers, "If Bill's a girl then I must be a woman. Say, I'd part with a hundred dollars to see Bill in girl's clothes. 'He' certainly must be a sight. All us chaps down here ought to go away back to be fooled like that. Why, he—I simply can't got used to saying 'she' when I'm talking about Bill—was as manly as any young fellow I ever saw. Why he—she—or rather he—Oh, what's the use—I'll never get used to calling Bill she."[95] Bill's landlady was similarly astonished: "The revelation has dumfounded me. My husband and I will both swear that 'Bill' Winters always acted to perfection the part of a natural man. The idea of 'him' turning out to be a woman. I can scarcely believe it."

The Howards, Bill's adopted family from Quincy, could not believe it themselves. Mary, his sister, was stunned. "I can't believe it at all. Mamma and papa would not believe it if 'Bill' told them so 'himself.' For a long time 'he' was seldom out of sight of any of us except while 'he' was at work, and if 'he' was only making believe 'he' certainly did it to perfection. My parents reared 'him,' one might say, and when my brother was at home they were like pals."[96] Mary recalled Bill using a razor to shave his face and taking photos with his girlfriends. She was left in awe of his appearance.

Bill wrote a short column for the *Post-Dispatch* summarizing his experiences. Like many trans men today, he explained that he was horrified at the way cis men treat women behind closed doors.

> I would not take $1000 a day for the experience I have gathered during the last nine years. I believe I have gained a more thorough knowledge in worldly ways than I could have obtained in any other school. I have learned the "way of man."
>
> I am convinced that man is not only not woman's superior but is not and never will be her equal. It is not the clothes that make a man. There are some good men in the world, but they are few and hard to find.
>
> A man treats his dog better than he does the woman who thinks enough of him to be his wife and slave.
>
> I am 22 years old now and it is barely possible that some day I may find a man who will convince me that he is good enough to be my husband. But it will take a long time for me to find that man, and I will have to forget a lot of things. One thing, he will have to consider me his equal.
>
> I am not a man-hater in any sense of the word. I sympathize with men in their brutal blindness. I am not basing my opinion on personal experience alone, but rather on the broad knowledge of mankind I was able to acquire while posing as a man. I may be called deceitful, or, perhaps, conceited, but believe me when I tell you that men are the very personification of deceit and conceit.[97]

Bill's self-narrative offers the contradiction of being trans among men. On one hand, he wanted to be known as male. On the other, to be known as male required being among men. The rampant misogyny and mistreatment of women were so disgusting that he claimed he did not want to go back.

Shortly before being outed, Bill went to a fortune teller. Following his arrest, police found his "Astro-psychic" reading. "February will bring you success," the fortune teller began.[98] "This would be a propitious month for you to start any new venture, as success would probably follow." Bill believed it came true as the judge set aside his fine, several families offered him a home, and he started a new journey without needing to hide his body. However, Bill's trans story does not end here.

The wrestling champion

Over the following two years, Bill continued to take up manual labor and began exercising like never before. By April 1911, he weighed nearly two hundred pounds and could lift more than most cis men. That same month, Officer William J. Schneider suggested bringing Bill to the city athletic headquarters as the "wrestling champion of the world."[99] A self-proclaimed Japanese jujutsu expert, Schneider believed that Bill was "the strongest woman in the world." Although he misgendered Bill, he continued to call him Willie. He told reporters of his plans to train the twenty-four-year-old: "I tested [him] with jiu jitsu holds and [he] never winced. I tried the thumb hold which will twist the strongest man under and [he] never even winced. [He] has consented to go into training and will start on handball." Of course, Bill could not meaningfully consent to any police request as they could arrest him at any moment for his past "crimes." Regardless of his feelings, he continued the athletic training regimens and joined several matches over the following months. He was set to wrestle champion wrestler Cora Livingston, the first women's world champion wrestler in history, for twenty-five dollars.[100] In May 1912, he wrestled the new champion, May Kelly, and easily won the match. They were set to have a second match for twice the wager, but the winner was not announced in the newspaper.[101]

Papers would excuse Bill's trans identity, chalking it up as his desire for manual labor. However, Bill continued the same work even after being outed. Traditionally, this is one reason why stories like his are cast out of trans history: there is a named ulterior motive for transness, suggesting it is just an act. Yet Bill was also under threat of direct punishment had he not explained his motives in a way that cisgender people could understand. Although he told the police he wanted to return to womanhood, he continued to use the name Bill for years to come. We cannot know his internal thought process for transitioning, but we can understand his story as an important contribution to trans history.

There is only sparse evidence of Bill after 1912. The census shows he worked as a machine operator for a screw company from 1910 to 1920 and lived in the same downtown boarding room during both decades. He then became a presser in a shoe factory in 1930. He appeared to live in St. Louis until his chosen and deadnames disappeared from written records later that decade.[102]

THE TEAMMATES: LÉON CAURLA AND PIERRE BRÉSOLLES

Léon Caurla and Pierre Joseph Brésolles were an unstoppable pair. Both record-breaking French sprinters, the two transitioned after competing together for the French national running team. Their narrative is a classic story of two teammates who not only transitioned genders but also transitioned from rivals to lovers.

Léon was born on September 4, 1926, in the small town of Étain, France. The commune in northern France was so rural that it did not chronicle much from the era and left few records about his childhood. Pierre, born on November 10, 1929, grew up in Occitanie in southern France. His early years received much attention for his impressive sportsmanship. Pierre's extraordinary speed was well documented since his teens.[103]

At age fifteen, Pierre broke the world record for the 400-meter dash. He made international news and gained the interest of French officials. His accomplishment was celebrated as a much-needed positive news story after the atrocities of World War II dominated the headlines. A photo of him running at an impressively vertical angle made its way across the continents. His grin and shoulder-length brown hair were seen around the world. Girls' sports were not enough for the young trans man, however, and he would compete in men's games in his hometown. He took up basketball and cross-country running alongside sprinting. Locals knew he was someone special and nurtured his athletic abilities.

Pierre joined the French national team around the same time as Léon in 1946. The two were quite different in physique: Léon, then nineteen, was larger than some of his cis male competitors. Pierre, then seventeen, was slim and small. Pierre had a "melodious" and energetic tone to his voice, while Léon had a gruff, rural accent. They were rivals and teammates during their first competition together at the 1946 European Athletic Championships in Oslo. The two joined famous athletes Anne-Marie Colchen and Monique Drilhon in the races.

The pair broke the French record for the 4 x 100–meter relay together and won the silver medal during the Oslo competition. Léon also won third in the 200-meter sprint and Pierre placed third in the 100-meter sprint, breaking the French national record on August 23, 1946.[104] Léon and Pierre found a quick interest in one another when the competition ended and began dating. There is little information about exactly how long they were together. The age of consent for same-sex couples at the time was twenty-one (while only fifteen for heterosexuals), meaning Léon could have faced legal action for dating Pierre, despite both being around the same age. Prosecutions were rare, but the chilling effect of the law influenced many queer and trans couples to stay quiet about their relationships.[105] The two remained relatively private, although Pierre announced his social transition a month after the 1946 tournament with the full support of his father. Léon soon followed, after winning first place in a 1947 British-French running competition.

Following much celebration, the two were recruited for the 1948 Summer Olympics. However, they refused to submit to gender testing, generating much controversy. There were conflicting reports about whether the two were also intersex.[106] They would both undergo surgeries over the following years. Pierre began his medical transition in 1948 and had a second—and final—operation in early 1949.[107] His transition made national news in France with both applause and occasional mockery. Far-right French politician and writer Pierre Descaves even made a radio play, *Le Sexe neutre* (*The Neutral Sex*), inspired by the young trans man's life.[108] Another paper celebrated his transition, comparing it to those of Lili Elbe, Dora Richter, and Zdeněk Koubek.[109] The publicity did not lead Pierre to quit sports. Instead, he signed up to play in the wing three-quarter position in AS Carcassonne, a semi-professional men's league based in Occitanie, France.

The French periodical *Qui? Detective* featured a long story on Pierre and other trans men in sports in 1951. Pierre wrote to the publication, complaining that his surgery was not 15,000 francs (equivalent to $441 today) as the writer claimed. Instead, it cost his father (who paid for his transition) 242,492 francs ($7,130 today).[110] His father was vocally supportive and traveled to Paris for his son's operation (see page 8 of the insert).

Pierre studied at the Université de Toulouse and earned two baccalaureates in history and geography. He later developed a talent for cooking with a particular love for cordon bleu, fine desserts, and pastries. He spent much time with his friends and loved to collect rare flowers and insects. He had a scientific mind that was filled with curiosity. He gave up professional sports in his later years but spent his time cycling on the streets of Aude and backpacking in the Pyrenees.

Léon's life was unusual for trans people at the time as he continued to openly transgress gender roles following his medical transition. The young man moved to Warcq, France, and became a coach for the AS Étain women's basketball team. There, he would wear kilts and gender-neutral tracksuits to the games. He still went out dancing in skirts, always surrounded by women interested in him (it is unclear if the French reporters were referencing gender-neutral kilts or feminine skirts). Papers noted he played basketball, but they did not mention for which team.

Léon was granted a change of his legal name and sex on February 13, 1952, paving the way for future French trans people. The *France-soir* newspaper caught up with him that year and he reported his pleasure in expressing himself.[111] The reporter, Maurice Josco, noted he was "born at the age of twenty-five with a glorious past." Indeed, Maurice appeared more eager to talk about Léon's past than his future.

"For him, life is as simple as it was for her. 'But you have friends. Don't you think they'll be a little embarrassed to call you "Léon"[?],'" the reporter mused.

"I've been given a nickname; it simplifies everything. My friends will continue to call me by my nickname, as they always have. There's no reason, I think, for me to change my nickname too," Léon explained. His nickname was *Fifille*, an informal term for "little girl." The irony was not lost on Léon, standing tall and broad.

"I'm still the same person," Léon explained. "I have a few feminine items. I'll wear them out." The young trans man went on to join the French air force as part of required military participation. An Aruban article described him as "a handsome young man with a mustache like Clark Gable and short curly locks."[112] A photo of Léon in the French military was leaked to the press in 1955. Reporters expressed surprise to see the world champion doing the work of a foot soldier but added, "he looks good."[113]

Although Léon and Pierre later broke up, the two had made their mark on French history. Léon returned to plow fields and live on his farm. He became a family man and a traveling florist in his later years. He died in 2002 in his hometown. Pierre went on to marry and raise a family. He also took up farming. He died peacefully in 2018 at age eighty-eight.

A NEW GENDER HISTORY

Historians begin by looking backward.
They often end by thinking backward.

—FRIEDRICH NIETZSCHE[1]

W hat do lost narratives of gender tell us about trans life? What do they teach us about the past? History—trans, cis, or otherwise—is mediated by forces that are too frequently disinterested in supporting our communities. It is not only "written by the winners," as historians often say, but echoed through our social body at every level. Institutions like governments, newspapers, and schools continue to regulate the basic historical facts we know. We repeat these facts as truths and drown out the broader scope of history in the process. History is not an objective science or static fact, as many are taught in school. When one fact is published and another is not, we must ask why such facts come into prominence while others fall into obscurity. Authority over our access to knowledge is the power to reproduce it. That is, our understanding of the world is regulated by those who seek to maintain their power rather than dismantle it. History has always been a malleable tool used for political ends. Only when we establish a widespread desire to teach the histories of the oppressed can we finally access the broader breadth of our human past and fight for a fairer future.

Activist José Rizal centered the case for history when he campaigned to decolonize the Philippines in the 1890s. The activist famously questioned racist Spanish historiography that portrayed native Filipinos as "savage" and unable to care for themselves. Spanish colonizers argued that they "civilized" the Indigenous population and used history, literature, and law to portray themselves as saviors of the people. Rizal's advocacy against their occupation scared the Spanish so much that they executed him in 1896. To this day, Rizal's writing echoes the experiences of the oppressed. Activists around the world still paraphrase his most well-known aphorism: "Know history, know self. No history, no self."[2] Rizal's writing was not only about Filipinos, just as this book is not only about trans people. Finding new ways to interpret history is vital for every social movement. Imagine children learning about their ancestors' revolutionary traditions. Imagine widespread education about the occupied land North Americans live on and the broken treaties that came to form the world's most powerful nations. Imagine a history for improving the world, rather than maintaining it. History is used to subjugate, but it may also be used to free us.

To "know self" goes beyond basic representation. It is not enough to say that trans people have always existed. Trans people thrived, prospered, and built communities. The world would be much different if schools taught the creative advocacy of Maude Milbourne, the courage of Okiyo, or the familial love of Ray Leonard. Children could learn that trans people have always been part of our communities, always present and always fighting for a better world. Today, transgender people are still forced to produce evidence of their identities from the past. Pundits challenge trans activists to detail gender history seemingly at every turn during every debate. It is my hope that this book will be a resource to defend the trans movement for years to come.

The struggles of trans children, activists, workers, and athletes are nothing new. Their achievements are not new either. Although it was certainly not easier in the past, trans people discovered ways to live in peace. Trans children were often supported by their parents. Trans activists frequently rallied their communities to action. Trans workers found jobs that suited them. Trans athletes competed and won. We cannot forget the past if we want to move toward a better future.

We are left wondering just how many more transgender histories are out there; so an enormous amount of research is required to share the histories of those outside the wealthiest and most powerful nations. Thousands of stories still await us in the archives. With new forms of digitization and research tools, we may soon recover even more stories that radically change our understanding of the world. History does not live exclusively in the past but shapes the present with each new echo of the lives that came before us.

ACKNOWLEDGMENTS

I owe my gratitude to the dozens of people who made this book possible. Speaking with Kate Bornstein, Marcia Ochoa, Jules-Gill Peterson, Sandy Stone, and Susan Stryker helped inspire the details and quirks of each chapter. I would also like to thank everyone at the First Tuesday Queer History Meet-up at The LGBTQ Center in New York City, particularly Tyler Albertario, Lisa Davis, Jonathan Ned Katz, Lou McCarthy, and Michael Waters, who helped me find sources and get inspired. Devlyn Camp and Randy Wicker's enthusiastic documentation of queer and trans history was also key to completing this project. I owe my literary agent at Sandra Dijkstra Literary, Jill Marr, and my editor at Beacon Press, Maya Fernandez, my full appreciation, as well.

Dozens of individuals and institutions helped me locate specific details, texts, and artifacts in this book. In chapter order: Ian Darnell for Effie Smith; Marwan Kaabour and Suneela Mubayi for Masoud El Amaratly; the Rhode Island Historical Society for Mabel Stanley; the National Museum of African American History and Culture for Sally-Tom; archivists at the Klamath County Museum, the Oregon Institute of Technology, and the Oregon State University for Muksamse'lapli; Nico K. for Maude Milbourne; Casey J. Hayes and Zavier Nunn for Gerda von Zobeltitz; and Ladislav Jackson of the Společnost pro queer paměť for Albín Pleva and Stefan Pekar.

I also owe appreciation to my friends Jessa Alexander, Joey Bradley, Kai Breaux, Adoh Brown, Erin Day, Forest Durwin, Amber Field, Ethan Fraschilla, Max Gregg, Logan Hoffman-Smith, Ivan Hsiao, K Iver, Maia Kobabe, Taylor Page, Dahlia Pham, and Harper Rubin for listening to me get excited about trans history all day.

NOTES

INTRODUCTION: REWRITING THE NARRATIVE

1. Jules Gill-Peterson, *Histories of the Transgender Child* (Minneapolis: University of Minnesota Press, 2018), 2.

2. Trump quoted in Christopher Kane, "Trump to Weaponize Feds Against Trans Americans If Reelected," *Los Angeles Blade*, Feb. 1, 2023. (Emphasis mine.)

3. John Money is often credited as coining the term *gender* in 1955. However, he did not invent the word or the sex/gender distinction. The infamous sexologist helped popularize it that year and the word was infrequently used in the modern sense until then. Earl Hinsie and Madison Bentley both published on the English term in 1945, a full decade before Money adopted it. I owe gratitude to Susan Stryker for bringing this to my attention. James K. Beilby and Paul Rhodes Eddy, *Understanding Transgender Identities: Four Views* (Grand Rapids, MI: Baker Academic, 2019); Diederik F. Janssen, "Sex/Gender: Did John Money Borrow the Distinction from Leland Earl Hinsie?" *Archives of Sexual Behavior* 49, no. 7 (2020): 2223–26.

4. Brian Lauter, "How to Read a New York Times Story About Trans Kids," *Outward* podcast, *Slate*, Nov. 22, 2022, https://slate.com/transcripts/c1ZtbWJKS 3ZLajlKSWpmNoxhVDkzMmo2bUNxRHJqcEhYSlRKOHIraHdGUTo=.

5. This is not to say that Mark was definitively the first minor to take hormones but that there were no earlier cases that were publicly known when I located the story. There is at least one other named teenager to have medically transitioned before Mark and David. Gerd Katter of Germany had a double mastectomy at age eighteen in 1928. Alexandre Hohl, *Testosterone: From Basic to Clinical Aspects* (Gewerbestrasse: Springer International Publishing, 2017); Andrea Rottmann, *Queer Lives Across the Wall: Desire and Danger in Divided Berlin, 1945–1970* (Toronto: University of Toronto Press, 2023).

6. Before this point, trans people were often categorized as *inverts, androgynes, urnings, transvestites, men-women, bisexuals,* and *homosexuals,* among many other English terms. Susan Stryker, *Transgender History: The Roots of Today's Revolution* (Berkeley: Seal Press, 2017), 37; David Oliver Cauldwell, "Psychopathia

Transexualis," in *The Transgender Studies Reader*, ed. Susan Stryker and Stephen Whittle (New York: Routledge, 2006).

7. Aimé Césaire, "Culture and Colonization," *Social Text* 28, no. 2 (2010): 130.

Pop History

8. A few popular authors who argue the trans movement is completely new include Richard Dawkins, Helen Joyce, and Abigail Shrier.

9. Mirjam Zadoff and Karolina Künn, *To Be Seen: Queer Lives 1900–1950* (Chicago: University of Chicago Press, 2022), 387.

10. Other books delve into specific subjects or topics. C. Riley Snorton's *Black on Both Sides*, offers a groundbreaking and theoretical perspective on how anti-Black racism shaped trans identity today. Gill-Peterson's *Histories of the Transgender Child* (Minneapolis: University of Minnesota Press, 2018) focuses on several narratives outlining the political construction of trans identity through age, race, and media. Other books, like Leslie Feinberg's *Transgender Warriors: Making History from Joan of Arc to Dennis Rodman* (Boston: Beacon Press, 1997) and Jonathan Ned Katz's *Gay American History* (New York: Thomas Y. Crowell, 1976), provide something similar to *Before Gender*. Both texts gather queer and trans biographies—sometimes ones not as well-known—to discuss contemporary gender and sexuality politics. Still, these books center moments of heightened visibility like Stonewall while only providing a sentence or two on lesser-known figures. These texts canonize certain parts of trans history while, as books with limited pages, leave out others.

11. See Snorton, *Black on Both Sides* and Gill-Peterson, *Histories of the Transgender Child*.

12. Liesl Theron and Tshepo Ricki Kgositau, "The Emergence of a Grassroots African Trans Archive," *Transgender Studies Quarterly* 2, no. 4 (2015): 578–83.

13. Other examples include the works of Jen Manion, Rachel Mesch, Henry Rubin, Kerry Segrave, and Alison Oram.

14. Historically, a disproportionate number of academics studying the trans community in the humanities are white trans men and queer cisgender women. These academics understandably want to write about others who have similar histories to them. For more discussion on the gender of trans studies, see Z. Nicolazzo, "Ghost Stories from the Academy: A Trans Feminine Reckoning," *Review of Higher Education* 45, no. 2 (2021): 125–48.

15. Alison Oram's *Her Husband Was a Woman!* is a similar offender, going as far as deadnaming and misgendering people who had undergone gender-affirming surgery. This was not an issue of publication year (2007), when deadnaming was already considered an unethical practice among historians.

16. Two other examples are those of Basque conquistador Antonio de Erauso and Badë, an Albanian Muslim *virdzine* (sworn virgin). Gabriela Cano,

"Unconcealable Realities of Desire: Amelio Robles's (Transgender) Masculinity in the Mexican Revolution," in *Gender, Politics, and Power in Modern Mexico*, ed. Mary Kay Vaughan et al. (Durham, NC: Duke University Press, 2006); René Grémaux, "Woman Becomes Man in the Balkans," in *Third Sex, Third Gender: Beyond Sexual Dimorphism in Culture and History*, ed. Gilbert Herdt (New York: Zone Books, 1996).

17. Sandy Stone, "The Empire Strikes Back: A Posttranssexual Manifesto," in *The Transgender Studies Reader*, ed. Susan Stryker and Stephen Whittle (New York: Routledge, 2013), 295–96.

18. The FBI was aware of Murray's request for hormones, although they never released the information publicly until after his death, upon request of researcher William J. Maxwell. Christina G. Bucher, "Pauli Murray (1910–1985)," in *Encyclopedia of African American Women Writers Vol. 2*, ed. Yolanda Williams Page (Westport, CT: Greenwood Publishing Group, 2007), 3; Federal Bureau of Investigation, "BS 140–3891, Pauli Murray FBI File," https://web.archive.org/web/20230424191729/http://omeka.wustl.edu/omeka/exhibits/show/fbeyes/murray; Simon D. Elin Fisher, "Challenging Dissemblance in Pauli Murray Historiography, Sketching a History of the Trans New Negro," *Journal of African American History* 104, no. 2 (2019): 176–200.

19. Kenneth W. Mack, *Representing the Race: The Creation of the Civil Rights Lawyer* (Cambridge, MA: Harvard University Press, 2012); Simon D. Elin Fisher, "Pauli Murray's Peter Panic: Perspectives from the Margins of Gender and Race in Jim Crow America," *TSQ* 3, nos. 1–2 (2016): 95–103.

20. Naomi Simmons-Thorne, "Pauli Murray and the Pronominal Problem: A De-essentialist Trans Historiography," *Activist History Review* (May 30, 2019); Rahel Gebreyes, "How 'Respectability Politics' Muted the Legacy of Black LGBT Activist Pauli Murray," *HuffPost*, Feb. 10, 2015.

Trans Before Gender

21. To identify is to internally and/or externally pronounce oneself as a different gender than what they were assigned at birth.

22. Emily Skidmore, "Recovering a Gender-Transgressive Past: A Transgender Historiography," in *A Companion to American Women's History*, ed. Nancy A. Hewitt and Anne M. Valk (Hoboken, NJ: Wiley, 2020).

23. *Oxford English Dictionary*, "woman," https://www.oed.com/search/dictionary/?scope=Entries&q=woman, accessed July 1, 2024.

24. I approach this book through what Emily Skidmore calls "transgender historiography" in her essay "Recovering a Gender-Transgressive Past." Historiography studies how history is written. Transgender historiography is the idea that readings of (gendered) history are malleable, localized, and subjective. That is, terms change over time and our current interpretation of history is entirely based on our own subjective experiences. Transgender historiography applies

present terms to past conditions and rejects the idea that today's descriptions are only contained to contemporary figures. Put differently, I am applying a foundational poststructuralist reading of history in a trans context. This is following the works of Michel Foucault, Jules Gill-Peterson, Susan Stryker, and Hayden White.

25. It is also worth mentioning the idea that there is not a purely modern mode by which trans people may "challenge gender categories." Even seemingly new features of trans life, like gender-affirming surgery, have existed for millennia. As you will read, gender categories are constantly changing but bear similarities between time periods. Genny Beemyn, "A Presence in the Past: A Transgender Historiography," *Journal of Women's History* 25, no. 4 (2013): 113–21; David Hudson, *History of Jemima Wilkinson: A Preacheress of the Eighteenth Century; Containing an Authentic Narrative of Her Life and Character, and of the Rise, Progress and Conclusion of Her Ministry* (Geneva: S. O. Hull, 1821); Scott Larson, "'Indescribable Being': Theological Performances of Genderlessness in the Society of the Publick Universal Friend, 1776–1819," *Early American Studies* 12, no. 3 (2014): 581–82.

26. Evan B. Towle and Lynn M. Morgan, "Romancing the Transgender Native: Rethinking the Use of the 'Third Gender' Concept," *GLQ* 8, no. 4 (2002): 469–97.

27. *Oxford English Dictionary*, "gay," https://www.oed.com/search/dictionary/?scope=Entries&q=gay, accessed July 1, 2024; *Oxford English Dictionary*, "Latina," https://www.oed.com/dictionary/latina_n?tab=factsheet#10782610, accessed July 1, 2024.

28. Mona Charen, "Are High School Kids Gay?" *Baltimore Sun*, July 22, 1993; Emily Priest, "It's Time to Share the Spotlight: Exploration of Trans Visibility Over the Years," *Gale Review*, Mar. 31, 2019.

29. It is also important to recognize that intersex and trans are not a binary. Today, many intersex people identify as trans. Trans and intersex people share a history. I chose to not include intersex people because of how intersex existence is used to argue against trans healthcare. Mark and David Ferrow, for example, claimed to have cracking voices during puberty (which is a symptom of common polycystic ovary syndrome among a host of other non-intersex conditions). With the single mention of cracking voices, anti-trans commenters declared the brothers had a rare intersex condition and were not transgender at all. Regardless of whether these conditions were actually present, the siblings transitioned as teens and would most likely be considered transgender today. Anti-trans pundits often consider intersex people as worthy of (nonconsensual) healthcare while non-intersex trans people as unworthy. During the 2020s trans panic, intersex surgeries were almost universally carved out from bills attempting to ban trans healthcare, medical funding, and research. These policies certainly harmed intersex people, too. However, the fixation on young non-intersex people

obtaining surgery led me to not include intersex stories in this book. Instead, I seek to focus on those deemed by these attacks as the least deserving of recognition: non-intersex trans people of color and minors. See Kiara Alfonseca and Mary Kekatos, "Amid Transgender Care Bans, Exceptions Made for Surgery on Intersex Children," ABC News, July 18, 2023.

30. Many trans people did gain economic status by transitioning (mostly trans men). I likely excluded some stories because the individual excused their gender for economic reasons but were still trans.

31. I also ensured their story was in the correct time period and qualified as "underreported":

1. Did they transition between 1850 and 1950?
2. Is contemporary reporting on them insufficient?
3. Is there enough information to make conclusions about their identity and form a true story of their life?

If the answer was yes to all these questions, then they would be included. I still had to leave out dozens of cases for space—largely those of white trans men who had similar stories already included in the book.

Lessons from Lost Trans History

32. George Santayana, *The Life of Reason or the Phases of Human Progress* (New York: Charles Scribner's Sons, 1920), 284.

33. Robert Beachy, *Gay Berlin: Birthplace of a Modern Identity* (New York: Vintage, 2014), 172–73.

34. Hil Malatino, "The Promise of Repair: Trans Rage and the Limits of Feminist Coalition," *Signs: Journal of Women in Culture and Society* 46, no. 4 (2021): 827–51.

35. Tom Scocca, "Why Is the New York Times So Obsessed with Trans Kids?" *Popula*, Jan. 29, 2023, https://popula.com/2023/01/29/the-worst-thing-we-read-this-week-why-is-the-new-york-times-so-obsessed-with-trans-kids/.

36. "A Young Kentucky Girl," *Akron Beacon Journal*, Aug. 14, 1891.

37. "Can She Wear Bloomers?" *St. Louis Post-Dispatch*, Sept. 9, 1895.

38. C. Riley Snorton makes this a key argument of his 2017 monograph, *Black on Both Sides*.

39. "The Man Who Lived 30 Years as a Woman," *Ebony*, Oct. 1951, 23.

40. Alex Bakker, Annette F. Timm, Michael Thomas Taylor, and Rainer Herrn, *Others of My Kind: Transatlantic Transgender Histories* (Calgary: University of Calgary Press, 2020), 1–2.

41. Martin Duberman, *Stonewall* (New York: Dutton, 1993), xix, emphasis in original.

42. New York Public Library, ed., *The Stonewall Reader* (New York: Penguin Books, 2019), xv.

43. It remains unclear exactly how many of each group actively fought one another. Paul Weber, "Haben die Schupobeamten die Homosexuellen planmäßig überfallen?" *Die Freundin*, July 23, 1930.

44. There are even earlier mass arrests provoked by anti-trans sentiment that parallel Stonewall. Mexico's "Dance of the Forty-One," a 1901 police raid on a private home in Mexico City, is one of the earliest. Nineteen of the arrested individuals were assigned male at birth and dressed in clothing designed for women. The government attempted to cover up the incident as some participants were connected to politicians and businessmen. However, this event does not quite meet the definition of riot or resistance. There were no reports of arrestees fighting back. Regardless, as more trans history is uncovered, we will continue to find more past uprisings that were lost to time. Robert Franco, "'Todos/as somos 41': The Dance of the Forty-One from Homosexual Reappropriation to Transgender Representation in Mexico, 1945–2001," *Journal of the History of Sexuality* 28, no. 1 (2019): 66–95.

45. Katie Sutton, "'We Too Deserve a Place in the Sun': The Politics of Transvestite Identity in Weimar Germany," *German Studies Review* 35, no. 2 (2012): 335–54.

46. Sarah Boslaugh, *Transgender Health Issues* (Santa Barbara: ABC-CLIO, 2018), 168.

47. Mathew Kuefler, *The Manly Eunuch: Masculinity, Gender Ambiguity, and Christian Ideology in Late Antiquity* (Chicago: University of Chicago Press, 2001); Will Roscoe, "Priests of the Goddess: Gender Transgression in Ancient Religion," *History of Religions* 35, no. 3 (1996): 195–230.

48. Bakker et al., *Others of My Kind*, 1.

49. Historian Rainer Herrn identified the individual as Gerd Katter, but this claim is contradicted by Katter's autobiography, which provides a different date and surgeon for his operation. I could not locate any other evidence for the existence of the sixteen-year-old outside Levy-Lenz's 1951 biography. University of Sussex PhD student Samson Dittrich pointed out this discrepancy to me and identified Herrn as the original source, arguing that Herrn made an incorrect assumption connecting the two trans men. Both trans men would have been around the same age and were both apprentices to woodcutters (a common job at the time). Samson Dittrich, "Gerd Katter (1910–1995)—Trans-Mann, Patient und Lobbyist," *Mitteilungen der Magnus-Hirschfeld-Gesellschaft* 64 (Feb. 2020): 18–25.

50. Pagan Kennedy, *The First Man-Made Man: The Story of Two Sex Changes, One Love Affair, and a Twentieth-Century Medical Revolution* (New York: Bloomsbury, 2008).

51. Some others cite Lili Elbe and Dora Richter as the first recipients of vaginoplasty (construction of the vulva and/or vagina) specifically, which is also not correct. John T. McQuiston, "Christine Jorgensen, 62, Is Dead; Was First to Have a Sex Change," *New York Times*, May 4, 1989; Stryker, *Transgender History*.

52. Rainer Herrn is one of the few researchers to highlight that Richard Mühsam provided early surgeries in 1920–21. Rainer Herrn, *Schnittmuster des Geschlechts: Transvestitismus und Transsexualität in der frühen Sexualwissenschaft* (Gießen: Psychosozial-Verlag, 2005), 167–75; Karl Otto Kankeleit, "Selbstbeschädigungen und selbstverstümmelungen der geschlechtsorgane," *Zeitschrift für die gesamte Neurologie und Psychiatrie* 107, no. 1 (1927): 414–81; Richard Mühsam, "Chirurgische Eingriffe bei Anomalien des Sexuallebens," *Therapie der Gegenwart* 67 (1926): 451–55; Stryker, *Transgender History*, 38–40; Weller Van Hook, "A New Operation for Hypospadias," *Annals of Surgery* 23, no. 4 (1896): 378–93.

53. Mühsam, "Chirurgische Eingriffe bei Anomalien des Sexuallebens," 451–55.

54. Nazis destroyed Baer's medical records along with the Institute for Sexual Science in 1933. Ofer Aderet, "Recalling the First Sex Change Operation in History: A German-Israeli Insurance Salesman," *Haaretz*, Dec. 5, 2015, https://www.haaretz.com/israel-news/2015-12-05/ty-article/.premium/the-first-sex-change-surgery-in-history/0000017f-f3fd-d5bd-a17f-f7ffa4970000; Guy Polat, "Karl M. Baer: First Transgender Person to Undergo Female-to-Male (FTM) Surgery," *Let Her Fly*, Oct. 10, 2022, https://letherfly.org/karl-m-baer-the-first-person-in-the-world-to-undergo-sex-change-surgery/.

55. Elizabeth Reis, *Bodies in Doubt: An American History of Intersex* (Baltimore: Johns Hopkins University Press, 2021), 46–47.

56. I found this phrase used in dozens of books, websites, and newspapers.

57. "Daring Agnes Rankin," *The Tennessean*, Sept. 27, 1891.

58. Stryker, *Transgender History*, 62.

59. "Legislation," *Mendocino Beacon*, Jan. 18, 19.

60. Outing brings up contentious ethical questions that are not addressed at length in this book. It is important to consider the harm caused by the powerful individuals whom Effie outed, which requires a more nuanced analysis than there is room for in her chapter.

61. James Barron, "How the Brooklyn Library Helped Fight Book Bans in Oklahoma," *New York Times*, Sept. 12, 2022.

62. Susan Stryker, for instance, claims "not until the middle of the twentieth century did social networks of transgender people begin to interconnect with networks of socially powerful people in ways that would produce long-lasting organizations and provide the base of a social movement." This is arguably true depending on how we define "powerful," but other historians might contest that a more accurate timeframe would be the nineteenth or early twentieth century. Stryker, *Transgender History*, 41.

63. There are notable debates over the accuracy of Herodotus's depictions of the Enarei that I do not contend with in this book. Herodotus, *The Histories* (New York: Penguin, 2003), 49, 261; Diederik F. Janssen, "Transgenderism Before Gender: Nosology from the Sixteenth Through Mid-Twentieth Century," *Archives of Sexual Behavior* 49, no. 5 (2020): 1415–25.

64. Stryker, *Transgender History*, 41.

65. Thomas J. Billard, "'Gender-Critical' Discourse as Disinformation: Unpacking TERF Strategies of Political Communication," *Women's Studies in Communication* 46, no. 2 (2023): 235–43.

66. Snorton, *Black on Both Sides*, 150.

67. Kennedy, *The First Man-Made Man*.

THE KIDS

1. From *We Both Laughed in Pleasure: The Selected Diaries of Lou Sullivan, 1961–1991*, ed. Ellis Martin and Zach Ozma (Brooklyn, NY: Nightboat Books, 2019), Gay, Lesbian, Bisexual, Transgender Historical Society, Louis Graydon Sullivan Papers, 40. Reprinted with permission.

2. Jules Gill-Peterson, *Histories of the Transgender Child* (Minneapolis: University of Minnesota Press, 2018), 11.

3. Elagabalus's political enemies wrote these accounts, so they must be understood with some skepticism. Martijin Icks, *The Crimes of Elagabalus: The Life and Legacy of Rome's Decadent Boy Emperor* (Cambridge, MA: Harvard University Press, 2012), 100.

4. Icks, *Crimes of Elagabalus*, 52, 118.

5. Eric R. Varner, "Transcending Gender: Assimilation, Identity, and Roman Imperial Portraits," *Memoirs of the American Academy in Rome. Supplementary Volumes* 7 (2008): 200–201.

6. "Another Female Impersonator in Trouble," *Glasgow Herald*, Aug. 21, 1877.

7. Gill-Peterson, *Histories of the Transgender Child*, 7.

8. Ludwig Levy-Lenz, *The Memoirs of a Sexologist: Discretion and Indiscretion* (New York: Cadillac Publishing Co., 1954), 463.

9. "A Girl's Sad Life Story," *Wheeling Register*, Aug. 19, 1893.

10. "Transportation to Geneseo," *Morning Democrat*, Nov. 18, 1893; "May Be Insane," *Quad-City Times*, Nov. 24, 1893.

11. Travis L. Dixon, *A Dangerous Distortion of Our Families: Representations of Families, by Race, in News and Opinion Media* (Oakland, CA: Color of Change, 2018); Emily Tomasik and Jeffrey Gottfried, "U.S. Journalists' Beats Vary Widely by Gender and Other Factors," Pew Research Center, Apr. 4, 2023.

The Brothers: Mark and David Ferrow

12. "Two Sisters Become Brothers: Sex Changed," *Barrier Miner*, Jan. 5, 1940; "Grey-Haired 'Lady' Witness Was Man," *Daily Herald*, Feb. 12, 1942; "2 Sisters Become Brothers," *Daily Mirror*, Aug. 26, 1939; *1939 Register*, 101/6492c, National Archives of the UK, https://www.fold3.com/record/749633834/ferrow-j-wwii-daily-reports-missing-dead-wounded-and-pows-1939-1947; "They Now

Smoke Pipes: 'Sisters' Return Home Boys," *Nottingham Evening Post*, Aug. 25, 1939; Clare R. Tebbutt, "Popular and Medical Understandings of Sex Change in 1930s Britain," PhD diss., University of Manchester, 2014.

13. "2 Sisters Become Brothers," *Daily Mirror*; "Two Sisters Are Brothers Now," *Yass Tribune-Courier*, Feb. 29, 1940.

14. "Inter-Departmental Committee on Civil Defence Gallantry Awards: Minutes and Recommendations," Class HO 250, Piece 31, National Archives of the UK.

15. "Case Number: 1270B," Home Office Records, National Archives of the UK, https://discovery.nationalarchives.gov.uk/details/r/C14150626.

16. "UK Army List, April 1941," Fold3, https://www.fold3.com/publication /1314/uk-army-list-april-1941, accessed July 2024; "Army Roll of Honour, 1939–1945, Ferrow, James" and "WWII, Daily Reports: Missing, Dead, Wounded and POWs, 1939–1947," National Archives of the UK.

17. "2 Sisters Become Brothers," *Daily Mirror*; "200 Exhibits in City Art Show," *Leicester Evening Mail*, Apr. 22, 1955.

18. "Volume 7a" and "Volume 9, 1316," General Register Office; "To Be Painted," *Leicester Evening Mail*, July 13, 1960; "David Gower," National Portrait Gallery, https://www.npg.org.uk/collections/search/portrait/mw40046/David -Gower, accessed Sept. 10, 2024.

19. Tebbutt, "Popular and Medical Understandings of Sex Change"; "Vanished Sisters Return as Boys," *Daily Herald*, Aug. 25, 1939; General Register Office, vol. 9.

The Outlaw: Effie Smith

20. "Effie Was Fred," *Wichita Beacon*, Nov. 3, 1893.

21. Kansas's only child labor regulation in 1891 restricted those under twelve years old from mining and those under fourteen from circus and street work. Everything else was allowed. Domenico Gagliardo, "A History of Kansas Child-Labor Legislation," *Kansas Historical Quarterly* 1, no. 4 (1932): 379–401.

22. "A Young Burglar," *Wichita Beacon*, Nov. 12, 1891.

23. "Effie Was Fred," *Wichita Beacon*.

24. The only contemporary report on Effie comes from this 1892 Chicago arrest. A few sentences in historian Jim Elledge's 2018 *The Boys of Fairy Town* unintentionally misgender Effie and incorrectly identified Smith by a pseudonym. "James Jones and Frank Smith," *Inter Ocean*, Nov. 23, 1892.

25. "Clever Method of Shoplifting," *Chicago Tribune*, Nov. 22, 1892.

26. "Frank Smith's Queer Confession," *St. Louis Post-Dispatch*, Mar. 7, 1895.

27. "Alton, Ill," *St. Louis Globe-Democrat*, Aug. 11, 1893.

28. "Where She Was Bound For," *St. Louis Post-Dispatch*, Aug. 14, 1893.

29. "A Girl's Sad Life Story," *Wheeling Register*, Aug. 19, 1893.

30. Michelle Jones and Lori Record, "Magdalene Laundries: The First Prisons for Women in the United States," *Journal of the Indiana Academy of the Social Sciences* 17, no. 1 (2014): 173.

31. The Chicago World's Fair was occurring at this time and would certainly give Effie more economic opportunities. Although, there is no mention that this is the reason she sought to travel to the city. The fair brought in over twenty-five million new people from fifty-one nations to the city in 1893. Norm Bolotin and Christine Laing, *The World's Columbian Exposition: The Chicago World's Fair of 1893* (Chicago: University of Illinois Press, 2002), 20.

32. "She Was a Man," *Newark Advocate*, Oct. 31, 1893; "Effie Smith Proves to Be a Man," *The Times*, Oct. 30, 1893; "Don Juan in a Workhouse," *Weekly Pantagraph*, Nov. 3, 1893.

33. "Effie Was Fred," *Wichita Beacon*.

34. "Effie," *Morning Democrat*, Nov. 18, 1893.

35. "Transportation to Geneseo," *Morning Democrat*, Nov. 18, 1893; "May Be Insane," *Quad-City Times*, Nov. 24, 1893.

36. "Has Reformed," *Wichita Beacon*, June 30, 1894.

37. "Smith's Revolting Story," *St. Louis Post-Dispatch*, May 22, 1895.

38. "Den of Vice and Vileness," *St. Louis Post-Dispatch*, May 18, 1895.

39. "Trial of a Female Impersonator," *St. Louis Globe-Democrat*, Mar. 7, 1895; "Smith's Wild Threat," *St. Louis Globe-Democrat*, Mar. 9, 1895.

40. "Queer Confession," *St. Louis Post-Dispatch*.

41. "Dacons Has Skipped Out," *St. Louis Post-Dispatch*, May 21, 1895.

42. "For the Grand Jury," *St. Louis Post-Dispatch*, May 19, 1895.

43. "St. Louis' Oscar Wilde," *Quincy Daily Herald*, May 20, 1895.

44. "Sensation in St. Louis," *Evansville Courier*, May 19, 1895; "Dacons Has Skipped Out," *St. Louis Post-Dispatch*.

45. "Smith's Revolting Story," *St. Louis Post-Dispatch*.

46. "Eine von der schwarzen 'kunßt,'" *Anzeiger des Westens*, Sept. 8, 1895.

47. "Fifty Years Ago Today," *Battle Creek Enquirer*, Oct. 10, 1946; "Death Records, 41: Wayne-Wexford, 1895, Alcona-Kent, 1896," Michigan Department of Community Health, Division for Vital Records and Health Statistics, 156; "An Interesting Story of Real Life," *True Northerner*, Oct. 21, 1896.

48. In the 1920s, Frank began selling Ferraline, a questionable drug made from a mixture of iron and water. This was the only subsequent mention of Frank I could locate. "A Friend of American Youth," *Nashville Banner*, July 24, 1920.

49. "Miss Inez Hoyt," *The Intelligencer*, Jan. 2, 1896; "'Inez Hoty's' Capers," Jan. 9, 1896; "Frank Smith Again in Trouble," *St. Louis Globe-Democrat*, Jan. 3, 1896.

50. "In Female Attire," *Quincy Weekly Whig*, Jan. 9, 1896.

51. Brianna Coppersmith, "When 'Empty Is Not Closed': Organizing Efforts to (Officially) Close St. Louis' Infamous Workhouse," *Saint Louis University Law Journal* 76 (2021); Nicholas Karr, "Annual Report of the City Workhouse,

for the Fiscal Year Ending April 13, 1896," in *Mayor's Message: With Accompanying Documents to the Municipal Assembly of the City of St. Louis, for the Fiscal Year Ending April 13, 1896* (St. Louis: Nixon-Jones Printing Co., 1897), 57–62.

52. "Frank Smith," Missouri State Penitentiary Database, Missouri Office of the Secretary of State, https://s1.sos.mo.gov/records/archives/archivesdb/msp/Detail.aspx?id=19716, accessed Aug. 15, 2024.

The Singer: Masoud El Amaratly

53. Marwan Kaabour, "Recovering Arab Trans History: Masoud El Amaratly, the Folk Music Icon from Iraq's Marshes," Ajam Media Collective, June 26, 2023, https://ajammc.com/2023/06/26/iraq-trans-history-masoud-amaratly/.

54. This is the Al-Kahla District of the Maysan Governorate today. There are debates around his year of birth, with some sources listing it as anywhere between 1893 and 1901. There are also debates around the location of his birth, with some placing it in nearby Amara. Salman Kayoush lists the year as 1897 and appears to be the most reputable source.

55. "Massouda El Amaratly," *Dom Tak*, SOWT, 2019, https://www.sowt.com/en/podcast/dom-tak-dm-tk/mswdt/transcript/630.

56. Salman Kayoush, "Masoud El Amaratly . . . The Story of a Picture," *Al Iraqiya*, 2017.

57. Wilfred Thesiger, *The Marsh Arabs* (New York: Penguin, 2008), 165.

58. Amara quoted in Thesinger, *Marsh Arabs*, 166. As a British researcher, Wilfred's account must be taken with a lens of doubt. However, Amara's account of mustarjil aligns with other local descriptions, including that of Masoud El Amaratly. Masoud, like many of his mustarjil brethren, was fully supported by his community. It was not until later colonial governance that the mustarjil community began to fade.

59. Amer Badr Hassoun, "Masoud El Amaratly: A Woman Who Changed Her Clothes and Name to Sing!" *Al Iraqiya*, 2018.

60. El Amaratly quoted in Hassoun, "Masoud El Amaratly."

61. Rahma Hajjah, "Masoud El Amaratly . . . On an Iraq That Embraced Gay People and Valued Their Creativity," *Raise Your Voice*, Aug. 23, 2019.

62. Reeva Spector Simon and Eleanor H. Tejirian, *The Creation of Iraq, 1914–1921* (New York: Columbia University Press, 2004).

63. Kaabour, "Recovering Arab Trans History."

64. Another story puts Masoud meeting Isa Ibn Huwaila in Baghdad while he sang at cafés. In both tellings, he began recording in 1925. "Massouda El Amartaly," *Dom Tak*.

65. Kayoush, "Masoud El Amaratly."

66. Habib Zahir al-Abbas, *Manhal: The Inquirer's Guide to Music and Singing News in Twentieth-Century Iraq* (Baghdad: House of Culture and Publishing Kurdish, 2012), 332.

67. Hajjah, "Masoud Al-Amaratly."

68. Hassoun, "Masoud El Amaratly."

69. "Massouda El Amartaly," *Dom Tak.*

70. Hassoun, "Masoud El Amaratly."

71. Kariri Al-Salman quoted in Kayoush, "Masoud El Amaratly."

72. "After Kazim al-Ghazali," *Al-Rai*, June 30, 1997.

73. Kayoush quoted in Alaa Hussein, "The Good Generation," TV episode, UTV, 2021.

The Shoemaker: Ray Leonard

74. "Woman in Disguise," *Coos Bay Times*, Sept. 30, 1911; "Woman Lived 49 Years as Man," *Eugene Guard*, Sept. 27, 1911.

75. "Jos. Leonard & Son," *Lebanon Express*, July 26, 1889.

76. Mary Canaga Rowland, *As Long as Life: The Memoirs of a Frontier Woman Doctor, Mary Canaga Rowland, 1873–1966* (Seattle: Storm Peak Press, 1994), 107.

77. Rowland, *As Long As Life*, 108.

78. "On Tuesday," *Lebanon Express*, July 11, 1902.

79. Twelfth Census of the United States, 1900, T623, National Archives and Records Administration (hereafter NARA), Washington, DC.

80. Rowland, *As Long as Life*, 107.

81. "She Wore the Pants 49 Years," *Capital Journal*, Sept. 26, 1911.

82. Rowland, *As Long as Life*, 107.

83. "Woman Lived 49 Years as Man," *Eugene Guard*.

84. "Ray Leonard May Go on Bench Again," *East Oregonian*, Nov. 1, 1911.

85. Rowland, *As Long As Life*, 108 (censored in original).

86. "Miss Ray Leonard," *Lebanon Express*, Jan. 24, 1917.

87. Fourteenth Census of the United States, 1920, microfilm publication T625, Records of the Bureau of the Census, Record Group 29, sheet 49B, NARA.

88. "County Birth and Death Records, 1855–1962, Ray Leonard," box 1, certificate 7, Oregon State Archives.

The Lover: Mabel Stanley

89. Massachusetts Vital and Town Records, Holbrook Research Institute Jay and Delene Holbrook, Town and City Clerks of Massachusetts, 46; Massachusetts Vital Records, 1840–1911, New England Historic Genealogical Society, 942.

90. "Masquerading as a Woman," *Lancaster Intelligencer*, Oct. 3, 1888.

91. The *Chicago Tribune* reported the man's name was John while the *Boston Globe* and *Pittsburgh Daily Post* reported the man's name was Leon. I could not locate records of him either way.

92. "Wore a Dress for Years," *Boston Globe*, Sept. 26, 1888.

93. "Mabel Stanley," *Boston Globe*, Apr. 11, 1884; "Mabel Stanley, for Being Idle," *Boston Globe*, Oct. 5, 1885; "Mabel Stanley and Ethel Arlington," *Boston Globe*, Nov. 25, 1885.

94. "She Proved to Be a Man," *Pittsburgh Daily Post*, Sept. 27, 1888.

95. "Frank Norcross," MSS 231 sg 1, series 1, vol. 4, Rhode Island Historical Society.

96. "Alcoholism Causes a Man's Death," *Boston Evening Transcript*, May 15, 1897; Bureau of the Census, Twelfth Census of the United States, 1900, T623, 23, NARA.

97. Bureau of the Census, Thirteenth Census of the United States, 1910, T624, Record Group 29. NARA; "Massachusetts State Vital Records, 1841–1925," Deaths, v. 1, Boston, file no. 1-6006, Jan.–June 1916, Registry of Vital Records.

The Girl Bandit: Emma Heinrich

98. "Girl Bandit Case Puzzle for Judge," *Meriden Daily Journal*, Jan. 4, 1906.

99. State Census of New Jersey, 1905, Reference Number: L-07, Film Number: 2, New Jersey State Archive.

100. "Little Girl Is Sent to Jail for Stealing Coal," *Passaic Daily News*, Nov. 13, 1905.

101. "'Bold Girl' a Boy," *Boston Globe*, Jan. 1, 1906.

102. "'Tomboy Burglar' Weeps," *Bellingham Herald*, Dec. 23, 1905.

103. "Girl Burglar at Fourteen," *Passaic Daily News*, Nov. 21, 1905.

104. "Little Girl," *Passaic Daily News*.

105. "One Girl, Two Boys, Burglars," *Passaic Daily Herald*, Nov. 21, 1905.

106. "'Tomboy Burglar,'" *Bellingham Herald*.

107. "Girl Burglar Sent to Home," *Passaic Daily News*, Dec. 14, 1905.

108. "'Bold Girl' a Boy," *Boston Globe*.

109. "'Tomboy Burglar,'" *Bellingham Herald*.

110. "Girls in State Home Locked in a Dungeon," *New York Times*, Nov. 30, 1908.

111. "Girl Burglar a Boy," *Passaic Daily News*, Jan. 2, 1906.

112. "'Bold Girl' a Boy," *Boston Globe*.

113. "'She's a Boy,' the Doctor Reported," *Morning Call*, Jan. 1, 1906.

114. "Emma Will Don Trousers," *Passaic Daily News*, Jan. 25, 1906.

115. "'Emma' Heinrich in Toils Again," *Passaic Daily News*, Mar. 11, 1907.

The Horse Thief: Willie Ray

116. Willie Ray was briefly featured in Emily Skidmore's 2017 *True Sex: The Lives of Trans Men at the Turn of the Twentieth Century* about his time in Mississippi. Skidmore's book provided an interesting basis for Willie's later life. However, due to his various names, she left out his remarkable teenage years. In fact, nobody has connected his many aliases in over 120 years.

117. Over the years, Willie had many aliases. I only call him Willie because it was the final name I could locate for him and the one he used the longest. During his time in Tennessee, however, he went by Ed Jones. He also used the names Ed Rankin, Willie Rankin, Will Osborn, Willie Craig, and Charles E. Jones, among others. I purposely changed all previous names to Willie for the sake of clarity. Tennessee City Death Records: Nashville, Knoxville, Chattanooga, Memphis 1848–1907, Tennessee State Library and Archives, 187.

118. Ben M. Barrus, Milton L. Baughn, and Thomas H. Campbell, *A People Called Cumberland Presbyterians: A History of the Cumberland Presbyterian Church* (Eugene, OR: Wipf and Stock Publishers, 1998); Tenth Census of the United States, 1880, Sharon Station, Weakley, Tennessee, Roll 1285, page 253B, Enumeration District 171, 38, Bureau of the Census; Civil War Pension Index, General Index to Pension Files, 1861–1934, NAI Title: General Index to Civil War and Later Pension Files, California, 1949; NAI Number: 563268, Record Group Title: Records of the Department of Veterans Affairs, 1773–2007; Record Group Number: 15; Series Number: T288; Roll: 384, NARA.

119. William Henry Glasson, *Federal Military Pensions in the United States* (New York: Oxford University Press, 1918); Stanley Lebergott, "Labor Force and Employment, 1800–1960," in *Output, Employment, and Productivity in the United States after 1800*, ed. Dorothy S. Brady (New York: National Bureau of Economic Research, 1966).

120. "Daring Agnes Rankin," *The Tennessean*, Sept. 27, 1891.

121. "Sorry She Wasn't a Man," *Norfolk Landmark*, Sept. 23, 1890.

122. "Daring Agnes Rankin," *The Tennessean*, Aug. 14, 1891.

123. It is worth noting that neither Annie nor Marion kept track of their birth dates. Annie was born in 1873, which is confirmed through Willie's records. However, she entered the wrong year on her census forms nearly every decade. The year 1875 appears on her death certificate but 1867 is on her gravestone. Marion's adjoined grave states his birth year as 1860. In 1900, however, he listed his birth year as 1873, making him the same age as Annie. Twelfth Census of the United States, 1900, Civil District 12, Lauderdale, Tennessee, Roll 1583, 14, Enumeration District 0094, Bureau of the Census; Find a Grave, "Fannie Lauderdale," https://www.findagrave.com/memorial/11662096/fannie-lauderdale, accessed Sept. 19, 2024.

124. "She's One of the Boys," *Memphis Avalanche*, Mar. 21, 1890.

125. "A Young Kentucky Girl," *Akron Beacon Journal*, Aug. 14, 1891.

126. One article stated the governor pardoned Willie on account of his age. The reporter did not provide evidence. Robert M. Ireland, "Law and Disorder in Nineteenth-Century Kentucky," *Vanderbilt Law Review* 32 (1979): 281–99; "A Girl Accused," *Memphis Weekly Commercial*, Sept. 24, 1891; "Agnes Rankin Pardoned," *The Tennessean*, Sept. 10, 1890.

127. This particular decision is how we may surmise he would be trans today: He had nothing to gain other than gender affirmation from wearing men's clothing. He was outed and everyone knew of his assigned sex, yet he continued to wear pants and his casual sack suit. "News from Union City," *Nashville Banner*, Sept. 27, 1890.

128. "Agnes Rankin Arrested," *Nashville Banner*, Oct. 3, 1890.

129. "Advantages of Being a Man," *Free Press*, Nov. 8, 1890.

130. "A Young Kentucky Girl," *Akron Beacon Journal*.

131. "Miss Agnes Rankin," *Los Angeles Times*, Aug. 27, 1891.

132. "Daring Agnes Rankin," *The Tennessean*.

133. "Agnes Rankin," *Public Ledger*, Aug. 18, 1891.

134. Reporters also named his employer as the owner of the horse and its original location as Gates, Tennessee. There was no explanation for this discrepancy between media outlets. "Directors Elected," *Memphis Daily Appeal*, June 15, 1888; "A Girl Accused," *Memphis Weekly Commercial*, Sept. 24, 1891.

135. "Daring Agnes Rankin," *The Tennessean*.

136. "Agnes Rankin," *The Tennessean*, Oct. 5, 1891.

137. "Miss Agnes Rankin," *Los Angeles Times*.

138. "Dressed in Male Attire," *Memphis Commercial*, Sept. 17, 1893.

139. Twelfth Census of the United States, 1900, Bureau of the Census, Civil District 7, Obion, Tennessee, Roll 1591, page 13, Enumeration District 0102, NARA; "William Stanley," *Paducah Sun-Democrat*, Jan. 25, 1915; William Stanley, "Last Will and Testament of William Stanley," Tennessee, Wills and Probate Records, 1779–2008.

140. Gatlin was the son of a Confederate prisoner of war who was released from Union capture in a prisoner exchange four years before James was born. We can only imagine how residual Civil War tensions between their fathers exacerbated this conflict. "Miss Ray's Case," *Birmingham News*, July 20, 1903; "Supposed Man Really Girl," *Davenport Morning Star*, July 24, 1903; "Will Stick to Her Trousers," *The Leader*, Aug. 15, 1903.

141. "Willie Ray of Booneville," *Aberdeen Weekly*, Apr. 10, 1908.

142. Thirteenth Census of the United States, 1910, microfilm publication T624, Bureau of the Census.

143. "Willie Ray," *Aberdeen Weekly*, Sept. 7, 1907; "Poor Willie," *Daily Corinthian*, Sept. 7, 1907.

144. "Fannie Lauderdale," Find a Grave, "Tennessee Death Records, 1908–1958," Tennessee State Library and Archives.

THE ACTIVISTS

1. "Legislation," *Mendocino Beacon*, Jan. 18, 1941.

2. Top scholars within transgender studies like Sally Hines repeat this "first" claim. See Sally Hines, "Riding the Waves: Feminism, Lesbian and Gay Politics,

and the Transgender Debates," in *1968 in Retrospect: History, Theory, Alterity*, ed. Gurminder K. Bhambra and Ipek Demir (London: Palgrave Macmillan, 2009), 150.

3. Zein Murib makes this claim in their popular essay "Transgender: Examining an Emerging Political Identity Using Three Political Processes," *Politics Groups and Identities* 3, no. 3 (May 2015): 1–17, for example.

The Freed Woman: Sally-Tom

4. "Sally-Tom," *St. Louis Globe-Democrat*, Apr. 14, 1889.

5. "Sally-Tom," *St. Louis Globe-Democrat*.

6. Randy Finley, *From Slavery to Uncertain Freedom: The Freedman's Bureau in Arkansas 1865–1869* (Fayetteville: University of Arkansas Press, 1996).

7. There were no indications she was intersex.

8. "Candidate Stevens," *Albany Weekly Herald*, May 14, 1892; "Mr. Cleveland's Mistake," *Albany Weekly Herald*, Feb. 18, 1893.

9. "Disguised as Woman," *Waycross Journal*, Mar. 6, 1908.

10. J. L. Walker, *History of Ware County, Georgia* (Greenville: Southern Historical Press, 2017), 93, 322.

The Countess: Gerda von Zobeltitz

11. "A German Baron Now a Countess by Court Decree," *Asheville Citizen-Times*, Aug. 11, 1912.

12. Including a chapter about Gerda was complicated. I found her to be one of the most well-documented trans figures in this book. However, the writing about her was almost exclusively in German and focused more on her family than her accomplishments. Katja Koblitz, a historian who runs the Spinnboden Lesbenarchiv und Bibliothek Berlin (the largest lesbian library and archive in Europe), published a thorough twenty-two-page biography of Gerda in 2009. Koblitz used an impressive number of oral histories, legal documents, and news reports to detail the narrative. I built off of this existing information to string together the most important aspects of Gerda: the key moments of her life, the Rauchfangswerder riots, and what is excluded from Koblitz's existing work. Katja Koblitz, "In ihm hat die Natur das berühmte dritte Geschlecht geschaffen'. Gerda von Zobeltitz, ein Transvestit aus Weißensee," in *Verzaubert in Nord-Ost: Die Geschichte der Berliner Lesben und Schwulen in Prenzlauer Berg, Pankow und Weißensee*, ed. Jens Dobler (Berlin: Bruno Gmünder, 2009).

13. Landesarchiv Berlin, Personenstandsregister Geburtsregister, 1916, Laufendenummer 153.

14. Gerda von Zobeltitz, "Die Welt der Transvestiten," *Die Freundin* 31 (1930): 5–6.

15. "Lokales und Vermischtes," *Berliner Tageblatt*, Feb. 27, 1912.

16. Translated by Robert Beachy. Robert Beachy, *Gay Berlin*, 172.

17. Koblitz, "In ihm hat die Natur," 62.

18. Beachy, *Gay Berlin*, 172–73.

19. "Der Jüngling in Frauenkleidern," *Das interessante Blatt*, Apr. 3, 1913.

20. The paper used the German term *"dritte Geschlecht,"* which roughly translates to "third gender" or "third sex." "Der Jüngling in Frauenkleidern," *Das interessante Blatt*, 6.

21. Koblitz, "In ihm hat die Natur."

22. Landesarchiv Berlin, Personenstandsregister Heiratsregister, 1891, D. 719.

23. Landesarchiv Berlin, Personenstandsregister Heiratsregister, 1919, B. 156.

24. Landesarchiv Berlin, Personenstandsregister Heiratsregister, 1919, B. 2057.

25. Dr. Casey J. Hayes coined this exact phrase in the early 2020s. However, German historian Jens Dobler initially declared "Rauchfangswerder was a riot" in his 2020 book on anti-queer policing in the Weimar Republic. Unfortunately, Dobler's short piece only cited Koblitz's 2009 biography of Gerda von Zobeltitz, which left much to be explained about exactly what made Rauchfangswerder a riot, who fought one another, and how queer people resisted. After speaking with Casey, I went back to the primary sources and found that there were far more details from the incredible story of Rauchfangswerder that have not been published in over ninety years. Jens Dobler, *Polizei und Homosexuelle in der Weimarer Republik: zur Konstruktion des Sündenbabels* (Berlin: Metropol, 2020).

26. Jens Dobler and Kristine Schmidt, "Die Bewegung der Weimarer Republik beginnt in Pankow," in *Verzaubert in Nord-Ost: Die Geschichte der Berliner Lesben und Schwulen in Prenzlauer Berg, Pankow und Weißensee*, ed. Jens Dobler (Berlin: Bruno Gmünder, 2009); Javier Samper Vendrell, *Seduction of Youth: Print Culture and Homosexual Rights in the Weimar Republic* (Toronto: University of Toronto Press, 2020).

27. "Ihre Freundin und Sie," *Bund für Menschenrecht, Die Freundin*, June 25, 1930.

28. I use gender-neutral they/them pronouns due to the lack of analogous forms of pronoun self-identification during Hahm's lifetime.

29. Ingeborg Boxhammer and Christiane Leidinger, "Offensiv—strategisch—(frauen)emanzipiert: Spuren der Berliner Subkulturaktivistin* Lotte Hahm (1890–1967)," *Gender—Zeitschrift für Geschlecht, Kultur und Gesellschaft* 1 (2021): 91–108; "Transvestitengruppe," *Die Freundin*, Oct. 1, 1930; Rainer Herrn, *Schnittmuster des Geschlechts: Transvestitismus und Transsexualität in der frühen Sexualwissenschaft* (Gießen: Psychosozial-Verlag, 2005), 149–50.

30. Paul Weber, "Haben die Schupobeamten die Homosexuellen planmäßigüberfallen?" Die Freundin, July 23, 1930.

31. It is possible an overlapping event may have saved some of the potential victims from police violence. In 1902 the upscale Dorian Gray Café opened its doors in Berlin. The café hosted its annual summer festival with free entry for women the same evening as the boat trip. It is unclear how the events may have influenced one another but likely meant fewer BfM travelers to Rauchfangswerder. "Conzert-Café, Dorian Gray," *Liebende Frauen* 5, no. 27 (1930): 8; Jöng Niendorf, "Letzter Halt Rauchfangswerder," *Berliner Morgenpost*, Aug. 26, 2012; Beachy, *Gay Berlin*, 60.

32. Fredrich Radszuweit, "Homosexuelle schlagen Polizei beamtenieder!" *Die Freundin*, July 30, 1930.

33. Weber, "Haben die Schupobeamten die Homosexuellen planmäßig überfallen?"

34. Hsi-Huey Liang, *The Berlin Police Force in the Weimar Republic* (Berkeley: University of California Press, 1970).

35. There is no conclusive evidence that this specific BfM attack on the police actually happened. Nor is there evidence of what would have sparked such a conflict, outside of the Schupo's ongoing harassment of the group.

36. "Zu der Schupo-Brügelei bei Berlin," *Coburger Zeitung*, July 9, 1930; "Polizei genen Polizei," *Salzburger Chronik für Stadt und Land*, July 8, 1930.

37. Weber, "Haben die Schupobeamten die Homosexuellen planmäßig überfallen?"

38. "Sonntags Bergnügen bei Berlin," *Ingolstädter Anzeiger*, July 9, 1930.

39. "Menn Polizitten Gegen 'Menschenrechte' kämpfen," *Grafinger Zeitung*, July 9, 1930.

40. "Schlägerei mit Tanzvergnügen," *Vorwärts*, July 8, 1930.

41. Radszuweit, "Homosexuelle schlagen Polizei beamtenieder!"

42. "Menn Polizitten gegen," *Grafinger Zeitung*.

43. At the time, the negative opinions of sex workers centered the fear of outing. A moral panic emerged within the respectable gay movement that queer sex workers could blackmail wealthy gay men. Friedrich Radszuweit wrote an entire novel on the topic in 1931, *Männer zu verkaufen*. For more on Radszuweit's work against supporting right-wing politics, see Huw Lemmey and Ben Miller, *Bad Gays: A Homosexual History* (New York: Verso Books, 2022), 154–60; Ben Miller, "In the Archives," *OutHistory*, Mar. 29, 2017.

44. Bernd-Ulrich Hergemöller, *Mann für Mann: Biographisches Lexikon zur Geschichte von Freundesliebe und mannmännlicher Sexualität im deutschen Sprachraum* (Hamburg: MännerschwarmSkript, 2010), 947–48.

45. Marie Weis, "Der Transvestit," *Gargonne* 4 (1930).

46. "Every transvestite who wants more, every transvestite who is concerned that the conditions of their soul are not disputed, who demands respect for their individuality as it is, must be clear that the achievement of these wishes can only be guaranteed by an organization that places itself exclusively at the service of these wishes and at the same time has enough reputation in public to be heard,"

Marie Weis wrote. Rainer Herrn, *Das 3. Geschlecht-Reprint der 1930–1932 erschienen Zeitschrift für Transvestiten* (Hamburg: MännerschwarmSkript, 2016), 255; Marie Weis, "Der Transvestit," *Liebende Frauen* 5, no. 29 (1930).

47. Heike Bauer, *The Hirschfeld Archives: Violence, Death, and Modern Queer Culture* (Philadelphia: Temple University Press, 2017), 86.

48. Kai Struve, *Deutsche Herrschaft, ukrainischer Nationalismus, antijüdische Gewalt: Der Sommer 1941 in der Westukraine* (Oldenbourg: De Gruyter, 2015), 592; "German Pogroms: Atrocities of the Waffen-SS Division 'Wiking' in Eastern Galicia in July 1941," *MORESHET: Journal for the Study of the Holocaust and Antisemitism* 19 (2022): 55.

49. Diane Reynolds, *The Doubled Life of Dietrich Bonhoeffer* (Cambridge: James Clarke & Co., 2017), 269.

50. Directorate of History, *Report No. 69* (Ottawa: Directorate of History, 1986), 65–66.

51. Koblitz, "In ihm hat die Natur," 76.

52. Koblitz, "In ihm hat die Natur," 77.

53. Koblitz, "In ihm hat die Natur," 78.

54. Zavier Nunn, "Trans Liminality and the Nazi State," *Past & Present* (2022).

55. Jens Dobler, Andreas Pretzel, and Christiane Leidinger, *Persönlichkeiten in Berlin 1825–2006: Erinnerungen an Lesben, Schwule, Bisexuelle, trans- und intergeschlechtliche Menschen* (Berlin: Landesstelle für Gleichbehandlung—gegen Diskriminierung, 2015).

The Petitioner: Carl Crawford

56. "Agreed to Do So No More," *Waco Times-Herald*, Aug. 19, 1902.

57. Peggy Howland Richard, "Stephen Palmer and Louisa Griswold Tipton," in *The Heritage of Grundy County, TN*, ed. Grundy County Heritage Book Committee (Marceline: Walsworth Publishing Co., 2004), 397; Social Security Applications and Claims, 1936–2007, Carl G. Crawford, SSN 264264984.

58. William L. Anderson, *Cherokee Removal: Before and After* (Athens: University of Georgia Press, 1992).

59. Richard, "Stephen Palmer and Louisa Griswold Tipton."

60. "Agreed to Do So No More," *Waco Times-Herald*.

61. "Tried," *Cincinnati Enquirer*, Oct. 24, 1903; "This Is a Hummer," *Sandusky Star-Journal*, Nov. 27, 1903.

62. Journalists at the time embellished stories like his with details of love and tragedy. Carl was never quoted mentioning his suicide attempt to the papers, so we cannot know if such dramatic reports were accurate.

63. Morrison & Fourmy, *Directory of the City of Waco, 1902–1903* (Dallas: Morrison & Fourmy Directory Co., 1902).

64. "Parading In Man's Attire," *Waco Times-Herald*, Aug. 18, 1902.

65. "A Statement," *Waco Times-Herald*, Aug. 25, 1902.

66. Circuit Court Clerk's Office, *Minute Books, Civil and Criminal*, Volume K, Dec. 1901–Oct. 1904, Tennessee State Library and Archives.

67. It is worth noting that all evidence points to Carl being non-intersex and no records of an intersex condition appeared. As mentioned, Carl was never examined by the doctor certifying his male status. "Sex Declared by County Court," *Nashville Banner*, July 4, 1904.

68. "Altamont, Tenn.," *Chattanooga News*, May 10, 1902; Tennessee State Marriages, 1780–2002, Tennessee State Library and Archives.

69. Fifteenth Census of the United States, 1930, Jacksonville, Duval, Florida, page 36A, Enumeration District 0046, FHL microfilm 2340049, Bureau of the Census; Fourteenth Census of the United States, 1920, Jacksonville Ward 6, Duval, Florida, Roll T625_217, page 10B, Enumeration District 52, Bureau of the Census; Sixteenth Census of the United States, 1940, Jacksonville, Duval, Florida, Roll m-t0627-00624, page 4A, Enumeration District 68-45, Bureau of the Census; Thirteenth Census of the United States, 1910, Jacksonville Ward 8, Duval, Florida, Roll T624_159, page 8b, Enumeration District 0088, FHL microfilm 13741721910, Bureau of the Census; World War I Selective Service System Draft Registration Cards, 1917–1918, US Selective Service System, M1509, NARA.

The Runaway: Mollie Wilson

70. "Dress Hid His Crimes: Negro Man Disguised as a Woman Dies in North End," *Kansas City Times*, Mar. 23, 1900; "The Police Were Fooled," *McAlester Capital*, Mar. 29, 1900.

71. "In Female Attire," *Weekly Standard*, July 14, 1899; "Mollie Wilson Fined for Streetwalking," *Leavenworth Times*, July 6, 1899.

72. "Mary Taylor Fined $10 for Street Walking," *Kansas City Gazette*, July 18, 1898.

The Healer: Muksamse'lapli

73. Muksamse'lapli used *female* to describe herself, and settlers typically used she/her pronouns for her. "White Cindy, Mystery Figure, Was Powerful Tribe Member," *Herald and News*, May 27, 1950.

74. W. M. Lorenz, "Early Days . . . 'July Grounds' Celebration," *Klamath Echoes* 1, no. 1 (1964): 33–39.

75. "A Pair of Dianas," *Democratic Times*, Dec. 24, 1886.

76. "Brown, Francis, July 5, 1980," *Horner Museum Oral History Collection, 1952–1993*, Series 2: Transcripts and Project Files, 1952–1992, Box-Folder 13.27: 8.

77. Contemporary Klamath activists like Shuína Skó use terms such as *two-spirit*, which they translate as *laap steínash shû'kla* ("two souls mixing

together"). Skó quoted in Derek DeForest, "Sacred Instructions: A Two-Spirit Klamath Tribal Member Connects with Her Voices and Visions," *Oregon Humanities*, Sept. 8, 2023, http://oregonhumanities.org/rll/beyond-the-margins/sacred -instructions/; Deward E. Walker Jr., *Handbook of North American Indians, V. 12, Plateau* (Washington, DC: Smithsonian Institution, 1998); Leslie Spier, *Klamath Ethnography* (Berkeley: University of California Press, 1930), 51.

78. Albert Samuel Gatschet, *The Klamath Indians of Southwestern Oregon* (Washington, DC: Government Printing Office, 1890), 25.

79. Thomas J. Connolly et al., "Looking Back, Looking Forward: Resilience and Persistence in a Klamath Tribal Community," *Journal of Anthropological Archaeology* 65 (2022): 1–17; Jefferson C. Davis Riddle, *The Indian History of the Modoc War* (Mechanicsburg, PA: Stackpole Books, 2004).

80. "'Sisters' White Cindy, Glass Eye Made Local History," *Herald and News*, Feb. 26, 1982; Marcella Rawe, "Missionary Tells of Pioneer Days," *Evening Herald*, Mar. 18, 1936; Edith R. McLeod, "White Cindy, Mystery Figure, Was Powerful Tribe Member," *Herald and News*, May 27, 1950.

81. Thirteenth Census of the United States, 1910. Klamath Indian Reservation, Klamath, Oregon; Roll: T624_1282, Page: 23b; Enumeration District: 0137, FHL microfilm: 1375295, Bureau of the Census; Indian Census Rolls, 1885–1940. Record Group: 75, Record Group Title: Records of the Bureau of Indian Affairs; Series: Microfilm Publication M595, NARA.

82. Frederick Vernon Coville, *Notes on the Plants Used by the Klamath Indians of Oregon. Vol. 5, No. 2* (Washington, DC: Government Printing Office, 1897).

83. McLeod, "White Cindy."

84. The meaning of nubia in this quote is unclear, although it may be referring to gold jewelry, the root of the word *Nubia*. "A Pair of Dianas," *Democratic Times*.

85. "Son of Chief Meets Death," *Klamath Republican*, Sept. 26, 1912; "Circuit Court Cases," *Klamath Republican*, Nov. 24, 1904; "Many Criminal Cases at Klamath," *Oregon Daily Journal*, Nov 10, 1904; "Big Cindy on War Path," *Weekly Rogue River Courier*, Oct. 27, 1904.

86. "Swings Indian by Necktie," *Los Angeles Times*, May 31, 1914; "White Cindy Is Given Liberty," *Evening Herald*, June 6, 1914.

87. "White Cindy Kills Aged Klamath Indian," *Medford Mail Tribune*, May 30, 1914.

88. "White Cinda [sic]," Death Certificate: Klamath, 1919, 40A-18, Oregon, Death Records, 1864–1967, Oregon State Archives.

89. McLeod, "White Cindy."

The Pacifist: Sadie Acosta

90. "Sadie No Lady, Says Physician at Fort Collins," *Greeley Daily Tribune*, Jan. 7, 1941.

91. "622 Maple," Fort Collins History Connection, https://fchc.contentdm
.oclc.org/digital/collection/bp/id/6815/rec/1; "Sadie Acosta," St. Louis, Missouri;
WWII Draft Registration Cards for Colorado, Oct. 16, 1940–Mar. 31, 1947,
Record Group: Records of the Selective Service System, 147, Box 1, National
Archives at St. Louis.

92. "Legislation," *Mendocino Beacon.*

93. Michelle Dietert and Dianne Dentice, "Transgender Military Experiences:
From Obama to Trump," *Journal of Homosexuality* 70, no. 6 (2023): 993–1010;
"Who Needs to Register," Selective Service System, https://web.archive.org
/web/20240617032008/https://www.sss.gov/register/who-needs-to-register/#p7,
accessed Sept. 12, 2024.

The Community Leader: Georgia Black

94. "The Man Who Lived 30 Years as a Woman," *Ebony*, Oct. 1951, 23.

95. Georgia's birth date is reported as anywhere between 1891 and 1906;
the year 1892 appears to be the most likely, as that is the one she personally
reported on her marriage certificate. She told the clerk she was twenty-five in
February 1918 when she married (one of her earliest records). Fifteenth Census
of the United States, 1930, Sanford, Seminole, Florida, page 32A, Enumeration
District 0001, FHL microfilm 2340067, Bureau of the Census; Fourteenth
Census of the United States, 1920, Sanford, Seminole, Florida, Roll T625_231,
page 9A, Enumeration District 181, Bureau of the Census; Seventeenth Census
of the United States, 1950, Sanford, Seminole, Florida, Roll 5855, page 10,
Enumeration District 59-15, Bureau of the Census; Sixteenth Census of the
United States, 1940, Sanford, Seminole, Florida, Roll m-t0627-00617, page
13A, Enumeration District 59-2, Bureau of the Census; Thirteenth Census
of the United States, 1910, Clermont, Lake, Florida, Roll T624_163, page 5a,
Enumeration District 0075, FHL microfilm 1374176, Bureau of the Census;
"County Marriages, 1916–1919, Georgia Sabb," Tallahassee and Clerk of
Courts, Florida State Archive.

96. "'Maid' Is Really Man," *Miami Herald*, Mar. 7, 1951.

97. Marriage Records, 1837–1974, vol. 3, Lake County, Alonzo Sabb, Jan. 14,
1912, 175, state of Florida.

98. Willie Sabb, "My Mother Was a Man," *Ebony*, June 1953, p. 75.

99. Sabb, "My Mother Was a Man," 76.

100. "The Man Who Lived 30 Years as a Woman," *Ebony*, 25.

101. "Florida Deaths, 1877–1939, Mustor Black," Oct. 25, 1925, Florida
State Board of Health; US Selective Service, World War I Selective Service
System Draft Registration Cards, 1917–1918, M1509, NARA.

102. Sabb, "My Mother Was a Man," 77.

103. Sabb, "My Mother Was a Man," 76.

104. "Sanford Negro 'Woman' Really a Man," *Bradenton Herald*, Mar. 8, 1951.

105. Sabb, "My Mother Was a Man," 80.

106. Sabb, "My Mother Was a Man," 80–82.

107. "The Man Who Lived 30 Years as a Woman," *Ebony*, 26.

108. Sabb, "My Mother Was a Man," 82.

109. Sabb, "My Mother Was a Man," 75.

110. Sabb, "My Mother Was a Man," 76.

111. Sabb, "My Mother Was a Man," 82.

112. C. Riley Snorton, *Black on Both Sides: A Racial History of Trans Identity* (Minneapolis: University of Minnesota Press, 2017), 156.

The Guardian: Okiyo

113. Surveys of past and present-day danshō generally find that they used terms like *women* to describe themselves. I use *trans* to depict her in the broadest sense of those identifying outside the Western gender binary. Hideko Abe, *Queer Japanese: Gender and Sexual Identities Through Linguistic Practices* (New York: Palgrave Macmillan, 2010), 55–57; Mitsuhashi Junko, "Sengo Nihon 'toransujendā' shakaishi no rekishiteki hensen no sobyō," in *Sengo Nihon josō/dōseiai kenkyū*, ed. Masami Yajima (Tokyo: Chūō University Press, 2006); Ishida Hitoshi and Murakami Takanori, "The Process of Divergence Between 'Men Who Love Men' and 'Feminised Men' in Postwar Japanese Media," *Intersections: Gender, History and Culture in the Asian Context* 12 (2006).

114. Oyama is also known as *onnagata* (female style). Keiichi Hirooka, *Sengo fūzoku taikei: Waga megami-tachi [A survey of entertainment after the war: My goddesses]* (Tokyo: Shōgakukan, 2007), 35.

115. Masanori Hirakawa and Tomohiro Shimohara, "387,000 Deaths Confirmed in WWII Air Raids in Japan; Toll Unknown in 15 Cities: Survey," *The Mainichi*, Aug. 23, 2020; Urban Areas Division, *Effects of Air Attack on Osaka, Kobe, Kyoto* (US Strategic Bombing Survey, 1947).

116. Edwin P. Hoyt, *Inferno: The Fire Bombing of Japan, March 9–August 15, 1945* (Lanham, MD: Madison Books, 2000); "Japan Surrenders," Office of Scientific and Technical Information, https://www.osti.gov/opennet/manhattan-project-history/Events/1945/surrender.htm, accessed Sept. 12, 2024.

117. Mark McLelland, *Love, Sex, and Democracy in Japan During the American Occupation* (New York: Springer, 2012), 62, 155.

118. Sheldon Garon, "The World's Oldest Debate? Prostitution and the State in Imperial Japan, 1900–1945," *American Historical Review* 98, no. 3 (1993): 710–32; Sarah Kovner, *Occupying Power: Sex Workers and Servicemen in Postwar Japan* (Redwood City, CA: Stanford University Press, 2020).

119. Hirooka, *Sengo fūzoku taikei*, 32; Todd Henry, "Between Surveillance and Liberation: The Lives of Cross-Dressed Male Sex Workers in Early Postwar Japan," in *The Transgender Studies Reader 2*, ed. Susan Stryker and Aren Aizura (New York: Routledge, 2013), 415–16.

120. Sarah Kovner, "Base Cultures: Sex Workers and Servicemen in Occupied Japan," *Journal of Asian Studies* 68, no. 3 (2009): 784.

121. National Diet Library, "Ueno Park," http://www.ndl.go.jp/scenery/e/column/ueno-park.html, accessed Sept. 12, 2024.

122. Abe, *Queer Japanese*, 169; Hirooka, *Sengo fūzoku taikei*, 36.

123. Abe, *Queer Japanese*, 53–54.

124. Henry, "Between Surveillance and Liberation," 416; Hirooka, *Sengo fūzoku taikei*, 36; Ōtani Susumu, *Ikite iru: Ueno chikadō no jittai* (Tokyo: Sengo Nihon Shakai Settaishi, 1948); Minami Takao, "Psycho-Medical Observations on Male Prostitution," *Medical Digest* 3, no. 4 (1948): 18–24; Michiko Takeuchi, "'Pan-Pan Girls' Performing and Resisting Neocolonialism(s) in the Pacific Theater: US Military Prostitution in Occupied Japan, 1945–1952," in *Over There: Living with the U.S. Military Empire from World War Two to the Present*, ed. Maria Höhn and Seungsook Moon (Durham, NC: Duke University Press, 2010).

125. McLelland, *Love, Sex, and Democracy in Japan During the American Occupation*.

126. Hideo Narutomo, *Criminal Investigation Record, No. 6* (Tokyo: Yuzankaku Publishers, 1963), 162–63.

127. "Eiichi Tanaka," *Japan Times*, Feb. 2, 1980; "Tanaka, Eiichi," National Diet Library, https://www.ndl.go.jp/portrait/datas/592/?_x_tr_hist=true, accessed Sept. 12, 2024.

128. This was not Tanaka's first failed roundup of sex workers. In May 1948 he arrested two hundred people he accused of selling sex. Many of them were simply bystanders. The police forced the detainees to pay 200 yen for sexually transmitted infection examinations. He was forced to testify in the National Diet about the failed operation but was not punished for his role in it. Tamotsu Murayama, "VD Examination by Police of Innocent Girls Probed," *Nippon Times*, July 2, 1948; "13th Diet House of Representatives Special Committee on Administrative Inspection No. 24," National Diet, May 17, 1952.

129. "About 30 Members," *Asahi Shimbun*, Nov. 23, 1948.

130. Hirooka, *Sengo fūzoku taikei*, 38.

131. Abe, *Queer Japanese*, 53–54.

132. "Danshō bakari no zadankai ijōshinri to hentai seiyoku o kaibō," *Shakai tanbō* (Apr. 1949): 32–37.

133. "About 30 Members," *Asahi Shimbun*.

134. Frederick Hulse, "Some Effects of the War on Japanese Society," *Far Eastern Quarterly* 7, no. 1 (1947): 40.

135. *Jiji Nenkan* (Tokyo: Jiji Press, 1950), 102.

136. Henry, "Between Surveillance and Liberation," 405.

137. Mitsuhashi Junko, "Japanese Female Fables [Vol. 14]: 'Okiyo,' the Male Prostitute Who Beat Up the Police Commissioner," Archive of Junko Mitsuhashi, https://zoku-tasogare-2.blog.ss-blog.jp/2020-07-24-13, accessed Sept. 12, 2024.

138. Eiichi Tanaka, *American Places* (Tokyo: Vigilante Association, 1954).

139. Peter J. Katzenstein, *Cultural Norms and National Security Police and Military in Postwar Japan* (Ithaca, NY: Cornell University Press, 2018).

140. Hirooka, *Sengo fūzoku taikei.*

The Professor: Maude Milbourne

141. "This Man Wants to Wear Regulation Clothes of a Woman," *Oakland Tribune*, May 30, 1905.

142. Seventh Census of the United States, 1850, Record Group Number 29, Series Number M432, Greenfield, Highland, Ohio, Roll 694, Page 142a, Bureau of the Census; Eighth Census of the United States, 1860, Record Group Number 29, Series Number M653, Greenfield, Highland, Ohio, Roll M653_986, page 90, Bureau of the Census; Find a Grave Index, "Wm. M. DeVoss," Find a Grave, Oct. 14, 2013, https://www.findagrave.com/memorial/118733485/william_matthews_devoss; County Marriage Records, 1774–1993, State of Ohio.

143. William Henry Chamberlin, *History of the Eighty-First Regiment Ohio Infantry Volunteers: During the War of the Rebellion* (Ann Arbor, MI: Gazette Steam Printing House, 1865); Historical Register of National Homes for Disabled Volunteer Soldiers, 1866–1938, Series M1749, NARA.

144. William Schuette and Myrna L. Armstrong, "Civil War Drummer Boys: Musicians, Messengers, and Medical Assistants," *Military Medicine* 184, nos. 1–2 (2019): 1–4.

145. Ninth Census of the United States, 1870, Concord, Fayette, Ohio, Roll M593_1199, page 400A, Bureau of the Census; "Mr. Randolph Milbourne," *Cyclone and Fayette Republican*, Nov. 26, 1884; "R. F. Milbourne," *Cyclone and Fayette Republican*, Apr. 15, 1885.

146. "Randolph Milburn," *Cyclone and Fayette Republican*, Mar. 21, 1883.

147. "Staunton," *Cyclone and Fayette Republican*, Oct. 23, 1885.

148. "R. F. Milbourne Has Returned," *Cyclone and Fayette Republican*, June 20, 1888; "R. F. Milbourne and Mother," *Cyclone and Fayette Republican*, Apr. 16, 1890; "Thursday Evening," *Cyclone and Fayette Republican*, June 25, 1890.

149. "Milbourne-Eberly," *Cyclone and Fayette Republican*, Feb. 25, 1897.

150. Louisa's first husband died in 1894, which may explain the description. Thirteenth Census of the United States, 1910, Lancaster Ward 1, Fairfield, Ohio, Roll T624_1179, page 7b, Enumeration District 0062, FHL microfilm 1375192, Bureau of the Census.

151. "The Will of the Late Mrs. Almira Hyer," *Cyclone and Fayette Republican*, May 24, 1900.

152. "Miss Maude Milbourne," *Cyclone and Fayette Republican*, Dec. 25, 1902; "Professor Randolph Milbourne," *Cyclone and Fayette Republican*, Dec. 11, 1902.

153. "Al Field Bequeaths Show. Will Requests Brother and Relative to Continue Minstrel Troupe," *New York Times*, Apr. 9, 1921.

154. "Maude Milbourne Gives an Entertainment at Dayton," *Cyclone and Fayette Republican*, Apr. 30, 1903.

155. "Prof. Milbourne in New Role," *Cyclone and Fayette Republican*, Apr. 7, 1904.

156. "Mrs. Milburn," *Ohio State Register*, Apr. 7, 1905.

157. "Randolph Milbourne of Washington C. H.," *Akron Beacon Journal*, Apr. 8, 1905; "The 'Prof.' Milbourne Does the Attorney General of the State of Ohio," *Ohio State Register*, Apr. 21, 1905.

158. Sharon M. Harris, *Dr. Mary Walker: An American Radical, 1832–1919* (New Brunswick: Rutgers University Press, 2009).

159. "Man Who Is Trying to Become a Woman and Woman Who Delights in Playing Man," *Atlanta Constitution*, May 21, 1905.

160. "Here Is the Human Limit," *Cincinnati Enquirer*, Oct. 20, 1906.

161. "Insists He Has a Right to Wear Women's Attire," *Cincinnati Enquirer*, Apr. 16, 1905.

162. "A Reversal of the Sexes," *Austin American-Statesman*, May 28, 1905.

163. "Wet and Dry," *Cyclone and Fayette Republican*, May 11, 1905.

164. "Well, This Is the Limit," *News-Democrat*, Nov. 4, 1906.

165. "Receives a Letter from a Follower in Iowa," *Cyclone and Fayette Republican*, June 1, 1905.

166. "Here Is the Human Limit," *Cincinnati Enquirer*.

167. "'Dress Reform Convention' to Be Held in This City," *Ohio State Register*, Dec. 14, 1906.

THE WORKERS

1. Leslie Feinberg, *Transgender Warriors: Making History from Joan of Arc to Dennis Rodman* (Boston, Beacon Press, 1997), 118.

2. Eric Marcus, "Coming of Age During the 1970s—Chapter Four: Respectable," *Making Gay History*, podcast, May 25, 2023.

3. Dean Spade, *Normal Life: Administrative Violence, Critical Trans Politics, and the Limits of Law* (Durham, NC: Duke University Press, 2015), 14.

4. David Baboolall et al., "Being Transgender at Work," *McKinsey Quarterly* (2021); Bianca D. M. Wilson et al., *LGBT Poverty in the US: Trends at the Onset of COVID-19* (Los Angeles: Williams Institute, UCLA School of Law, 2023).

5. David Leonhardt, "The Black-White Wage Gap Is as Big as It Was in 1950," *New York Times*, June 25, 2020.

6. "This Girl Would Prefer to Be Boy," *Washington Times*, Jan. 25, 1905.

The Maid: Josephine Robinson

7. "Accident Revealed Chicago Society Ladiesmaid a Man," *St. Louis Post-Dispatch*, July 4, 1909.

8. Thirteenth Census of the United States, Chicago Ward 7, Cook, Illinois, Roll T624_248, page 11a, Enumeration District 0431, FHL microfilm 1374261, Bureau of the Census.

9. "Why He Donned Female Attire," *Buffalo Enquirer*, June 9, 1909.

10. "Street Car Gallantry Receives an Awful Blow," *Inter Ocean*, June 10, 1909.

The Cobra Woman: Elsie Marks

11. "'Cobra Woman,' Killed by Snake, 'Man' with Husbands," *Greenville News*, Apr. 16, 1946.

12. A. Nadir and Isabella McCaul were Parsis, an Indian ethnoreligious group stemming from Zoroastrianism. There are impressively conflicting reports about Elsie's early life, including some reported by her directly. Almost all accounts, including her second marriage license, put her birth in India. However, her third marriage license claimed she was born in New Jersey and her father was named Theodore Y. Nader, not A. Nadir. It is possible the individual writing this particular license misheard her as there is no information regarding the discrepancy. It is also possible this was her father's English name. San Francisco County Records, 1824–1997, Marriage Licenses, microfilm, image 255, City and County of San Francisco.

13. A reporter made this claim in 1946, which appears to align with Elsie's documents. However, the reporter claims the 1923 wreck was in Michigan. There were only two circus train crashes that year. One was in Topeka and the other near Erie, Pennsylvania. The Hagenbeck-Wallace Circus crash was the only one that caused enough damage to destroy Elsie's records. The reporting on the crash also mentioned at least one snake charmer was present on the train in Kansas. While it is an interesting story, the reporter did not cite sources for the claim, and it is important to express skepticism of such dramatic events. "Tiger Hunt Follows Train Wreck," *Columbus Enquirer-Sun*, July 16, 1923; "P. T. Barnum's Protege," *Long Beach Independent*, Apr. 16, 1946; "Several Persons Hurt in Circus Train Wreck," *The Times*, July 16, 1923.

14. "Marriage Records, 1867–1952," film 172, image 511, Michigan Department of Community Health, Division of Vital Records and Health Statistics.

15. Fifteenth Census of the United States, 1930, Buffalo, Erie, New York, page 13B, Enumeration District 0265, FHL microfilm 2341165, Bureau of the Census; "Passenger Lists of Vessels Departing from Honolulu, Hawaii, Compiled 06/1900 –11/1954," NAI Number A3510; Record Group Title: Records of the Immigration and Naturalization Service, 1787–2004, Record Group Number RG 85, NARA.

16. "Pet Kills Cobra Woman," *Daily News*, Apr. 16, 1946.

17. San Francisco County Records, City and County of San Francisco.

18. "Passenger Lists of Vessels Arriving at Honolulu, Hawaii, Compiled 02/13/1900–12/30/1953," NAI Number A3422, Record Group Title: Records of

the Immigration and Naturalization Service, 1787–2004, Record Group Number RG 85, NARA.

19. "'Elsie, the Cobra Woman' a Man, Autopsy Shows," *Des Moines Register*, Apr. 16, 1946.

20. "'Cobra Woman' Bitten by Rattlesnake," *Long Beach Independent*, Apr. 14, 1946; "Rattlesnake That Killed Woman Was New to Show," *Los Angeles Evening Citizen News*, Apr. 15, 1946.

The Dancer: Albín Pleva

21. "Rychlá premèna dámy v muže," *Telegraf*, Jan. 22, 1937.

22. "Die Frau, die ein Mann war," *Reichenberger Zeitung*, Jan. 29, 1937.

23. "Muž v suknich," *Lidové noviny*, Feb. 12, 1937.

24. Chad Bryant, *Prague in Black: Nazi Rule and Czech Nationalism* (Cambridge, MA: Harvard University Press, 2007).

25. Jan Seidl, "Legal Imbroglio in the Protectorate of Bohemia and Moravia," in *Queer in Europe During the Second World War*, ed. Régis Schlagdenhauffen (Strasbourg: Council of European Publishing, 2018).

26. Rob Cameron, "Czechs Demolish Pig Farm on Nazi Concentration Camp for Roma," BBC, July 22, 2014; Michal Frankl, "Free of Controversy? Recent Research on the Holocaust in the Bohemian Lands," *Dapim: Studies on the Holocaust* 31, no. 3 (2017): 262–70; Markus Pape, *A nikdo vám nebude věřit: dokument o koncentračním táboře Lety u Písku* (Prague: GplusG, 1997).

27. Brian Kentey, "Lety u Pisku: The Politics Behind the 'Concentration Camp' Pig Farm," Radio Prague, May 19, 2005.

28. Ctibor Nečas, *The Holocaust of Czech Roma*, trans. Šimon Pellar (Prague: Prostor, 1999).

29. Helena Danielová, *Paměti romských žen: Kořeny I* (Brno: Muzeum romské kultury, 2002).

30. Aletta Beck, "Život v táboře v Letech," Institut Terezínské iniciativy, Mar. 17, 2021, https://www.holocaust.cz/dejiny/koncentracni-tabory-a-ghetta/cikanske-tabory/cikansky-tabor-v-letech/zivot-v-tabore-v-letech.

31. Nečas, *The Holocaust of Czech Roma*, 83.

32. Cikánsky tábor Lety u Pisku: Lety Concentration Camp Records, RG-04.076M, Aug. 31, 1942, 453–55, US Holocaust Memorial Museum.

33. "The Struggle for the Removal of the Pig Farm at the Former 'Gypsy Camp' Near Lety u Písku," European Holocaust Memorial Day for Sinti and Roma, https://www.roma-sinti-holocaust-memorial-day.eu/recognition/lety/, accessed Aug. 15, 2024.

34. *Deutsches Bühnen-Jahrbuch 55* (Berlin: Genossenschaft Deutscher Bühnen-Angehöriger, 1944), 120.

35. "Sinti and Roma (Gypsies) in Auschwitz," Auschwitz-Birkenau State Museum, https://web.archive.org/web/20240526181035/https://www.auschwitz

.org/en/history/categories-of-prisoners/sinti-and-roma-in-auschwitz/; "Genocide of European Roma (Gypsies) 1939–1945," *Holocaust Encyclopedia*, July 24, 2023, US Holocaust Memorial Museum.

36. Popular estimates of the Porajmos range from 250,000 (US Holocaust Memorial Museum) to 1.5 million (Romani scholar Ian Hancock). Ian Hancock, "Romanies and the Holocaust: A Re-evaluation and an Overview," in *The Historiography of the Holocaust*, ed. Dan Stone (New York: Palgrave Macmillan, 2005); "Genocide of European Roma (Gypsies) 1939–1945," *Holocaust Encyclopedia*.

37. "Lety u Písku: The Memorial to the Holocaust of the Roma and Sinti in Bohemia," Museum of Romani Culture, https://www.rommuz.cz/en/lety-u-pisku/, accessed Sept. 13, 2024.

38. Paul Polansky, *Black Silence: The Lety Survivors Speak* (Prague: GplusG, 1998), 16.

39. Peter Finn, "WWII Camp Still a Source of Suffering for Gypsies," *Washington Post*, Oct. 3, 1999.

40. Miroslav Broz, "A Battle for Roma History in the Czech Republic," Open Society Foundations, Aug. 1, 2014, https://www.opensocietyfoundations.org/voices/battle-roma-history-czech-republic; Cameron, "Czechs Demolish Pig Farm on Nazi Concentration Camp for Roma"; Czech News Agency, "Muzeum a architekti podepsali smlouvu na památník v Letech," *Archiweb*, Jan. 7, 2021, https://www.archiweb.cz/en/n/home/muzeum-a-architekti-podepsali-smlouvu-na-pamatnik-v-letec; "The Struggle for the Removal of the Pig Farm at the Former 'Gypsy Camp' Near Lety u Písku," European Holocaust Memorial Day for Sinti and Roma.

41. Tom McEnchroe, "Archaeologists Discover Graves of Roma Persecuted During WWII in Lety Camp," Radio Prague, Sept. 13, 2019.

42. Markus End, Hristo Kyuchukov, and Pia Laskar, *Antiziganism: What's in a Word?* (Newcastle upon Tyne, UK: Cambridge Scholars Publishing, 2015); Emma Townsend, "Hate Speech or Genocidal Discourse? An Examination of Anti-Roma Sentiment in Contemporary Europe," *PORTAL: Journal of Multidisciplinary International Studies* 11, no. 1 (2014): 1–23.

The Florist: John Berger

43. "Eine von der schwarzen kunßt," *Anzeiger des Westens*; "Can She Wear Bloomer?" *St. Louis Post-Dispatch*, Sept. 9, 1895; "Her Lover Is a Woman," *St. Louis Post-Dispatch*, Sept. 8, 1895.

44. "Her Lover Is a Woman," *St. Louis Post-Dispatch*.

45. "Joked About Her Sex," *St. Louis Post-Dispatch*, Sept. 10, 1895.

46. As noted in "Eine von der schwarzen kunßt," *Anzeiger des Westens*.

47. "Can She Wear Bloomers?," *St. Louis Post-Dispatch*.

48. "Scheint Mangel an Damen-Be-kanntschaft zu haben," *Anzeiger des Westens*, Dec. 15, 1895; "Anna Mattarstaig Fined $20," *St. Louis Post-Dispatch*, Sept. 10, 1895.

The Butler: Alfred Grouard

49. "Clue Sought Here to Woman Who Posed as Butler 14 Years," *Baltimore Sun*, Nov. 17, 1937; "Woman Who Posed as Male Butler 13 Years Is Dead," *Brooklyn Citizen*, Nov. 16, 1937; Fifteenth Census of the United States, 1930, T626, Bureau of the Census, NARA; "Only Death Reveals Butler Was Woman," *New York Times*, Nov. 16, 1937.

50. "Woman Chef in Male Disguise a Carlisle Girl," *The Sentinel*, Nov. 18, 1937.

51. "Death Reveals a Woman's Masquerade as a Man for 12 Years," *Daily Mirror*, Nov. 22, 1937.

52. "Death Holds Secret of Why Woman Masqueraded for 14 Years as Butler," *The News*, Nov. 17, 1937.

53. "Her Notes Give Clue to 'Butler,'" *Daily News*, Nov. 17, 1937.

54. "Clue Sought Here," *Baltimore Sun*.

55. "Death Reveals," *Daily Mirror*.

The Craftswoman: Ann Storcy

56. "Peg-Leg Annie's Disguise Hid Big Mystery," *News Palladium*, Sept. 13, 1961.

57. "Near Rush Lake," *St. Joseph Saturday Herald*, Apr. 18, 1885.

58. "'Peg Leg' Ann Just a Man," *Buffalo Enquirer*, Apr. 29, 1904; "Peg Leg Was a Man," *Herald-Palladium*, Apr. 28, 1904.

59. Sabine Lang, *Men as Women, Women as Men: Changing Gender in Native American Cultures* (Austin: University of Texas Press, 1998).

60. Ruth Landes, *The Prairie Potawatomi: Tradition and Ritual in the Twentieth Century* (Madison: University of Wisconsin Press, 1970), 196.

61. "'Peg Leg' Ann Just a Man," *Buffalo Enquirer*.

62. "True Life Story of Peg Leg Ann," *Herald-Palladium*, June 4, 1904; "Monsieur D'Arcey," *Herald-Press*, Apr. 30, 1904.

63. "Peg-Leg Annie's Disguise," *News Palladium*.

The Boy-of-All-Work: Frank Williams

64. "The Romance of a Girl-Boy," *St. Louis Post-Dispatch*, Apr. 23, 1905; "Lived Her Whole Life as a Boy," *Valley Spirit*, Mar. 29, 1905.

65. "Illness Reveals Girl Masquerading as Boy," *Daily Times*, Mar. 2, 1905.

66. "Lived Her Whole Life as a Boy," *Valley Spirit*.

67. "Iowa 'Man' a Woman," *Evening Times-Republican*, Jan. 25, 1905.

68. "This Girl Would Prefer to Be Boy," *Washington Times*.

69. "Girl Posed as a Boy," *Eagle River Review*, Mar. 3, 1905.

70. Iowa 'Man' a Woman," *Evening Times-Republican*.

71. "The Romance of a Girl-Boy," *St. Louis Post-Dispatch*.

72. "Illness Reveals Girl Masquerading as Boy," *Daily Times*.

73. "Worse," *Cincinnati Enquirer*, Feb. 7, 1905.

74. "Illness Reveals Girl Masquerading as Boy," *Daily Times*.

75. "This Girl Would Prefer to Be Boy," *Washington Times*.

76. Nixola Greenley-Smith, "Girls Will Be Boys," *Meriden Daily Journal*, Mar. 2, 1905.

THE ATHLETES

1. Andraya Yearwood quoted in Mirin Fader, "Andraya Yearwood Knows She Has the Right to Compete," *Bleacher Report*, Dec. 17, 2018, https://bleacherreport .com/articles/2810857-andraya-yearwood-knows-she-has-the-right-to-compete.

2. "Cronica La Reverte," *El País*, Oct. 1, 1905.

3. Neil Amdur, "Renee Richards Ruled Eligible for U.S. Open," *New York Times*, Aug. 17, 1977.

4. Lindsay Pieper, *Sex Testing: Gender Policing in Women's Sports* (Urbana: University of Illinois Press, 2016).

5. *"They're Chasing Us Away from Sport": Human Rights Violations in Sex Testing of Elite Women Athletes*, Human Rights Watch, Dec. 4, 2020.

6. "Another Wived Woman Who Passes as Man," *Leavenworth Times*, Oct. 6, 1901.

The Billiardist: Frances Anderson

7. "Champion Woman Billiardist Monday Night at the W. O. W. Home," *Daily Advertiser*, May 17, 1919.

8. "Orie Anderson," *Saturday Evening Kansas Commoner*, May 17, 1889.

9. "Orie Anderson, the Bright," *Newton Daily Republican*, July 12, 1887; "Orie Anderson Gave a Party," *Evening Kansan*, June 3, 1886; "Gun Club Shoot," *Evening Kansan*, July 14, 1888.

10. "Kansas Woman Thinks Dead 'Miss' Is Brother," *Fort Worth Record-Telegram*, Apr. 7, 1928.

11. "The Gamblers," *Newton Daily Republican*, July 20, 1893.

12. Missouri Marriage Records, 1890–1897, microfilm 815, Missouri State Archives; "Orie Anderson in a Hospital," *People's Voice*, Feb. 14, 1899; "Should Have Attention," *Sumner County Star*, Aug. 6, 1896.

13. "Border Bacchanals," *Daily Mail*, Apr. 15, 1898; "Another Joint Raided," *Hunnewell Reporter*, Apr. 15, 1898.

14. "Cocaine and Morphine Fiend," *Newton Daily Republican*, Feb. 14, 1899; "Orie Anderson," *People's Voice*.

15. "Newsboy Frank Strikes It Rich," *Des Moines Tribune*, Aug. 23, 1907.

16. "Fort Wayne Girl Shows Unusual Ability as Billiard Cue Artist," *Fort Wayne Sentinel*, Apr. 5, 1919; "Woman Cue Artist Was Virginia Nurse," *Macon Daily Telegraph*, Apr. 7, 1919.

17. "Champion Woman Billiardist," *Daily Advertiser*.

18. "He Posed as Woman for Years," *Sapulpa Herald*, Mar. 30, 1928.

19. "'Her' Secret Out in Death," *Los Angeles Times*, Mar. 30, 1928; "Orie Anderson Laid at Rest," *Hutchinson News*, Apr. 12, 1928.

The Matador: Agustín Rodríguez

20. See David Castro Devesa, "The Social and Legal Exclusion of Bull-fighter Women: A Symbol of the Consolidation of the Established Gender Order (1895–1910)," *ARENAL* 27, no. 1 (2020): 199–218.

21. "María Salomé," *Ahora*, Aug. 15, 1934; "Cronica La Reverte," *El País*.

22. José Aledón, "Un Toque de Clase: La mujer en los toros," *Avance Taurino* no. 26 (Dec. 8, 2020): 50; "Historia Que Parce Cuento: Hermafroditismo Y Toreria," *El Globo*, Aug. 26, 1911; Adrian Shubert, *Death and Money in the After-noon: A History of the Spanish Bullfight* (Oxford: Oxford University Press, 1999).

23. "La Unión 5 de Diciembre," *El Torreo*, Jan. 1, 1899.

24. "Cronica La Reverte," *El País*.

25. "La Reverte," *El Enano*, Jan. 15, 1899.

26. "Toreros Y Toros," *La Correspondencia de España*, Nov. 12, 1900.

27. "María Salomé," *Ahora*.

28. "Cronica La Reverte," *El País*.

29. "Escándalo en una Plaza de Toros," *El Correo español*, Aug. 5, 1907.

30. Shubert, *Death and Money in the Afternoon*.

31. "Atropello Incalificable," *El País*, June 26, 1908.

32. "'La Reverte' á lo contencioso," *El Mundo*, July 20, 1908; "La Reverte, contra Cierva," *El País*, July 20, 1908.

33. "Un Cambio en La Cabeza," *Gedeón*, Sept. 10, 1911.

34. "María Salomé," *Ahora*.

35. "La Reverte," *La Mañana*, Sept. 2, 1911; and "Reverte II," *La Mañana*, Sept. 18, 1911; "¿La Reverte es hombre ó mujer?" *Las Ocurrencias*, Sept. 8, 1911.

36. "Toros en Madrid y Vista Alegre," *El Mundo*, Sept. 29, 1912.

37. "María Salomé," *Ahora*.

38. "Spain's Women Bullfighters," *Nottingham Evening Post*, Aug. 25, 1934.

39. Muriel Feiner, *La mujer en el mundo del toro* (Madrid: Alianza Editorial, 1995).

40. Christopher Arnold, "Thus Began," *Miami Herald*, Nov. 20, 1963.

The Pentathlete: Stefan Pekar

41. "Uspesna nase atletka Stépánka Pekarova," *Venkov*, Aug. 1, 1937.

42. Alfred Janecký, *Slavné postavy naší atletiky* (Prague: Alfred Janecký, 1946), 576–77.

43. Michael Waters, *The Other Olympians: Fascism, Queerness, and the Making of Modern Sports* (New York: Farrar, Straus and Giroux, 2024), 65–67.

44. Zdeněk Koubek, "Zdeněk Koubek: The Story of a World Record Woman," trans. Meghan Forbes, *Pražský ilustrovaný zpravodaj*, nos. 7–9 (1936).

45. "Women's World Games," *The Advertiser*, Nov. 15, 1934.

46. Lída Merlínová, *Zdenin světový record* (Prague: Šolc a Šimáček, 1935), 185.

47. "Ženské světové hry v Londýn," *Moravská orlice*, July 27, 1934; "Zenske Družstvo Pro Londyn Jmenovano," *Národní osvobození*, Aug. 2, 1934; "Koubková A Pekarova Pojedou Do Londýna," *Národní osvobození*, May 7, 1934; "Jen 2 atletky na Světové hry," *Večer*, May 7, 1934.

48. "Londýn-Turin," *Polední list*, July 18, 1934.

49. I corrected the title of the book in the text to reflect Zdeněk's chosen name. The original title is *Zdenin světový rekord*.

50. "Čs. atletky na ženské světové hry zdk Praha 5. Srpna," *Lidové noviny*, Aug. 6, 1934; Merlínová, *Zdenin světový record*, 186.

51. Some archival sources report it was August 5, and Zdeněk's later retelling claims it was August 7.

52. Reporters and Zdeněk had slightly divergent narratives of the trip. They provided different numbers of attendees and modes of transportation. Waters, *The Other Olympians*, 103.

53. "Světové hry žen," *Lidové noviny*, Aug. 9, 1934; Merlínová, *Zdenin světový record*, 198.

54. It is unclear if this is exact, paraphrased, or invented dialogue by Merlínová (she does not cite sources). Merlínová embellished her nonfiction books and the scene undoubtedly raised the stakes in the narrative. The scores, weather, and eventual decisions in lineup match historical records, however. Merlínová, *Zdenin světový record*, 190.

55. "Zwischendurch," *Bergische Zeitung*, Aug. 27, 1934.

56. "FSFI Women's World Games," *Athletics Weekly*, http://www.gbrathletics.com/ic/fsfi.htm; Peter Matthews, *Historical Dictionary of Track and Field* (Lanham, MD: Scarecrow Publishing, 2012), 164.

57. This is according to Merlínová. I could not find any record stating he was injured. Merlínová, *Zdenin světový record*, 203.

58. Koubek, "Zdeněk Koubek."

59. "Mlle. Skalova," *Straits Times*, Sept. 18, 1934.

60. Pavel Hladík, *Mistrovství a Přebory v Atletice* (Prague: Český atletický svaz, 2015).

61. Československo Atletické Amatérské Unie, *Výroční zpráva Československé Atletické Amatérské Unie* (1935), 11.

62. Max Dohle, *"They Say I'm Not a Girl": Case Studies of Gender Verification in Elite Sports* (Jefferson, NC: McFarland and Co., 2020).

63. Stefan had a noticeably receding hairline and angular face, which led spectators to media commentators to question how hormones may have affected his body. Common conditions like PCOS (polycystic ovary syndrome) affect between 4 and 20 percent of the world's population and often produce these symptoms. They also disproportionately affect trans men (when compared to cis

women). But we can only speculate the influence of hormones on Stefan's body and athletic capabilities. Ritu Deswal et al., "The Prevalence of Polycystic Ovary Syndrome," *Journal of Human Reproductive Sciences* 13, no. 4 (2020): 261–71; Dohle, *"They Say I'm Not a Girl,"* 25; Minghao Liu, Swetha Murthi, and Leonid Poretsky, "Polycystic Ovary Syndrome and Gender Identity," *Yale Journal of Biology and Medicine* 93, no. 4 (2020): 529–37.

64. "Poslední slova Pekarové v sukních," *Polední list*, July 31, 1937.

65. Pavel, Kovář, *Příběh české rekordwoman: Zákulisí největšího sportovního skandálu první republiky*, (Prague: Pejdlova Rosička 2017), 206.

66. "Pekarová-Koublem Č. 2," *Polední list*, July 29, 1937.

67. Pavel Kovář, *Příběh české rekordwoman*, 206.

68. "What! Another!" *Montreal Daily Star*, Oct. 4, 1937.

69. Markéta Jančíková, "Zdena/Zdeněk Koubková/Koubek," *Encyklopedie Brna*, Sept. 18, 2022, https://encyklopedie.brna.cz/home-mmb/?acc=profil _osobnosti&load=11754; "What! Another!" *Montreal Daily Star*; "Pekarová byla včera operována," *Moravská orlice*, Mar. 13, 1938; "Pekarová-Koublem Č. 2," *Polední list*.

70. Janecký wrote, "[His] masculine tendencies were conspicuous, yet [his] life among the students did not suggest any change. On the contrary, [he] soon became popular with the students." Janecký, *Slavné postavy naší atletiky*, 577.

71. Books like Katie Sutton's *The Masculine Woman in Weimar Germany* (Oxford: Berghahn Books, 2011) and Robert Beachy's *Gay Berlin: Birthplace of a Modern Identity* discuss how the conflict led to the reinstitutionalization of gender norms via Nazi ideology.

72. Peter Demetz, *Prague in Danger: The Years of German Occupation, 1939–45* (New York: Farrar, Straus and Giroux, 2009); Petr Svoboda, "17. listopad 1939 je opředen mýty, říká historik Petr Koura," *IForum* (2005).

73. Bohuslav Chňoupek, *Generál se lvem* (Prague: Lidové nakladatelství, 1978), 207–8.

74. "Krematorium Sl. Ostrava," *Nová Svoboda*, June 24, 1983.

The Wrestler: Bill Winters

75. "How Lillian Winters Deceived Men," *St. Louis Post-Dispatch*, Feb. 21, 1909.

76. Newspapers reported Bill's birth year as 1887, but he self-reported 1883 to the census bureau. There is no explanation for the discrepancy. Fourteenth Census, Bureau of the Census, 1920, https://www.census.gov/library/publications /1921/dec/vol-01-population.html

77. In 1909 Bill reported the date as August 2, 1900. However, the Galveston flood occurred in September of that year. "True Sex Is Revealed," *Sedalia Democrat*, Feb. 15, 1909; Casey Edward Greene and Shelly Henley Kelly, *Through a Night of Horrors: Voices from the 1900 Galveston Storm* (College Station: Texas A&M University Press, 2002).

78. Texas birth and death records were not officially recorded before 1903, making it difficult to check the accuracy of Dick's claims. Regardless, the flood and lack of records left the details of Willie's earlier years somewhat of a mystery.

79. "Charming Boy Turns Out to Be a Feminine Masquerader," *Herald and Review*, Feb. 21, 1909.

80. Miriam Frank, *Out in the Union: A Labor History of Queer America* (Philadelphia: Temple University Press, 2014), 1.

81. "Willie Winters a Girl: Sweetheart Greatly Shocked," *St. Louis Post-Dispatch*, Feb. 15, 1909.

82. "Girl in 'Husband' Role," *St. Louis Globe-Democrat*, Feb. 16, 1909.

83. "How Lillian Winters Deceived Men," *St. Louis Post-Dispatch*.

84. There are two drastically different stories of how Bill was discovered. One attests he jumped backward off a train and was caught while someone was tending to his injuries. Another claims he was arrested at a speakeasy. No arrest or court records of him could be located in Missouri's archives. Bill's outing came at the same time as that of James Davis, who had a similar experience transitioning. Interestingly, their stories were confused in several newspapers, leading to the uncertainty over which story came by train and which by arrest. Both were St. Louis–based trans men who were outed within hours of one another. With the lack of records, there is no way to tell which is which with absolute certainty. I chose to center Bill's speakeasy arrest because it was reported in more papers than the other and allegedly included quotes from local officers (there is also no way to tell if the quotes are authentic). "The New Emancipated Woman," *St. Louis Post-Dispatch*, Apr. 18, 1909.

85. "Girl Poses Nine Years as a Boy," *Manhattan Mercury*, Mar. 9, 1909.

86. "How Lillian Winters Deceived Men," *St. Louis Post-Dispatch*.

87. "How Lillian Winters Deceived Men," *St. Louis Post-Dispatch*.

88. "Girl in 'Husband' Role," *St. Louis Globe-Democrat*.

89. "Willie Winters a Girl," *St. Louis Post-Dispatch*.

90. "Posed as a Man for Years," *New York Times*, Feb. 15, 1909.

91. "How Lillian Winters Deceived Men," *St. Louis Post-Dispatch*.

92. "Posed as a Man for Years," *Evansville Journal-News*, May 16, 1909.

93. "No Warrant for Girl-Boy," *St. Louis Globe-Democrat*, Feb. 18, 1909.

94. "The New Emancipated Woman," *St. Louis Post-Dispatch*.

95. "How Lillian Winters Deceived Men," *St. Louis Post-Dispatch*.

96. "Posed as a Man for Years," *Evansville Journal-News*.

97. "How Lillian Winters Deceived Men," *St. Louis Post-Dispatch*.

98. "Willie Winters a Girl," *St. Louis Post-Dispatch*.

99. "Police to Exploit Willie Winters as Strong Woman," *St. Louis Star and Times*, Apr. 22, 1911.

100. Pat Laprade and Dan Murphy, *Sisterhood of the Squared Circle: The History and Rise of Women's Wrestling* (Toronto: ECW Press, 2017).

101. "Jitsu Cop Is a Whirlwind of Sinew," *St. Louis Post-Dispatch*, Nov. 17, 1909; "Women Wrestlers Clash," *St. Louis Globe-Democrat*, May 16, 1912.

102. Fifteenth Census of the United States, 1930, St. Louis, St. Louis, Missouri, page 9B, Enumeration District 0351, FHL microfilm 2340966, Bureau of the Census; Fourteenth Census of the United States, 1920, (NARA microfilm publication T625), Record Group 29, 10, Bureau of the Census; Thirteenth Census of the United States, 1910, St. Louis Ward 6, St. Louis, Missouri; Roll T624_813, page 4b, Enumeration District 0103, FHL microfilm 1374826, Bureau of the Census.

The Teammates: Léon Caurla and Pierre Brésolles

103. Alain Bouillé, "Les Grandes Du Spring Féminin," in *Revue FFA 346*, NS5 (December 1991), Fédération française d'athlétisme, 32 ; "La Championne D'athlétisme Claire Bresoles Le Plus Recent Des Androgynes Du Sport," *Qui? Detective* (Aug. 1, 1951): 18–19.

104. "Première Journée Des Championnats D'Europe à Oslo," *L'Humanité*, Aug. 23, 1946.

105. Julian Jackson, *Living in Arcadia: Homosexuality, Politics, and Morality in France from the Liberation to AIDS* (Chicago: University of Chicago Press, 2019).

106. "Are Girl Athletes Really Girls?" *Life*, Oct. 7, 1966.

107. "Pierre Bressoles," *La Victoire*, Jan. 26, 1949.

108. "Claire Bressoles," *Las Presse*, Oct. 11, 1948; Christopher Todd, *Pierre Descaves: Temoin Et Pionnier De la Radio, Vol. 1* (Lewiston, ME: Edwin Mellen Press, 2000).

109. Raymond Vanker, "'Mademoiselle' Claire Bressoles pourra sans doute être 'papa,'" *ICI Paris Hebdo*, Oct. 18, 1943.

110. "M. Pierre Bressoles," *Qui? Detective*, Feb. 26, 1951.

111. Maurice Josco, "Pour Ne Pas Changer Ses Habitudes," *France-soir*, Mar. 4, 1952.

112. "Vrouw Bleek Man Te Zijn," *De Arubaanse Courant*, Mar. 5, 1952.

113. "Ce militaire a été . . . championne de France!" *L'Est républicain*, Feb. 3, 1955.

CONCLUSION: A NEW GENDER HISTORY

1. David Hackett Fisher, *Historians' Fallacies: Toward a Logic of Historical Thought* (New York: Harper and Row, 1970), 131.

2. This famous English-language proverb paraphrases José Rizal's original Tagalog writing, which better translates to "those who do not look back to where they came from will not reach their destination." The exact origin of the popular English phrase is unknown. Jose Rizal, *The Philippines a Century Hence* (Manila: Philippine Education Co., 1912).

INDEX

Mississippi: cross-dressing laws, 86;
   prohibition laws, 86; Willie Ray
   in, 85, 86, 237n116
Money, John, 6, 225n3
Morris, Jan, 6
Mühsam, Richard, 22–23, 231n52
Muksamse'lapli (White Cindy), 14,
   118–24, I–3
Murray, Pauli, 11, 227n18
Museum of Romani Culture, 164
mustarjil (becoming man), 60–62

Nashville Banner, Crawford coverage,
   114–15
Nazi Germany: antagonism to queer
   and transgender people, 100;
   anti-Romani ideology, 160; incon-
   sistent views about trans people,
   164; patriarchal gender norms,
   258n72; religiosity, 105
New Jersey: Heinrich in, 73
Newton, Kansas: Anderson family in,
   189–90
New York, New York: LGBTQ+
   history in, 6, 20, 171
New York Times: coverage of trans
   issues in, 17
noncompliance, as form of activism,
   25–26

O'Brien, M. E., 37
Ohio: Maude Milbourne in, 139,
   140, 141, 145-46; Storcy family in,
   177–78; Frank Williams in, 144,
   181, 182
Okiyo, 4, 8, 14, 21, 24–25, 88, 132,
   134–38, 220. *See also* danshō
Ondra, Anny, 201
orchiectomy (castration), 21, 31
Oregon territory, 120
Osaka, Japan: Okiyo's family in, 8,
   131–32

The Other Olympians (Waters), 188
outing: and employment challenges,
   150–52; ethical questions, 57,
   231n60; and self-advocacy, 88–89,
   179. *See also biographical sketches of
   specific individuals*
oyama (female style), 247n114

Parsis, 251n12
PCOS (polycystic ovary syndrome),
   257–58n63
Pekar, Stefan, 27, 164, 189, 198–206,
   257–58n63, I–7
Peterson, Jules-Gill, 34
phalloplasty, 22–23
Phelps, Michael, 188
Philadelphia, 25
Pleva, Albín, 4, 27, 159–61, I–4
Polansky, Paul, 164–65
police: in Berlin, 99–103; fear of
   in trans community, 98; in St.
   Louis, 46, 47, 48; Ueno Park riots,
   135–37
Porajmos (Romani Holocaust), 4,
   159, 164–65, 253n36
Posttransexual Manifesto (Stone), 10
Potawatomi Nation, 173, 176–77
Prague: Stefan Pekar in, 164, 198,
   199, 200, 201, 203, 204, 205; Albín
   Pleva in, 163
Providence, Rhode Island: Stanley
   in, 70–71
Public Universal Friend, 13–14

racism and trans oppression, 7–8, 19,
   36–37, 92, 95, 152
Radszuweit, Friedrich, 99–100,
   103–4, 242n43
Rankin, Joseph and Susan, 78, 85
Rauchfangswerder riots, 20, 93,
   96–103, 106, 241n25. *See also*
   Zobeltitz, Gerda von